Chicken Soup for the Soul®

Christian Kids

Our **101** BEST STORIES

Chicken Soup for the Soul: Christian Kids
Stories to Inspire, Amuse, and Warm the Hearts of Christian Kids and Their Parents
by Jack Canfield, Mark Victor Hansen & Amy Newmark

Published by Chicken Soup for the Soul Publishing, LLC   www.chickensoup.com

The publisher gratefully acknowledges the many publishers and individuals who
granted Chicken Soup for the Soul permission to reprint the cited material.

*Cover photos courtesy of © Radius Images/Alamy, iStockphotos.com/sunnyfrog. Interior
illustration courtesy of iStockphoto.com/Vjom*

Cover and Interior Design & Layout by Pneuma Books, LLC
For more info on Pneuma Books, visit www.pneumabooks.com

Distributed to the booktrade by Simon & Schuster. SAN: 200-2442

Publisher's Cataloging-in-Publication Data
(Prepared by The Donohue Group)

Chicken soup for the soul. Selections.
    Chicken soup for the soul : Christian kids : stories to inspire, amuse,
and warm the hearts of Christian kids and their parents / [compiled by] Jack
Canfield [and] Mark Victor Hansen ; [edited by] Amy Newmark.

    p. ; cm. -- (Our 101 best stories)

    ISBN-13: 978-1-935096-13-9
    ISBN-10: 1-935096-13-3

1. Christian children--Literary collections. 2. Christian children--Anecdotes. I.
Canfield, Jack, 1944- II. Hansen, Mark Victor. III. Newmark, Amy. IV. Title. V. Title:
Christian kids

PN6071.C58 C54 2008
808.89/282   2008935336

PRINTED IN THE UNITED STATES OF AMERICA
on acid∞free paper
16 15 14 13 12 10 09 08   01 02 03 04 05 06 07 08

Chicken Soup for the Soul

Christian Kids

Our 101 BEST STORIES

Stories to Inspire, Amuse,
and Warm the Hearts of
Christian Kids and Their Parents

Jack Canfield
Mark Victor Hansen
Amy Newmark

CSS

Chicken Soup for the Soul Publishing, LLC
Cos Cob, CT

Contents

❹

~This I Pray~

❺

~Family Time~

❻

~The People We Know in Heaven~

❼

~Giving~

❽

~Creatures Great and Small~

❾
~Send Me a Sign~

❿
~God's Angels~

⓫
~For Our Moms and Dads~

⑫
~Miracles Happen~

⑬
~The Wisdom of Children~

⑭
~We Believe~

A Special Foreword

by Jack and Mark

For us, 101 has always been a magical number. It was the number of stories in the first *Chicken Soup for the Soul* book, and it is the number of stories and poems we have always aimed for in our books. We love the number 101 because it signifies a beginning, not an end. After 100, we start anew with 101.

We hope that when you finish reading one of our books, it is only a beginning for you too — a new outlook on life, a renewed sense of purpose, a strengthened resolve to deal with an issue that has been bothering you. Perhaps you will pick up the phone and share one of the stories with a friend or a loved one. Perhaps you will turn to your keyboard and express yourself by writing a Chicken Soup story of your own, to share with other readers who are just like you.

This volume contains our 101 best stories and poems for Christian parents and their children. We share this with you at a very special time for us, the fifteenth anniversary of our *Chicken Soup for the Soul* series. When we published our first book in 1993, we never dreamed that we had started what became a publishing phenomenon, one of the best-selling series of books in history.

We did not set out to sell more than one hundred million books, or to publish more than 150 titles. We set out to touch the heart of one person at a time, hoping that person would in turn touch another person, and so on down the line. Fifteen years later, we know that it has worked. Your letters and stories have poured in by the hundreds of thousands, affirming our life's work, and inspiring us to continue to make a difference in your lives.

On our fifteenth anniversary, we have new energy, new resolve, and new dreams. We have recommitted to our goal of 101 stories or poems per book, we have refreshed our cover designs and our interior layout, and we have grown the Chicken Soup for the Soul team, with new friends and partners across the country in New England.

In this new volume, we have selected our 101 best stories and poems for Christian parents and their children from our rich fifteen-year history. We know that your connection and relationship with God are important to you, and that you enjoy sharing these values of faith, hope, love, charity, forgiveness, and devotion with your children.

We hope that you will find these stories as inspiring and supportive as we have, and that you will share them with your families and friends. Some of them are funny, and some will make you cry. We made sure that all of the selected stories are appropriate for sharing with children. We have also identified the 35 *Chicken Soup for the Soul* books in which the stories originally appeared, in case you would like to continue your family reading among our other titles. We hope you will also enjoy the additional titles for Christians and families in "Our 101 Best Stories" series.

With our love, our thanks, and our respect,
~*Jack Canfield and Mark Victor Hansen*

Psalm 23
Prayer for Children

1. *The Lord is my Shepherd; I shall not want.*

2. *He maketh me to lie down in green pastures; He leadeth me beside the still waters.*

3. *He restoreth my soul; He leadeth me in the paths of righteousness for His name's sake.*

4. *Yea, though I walk through the valley of the shadow of death, I will fear no evil; for Thou art with me; Thy rod and Thy staff, they comfort me.*

5. *Thou preparest a table before me in the presence of mine enemies; Thou anointest my head with oil; my cup runneth over.*

6. *Surely goodness and mercy shall follow me all the days of my life, and I will dwell in the house of the Lord forever.*

Christian Kids

Christian Kindness

Always try to be a little kinder than necessary.
~Sir James Matthew Barrie

My Little Buddy

The heart of the giver makes the gift dear and precious.
~Martin Luther

Most people's first jobs are pretty boring and anything but glamorous. Mine fit the stereotype exactly. But I stuck with it and plugged along day after day, year after year—for three years, six months and five days, to be exact. When asked how work was going, I had my typical responses: "I hate it," "I despise it," or my favorite, "It sucks." My first job wasn't as a waitress at the local diner or a cashier at Kmart. No, my working days started early. When I was ten years old, I became a delivery girl for the local paper.

It wasn't so much the work I hated. Who can complain about taking one hour out of each day to throw papers on porches? No, it wasn't hard work; it was just lonely. I barely had interaction with any of my customers, and it made my job seem pointless, or unappreciated at the very least. I delivered through pouring rain, scorching heat, snow and, even once, a hailstorm. I went through the motions day after day. I rarely got a hello from a friendly resident of the neighborhood; at times, I wondered if there even was a friendly resident beyond those porches. After one long June day of the same boring routine, I prayed—hard. I prayed that the job would liven up. For if it didn't, I was sure I was going to die of boredom and loneliness.

The next day, I raced home from school to get my paper route done so I could meet my friends later. I looked on my cover sheet and noticed two new customers. Ugghh, I thought. Just what I need today. I started my route as I would have any other day, dragging my feet and hanging my head. I came to the street of one of the new customers and searched for the house. It was the big, brick house with the SOLD sign still in the front lawn. I had walked past it many times as it stood dark and empty. It was nice to see that someone was making it a home again.

On the front porch, the new owners had hung a little wooden porch swing. And on that swing sat a little boy. He was so cute! His blond hair was neatly combed to the right side, and his big blue eyes shone like they held the stars in them. At first glance, I guessed he was five. He was so adorable, and I was happy to see his smiling face looking at me. I promptly forgot that I was in a hurry to finish my paper route. As I stretched out my arm to see if he wanted the paper, he smiled and said, "Hi!" I was pleasantly surprised; in this neighborhood, even the cats didn't seem friendly.

"Well, hi," I said. He scootched his little bottom off the swing and came to take the paper. As I stood there, arms still outstretched, he confidently moved toward me. He took the paper and, as if he had known me all his life, he put his arms around me in a hug and said, "Thank you, thank you, thank you," in a sing-songy voice. Standing there stunned, I watched as he turned and trotted back into the house yelling, "Mommy, Mommy, Mommy, the paper is here!" The rest of the route I smiled, held my head up and thought about this little boy who had just put a little happiness into my day and didn't even know it.

The next day when I began my route, I had high hopes of seeing my little buddy again. As I approached the house, I scanned the porch, hoping to see him sitting on the swing... to no avail. As I reached in my bag and pulled back to launch the paper, he emerged from his house with a plate of cookies in hand. He walked over to the top step of the porch and sat. He had the same radiant smile as the day before as he patted the spot next to him. Happy that he again wanted to have interaction with me, I went over to sit on the step next to him. He handed me a cookie, took one himself and we ate. No words were spoken until we had both finished our cookies.

"Thanks," I said.

"Did you like it? Those are my mommy's famous chocolate chip cookies. And they are the best."

"It was delicious," I said with a smile. "So, what's your name?"

"I'm Andrew. And who are you?" he asked, with wonder in his voice.

"Bethany. I'm Bethany."

After we ate our cookie, he took the paper, hugged me and in his song-like manner said, "Thank you, thank you, thank you."

After that day, I did my paper route with happiness in my heart and a smile on my face. Sure, I still had my bad days, but whenever I reached his house, my frown became a smile. If he was going to be at his grandma's the next day or shopping with his mom, he was sure to let me know the day before so I would know where he was. Monday was our conversation day. Every Tuesday he brought me one of his mom's famous cookies. Every Wednesday we drank a juice together. On Thursday, it was a piece of gum. On Friday, he gave me five cents. Sometimes it was five pennies, and sometimes it was a nickel, but it was always five cents to say thanks for delivering each day of the week.

On every holiday, he had a present for me, whether it was something his mom had bought for him to give or a picture he had colored himself. Without fail, he had something to present to me. My favorite gift was the one I received on Easter. It was a cross made out of Popsicle sticks that said, "Jesus loves me, this I know... and he loves you, too!" It wasn't an extravagant gift, but one that came from the heart and let me know I was appreciated.

Even if he wasn't going to be there, he left my treasure on the porch swing in a box. He became my "little buddy," and I became his "big buddy." Each day he was home, he would greet me with his "Hey, big buddy!" and wait for my reply of, "Hey, little buddy!" Then he would hand me my treasure, and we would exchange a few words about how his day was going or what he was up to. I would hand over his paper, and he would hug me and say, "Thank you, thank you, thank you." It never changed.

I'm sure my "little buddy" never realized what he did for me. I'm sure my "little buddy" had no idea that because of him I was able to hold my head high and smile for an hour each day, regardless of how bad the rest of the day had been. My "little buddy" taught me many things. The radiant smile that never left his face taught me how far a simple gesture can go. His presents taught me that big things really do come in small packages. And his hugs taught me that even the most insignificant jobs in life can mean something to someone.

~Bethany Couts
Chicken Soup for the Christian Teenage Soul

2

Caroline's Compassion

The capacity to care is the thing that gives life
its deepest meaning and significance.
~Pablo Casals

When my daughter, Caroline, was very young, we started saying a prayer every time we heard a siren from an ambulance or fire truck. It's a quick prayer, just, "God, please be with the people the ambulance (or fire truck) is going to help."

I always initiated the prayer, and sometimes, she would even whine, "I don't want to say it this time."

I just reminded her that someone was in need, and that if we were in need, we would want people to pray for us. I thought it was a good way to help her learn about compassion and how, as Christians, we love and care for others, even it we don't know them personally.

It's the same reason, I told her, that we pick up a few extra items at the grocery store and deliver them to our church's food pantry. And it's the reason we prepare care packages for missionaries and bag up clothes she has outgrown to take to a local ministry helping the poor.

But when she started kindergarten this year, I realized she might not fully comprehend the compassion thing.

When her class was collecting canned goods at Thanksgiving to benefit a local mission, we looked in our pantry to choose something to donate. She didn't want to give away the corn or sweet peas, because those were her favorites.

"Let's take the black beans and... here, kidney beans... yuck!" she proclaimed.

I realized that, to Caroline, this was more about cleaning out the pantry and getting rid of the foods she didn't like than it was about helping the needy.

Rationalizing that she was only five years old, we took the cans of "yucky" beans and off we went to school.

I was rather surprised to pass another mom in the hall that morning, carrying two huge bags laden with groceries.

"Ashlen insisted that we bring all of this," she told me. "I tried to pick out a few cans, but she just kept reminding me that the people were hungry and that we needed to give them more."

"That's so sweet," I told her, with what must have looked like a big, fake grin on my face.

Actually, I was thrilled that her daughter was so kind, but I had to wonder why mine, apparently, was not.

Through the holidays, I was determined more than ever, to teach my daughter about compassion. I told Caroline about all the monetary donations during the season, and we spent extra time focusing on the gifts we were going to give others, rather than what we might receive. We made extra deliveries to the food pantry, took flowers to the local nursing home and baked cookies and brownies for a few of our elderly neighbors.

One day at the grocery store, we saw a huge box for donated toys for underprivileged children.

I pointed the box out to Caroline and told her people were bringing toys to be given to children who might not otherwise get Christmas presents.

"Maybe we could bring something for the box," I suggested.

"Well, we could buy some toys, and if they are not something I like, we could bring them here," she told me, matter-of-factly.

Oh, boy. I realized we still weren't quite there yet. In earnest, I turned to God. I asked Him to help me find ways to teach Caroline to be more compassionate, and I asked Him to open her heart to better understand the importance of loving and helping people.

One day as I rushed through the house picking up toys and putting away laundry, I peeked in Caroline's room and noticed her sitting on her bed, head bowed and hands folded.

"Dear God," she said, "please be with the people the fire truck is going to help."

In all my busyness I had not even heard the siren.

But she did.

~Frances Pace Putman
Chicken Soup for the Christian Soul 2

And a Little Child Shall Lead Them

The setting was a McDonald's restaurant in a small community in central Pennsylvania. Most of us think of dining at McDonald's as "fast food." Not so for a lonely, retired eighty-year-old woman, whose physical and mental health was waning. Each day, she arrived early in the morning and sat at a back booth until late afternoon, seeking companionship and hoping to be included in the conversations of nearby patrons.

June was her name, and home was a second-floor apartment in the nearby college town. Despite the steep steps that were becoming increasingly difficult for her, the pleasant ambience of McDonald's drew her to the corner she called her "home away from home." Each day this proud woman sat bundled up in the same back corner, wearing a familiar babushka on her head, her eyes always hidden behind dark sunglasses, her heavy coat buttoned.

During the fall of 2001, my four-year-old granddaughter, Catie, attended preschool three days a week; I picked her up each day at the sitter's and took her to lunch before I dropped her off at school. Most children love "Mickey D's," and Catie was no exception! Catie's favorite seat was one table away from June on the same bench seat.

I must admit I became tired of eating hamburgers, and I would often ask Catie, "Could we please go somewhere else today?" Her answer was always an adamant: "No, Nana, I have to see June." Each day as we approached the parking lot, Catie's eyes would search for June's battered 1975 Monte Carlo, with the cluttered interior containing June's "treasures." When she spotted June's car in the handicapped space, she was elated. As soon as I got her out of her car seat, she would race ahead of me, bounding through the restaurant, craning her neck to see if June was in her spot. If she was, they played a little game. Catie would pretend to hide behind a display, peek around the corner, then race into June's arms. Many patrons watched for Catie and smiled tenderly as this adorable little blond child clasped her friend tightly, proving to all that friendship transcends age. As I reflect on this relationship, I realize that God planned for these two to meet and to bond.

Over the months, Catie would bring June small gifts: a key chain from her first trip to Disney World, a bouquet of flowers hand-carried to her apartment when June was sick, a mug for her birthday with a photo of Catie perched on June's lap in their favorite corner of McDonald's.

Unfortunately, in the fall of 2002, just as Catie entered kindergarten, June's health deteriorated to the point where she had to have dialysis treatments three times a week. Many days, her seat would be empty when we arrived at McDonald's. Catie always asked one of the clerks about her friend. Sometimes, the manager or one of the workers, who had also befriended June, would give us an update. Near Christmastime, Catie and I received the news that June had gone to a nursing home.

When we first found June's room, she was lying in bed with her eyes closed. June seemed to sense our presence, and, as her eyes opened, she spotted Catie. Catie walked over to the bed, June sat up and they hugged. Tears filled my eyes as I realized the power of the moment. They talked a mile a minute, and June showed Catie the birdfeeder outside her window. This visit was a ray of sunshine for June, whose life was far from sunny. Her diabetes was worsening; her beloved car had to be sold; and the outlook for the future was bleak.

Before we left that day, June opened Catie's Christmas present, a pink fleece blanket to keep June's feet warm. She loved it, and they hugged tightly once again. Over the next few months, school kept Catie busy, yet each time we went to McDonald's, Catie's eyes were drawn to that back corner.

Before Easter, I received a phone call from a McDonald's employee telling me that June's health was failing; they were going to have to amputate her leg. Catie sent a card to June, telling her she would pray for her. Soon, we got even worse news: June had passed away.

Catie would be in school on the day of June's funeral, but we sent two pink roses with some babies' breath. The morning of the visitation, I walked into the funeral home to pay my respects. Only two small flower arrangements were visible, and the people there were few. As I walked down the aisle, a woman who identified herself as June's niece approached me, wondering who I was. When I told her that I was the grandmother of Catie—June's friend from McDonald's—she grabbed my hand and led me to the casket. There lay this peaceful angel with her white babushka on her head and with Catie's two pink roses in her hands. I soon learned from her niece that roses had been June's favorite flowers. The pink fleece blanket covered her legs, and on top of the blanket were Catie's card and the photo of the two of them in the corner booth at McDonald's, Catie sitting on June's lap and June resplendent in her trademark dark glasses and babushka. Tears flowed from my eyes. In that moment, I truly came to see what a gift God had given the world in my granddaughter, whose genuine love had wholly embraced this lonely, elderly woman.

While taking Catie to school the day of June's funeral, we talked about my saying goodbye to June for her. She asked me about the memorial card that was lying on the seat next to me. I read it to her, and we talked about their birthdays both being in June, but that this year, June would be in heaven for hers. As she got out of the car, she wondered if she could take the card to school and I told her that was fine. She bounded up the sidewalk with her friend Carly, who asked her what she had in her hand. I heard her explain, "This is my best friend, June."

~Audrey Conway
Chicken Soup for the Girlfriend's Soul

The Hug of a Child

A hug delights and warms and charms,
that must be why God gave us arms.
~Author Unknown

As we drove across town, I prepared my two children for what they were about to see. A lady from our new church was dying of cancer, and I had volunteered to help her with the housework. "Annie has a tumor in her head, which has disfigured her face," I cautioned them.

Annie invited me to bring my children with me one day, as I had told her so much about them. "Most children are frightened by my appearance," she said. "So I will understand if they don't want to meet me."

I struggled for the words to describe Annie's appearance to my son and daughter. Then I remembered a movie I'd seen two years earlier with my son, when he was ten. I wanted him to understand that disabled people are like anyone else — their feelings can be hurt, too.

"David, remember the movie *Mask* about the boy with the facial deformity?"

"Yes, Mom. I think I know what to expect." His tone told me it was time to stop mothering him so much.

"What does a tumor look like?" Diane asked me.

Answering my nine-year-old daughter would be tricky. In order to prevent Diane's revulsion when she met Annie, I needed to prepare her just enough but not too much. I didn't want to frighten the child.

"Her tumor looks like the skin on the inside of your mouth. It sticks out from under her tongue and makes it hard for her to talk. You'll see it as soon as you meet her, but there's nothing to be afraid of. Remember, don't stare. I know you'll want to look at it... that's all right... just don't stare." Diane nodded. I knew she was trying to picture a tumor in her mind.

"Are you kids ready for this?" I asked as we pulled up to the curb.

"Yes, Mom," David said, sighing as only a preteen can.

Diane nodded and tried to reassure me. "Don't worry, Mommy. I'm not scared."

We entered the living room, where Annie was sitting in her recliner, her lap covered with note cards for her friends. I stood across the room with my children, aware that anything could happen next.

At the sight of my children, Annie's face brightened. "Oh, I'm so glad you came to visit," she said, dabbing a tissue at the drops of saliva that escaped from her twisted mouth.

Then it happened. I watched David stride across the room to Annie's chair, wrap his arms around her shoulders and press his cheek to her misshapen face. Smiling, he looked into her eyes and said, "I'm happy to meet you."

Just when I didn't think I could be more proud, Diane copied her big brother and gave Annie the precious, accepting hug of a child.

My throat tightened with emotion as I saw Annie's eyes well up with grateful tears. I had nothing to worry about.

~Victoria Harnish Benson
Chicken Soup for the Volunteer's Soul

5

Altar Boys

When they were young, life with my two sons was what would tactfully be called "challenging." For years, broken bones, stitches, notes from the school principal, torn jeans and numerous unusual pets hidden under their beds were part of our daily family life. But sometimes I would get a comforting glimpse of the fine young men Kevin and Eric would one day become, and suddenly the world would seem right.

One such glimpse came when Kevin and Eric befriended a new boy in the neighborhood. My sons were about ten and twelve that year, and Danny was somewhere in between. Danny was an intense child, thin and slightly built. But he couldn't run and jump and climb like the rest of the neighborhood children. Danny spent his days in a wheelchair.

Although there were dozens of children for blocks around, only Kevin and Eric took the time to meet Danny and spend time playing with him. Usually, they would go around the corner to his house. And once in a while, they would help Danny navigate the streets and sidewalks and bring him to our home.

As the boys' friendship with Danny blossomed, I was gratified to see that they accepted and loved Danny without seeing him as physically limited. More than that, they realized that Danny both needed and deserved to experience, as much as possible, all the things "normal" children could enjoy.

One Saturday, several months after Danny moved into the

neighborhood, Kevin and Eric asked if he could spend the night with us. My husband and I said that was fine, and we reminded them that we would attend church as usual the next morning. Danny was invited to sleep over, and to accompany us to church.

That night, the three boys had a great time playing games and watching television. When it was time for bed, my husband carried Danny upstairs to the boys' room, and we made certain he was comfortable for the night.

Dealing with a child in a wheelchair was a new and very humbling experience for us. Suddenly, a few scraped knees and broken arms seemed to be blessings—products of having healthy, active children. They were reasons to give thanks, rather than the purple hearts of parenthood we'd thought them to be.

The next day, with help from all of us, Danny was soon dressed and ready for church. Kevin and Eric helped Danny into the backseat of the station wagon, and we loaded the wheelchair into the cargo area. Once at the church, we unloaded everybody, and the boys happily wheeled Danny off to meet their friends.

At the time, our church had a rather pleasant tradition of letting the children in the congregation take turns each week being unofficial acolytes. Invariably, the children were excited when they were chosen to walk down the center aisle of the church carrying a long brass taper used to light the candles. We adults always enjoyed seeing how seriously the youngsters took their job, how slowly and tentatively they climbed the stairs to the altar and solemnly touched each candle, ever-so-lightly, until it caught flame.

After church school, we were preparing to enter the sanctuary when the minister approached us. Kevin and Eric had asked him if Danny could light the candles this week.

Concerned about the logistics of Danny navigating the stairs, the minister had tried to persuade them otherwise and had pointed out the obstacles. But my sons had insisted that Danny perform the honor, he said, and had assured him that they had figured out a plan. Wisely, the minister had given consent and left the situation in the boys' hands.

As the opening music began, I turned in my seat to see how my two unpredictable sons would make this miracle happen. Kevin and Eric stood behind the wheelchair, beaming from ear to ear. In front of them sat Danny, proudly and nervously holding the long brass rod that would set the candles blazing. Slowly walking to the music, the boys pushed the wheelchair down the aisle. Soon, all heads were turned to follow their progress. The entire congregation had just become aware of the challenge ahead: the series of steps Danny would have to climb to reach the altar.

As the wheelchair neared the altar, every breath in the room suspended. We had no idea how they were going to pull this off. Did they plan to carry that heavy wheelchair up those stairs? Would they try to pick him up and carry him? Was this fast becoming a disaster?

Kevin and Eric rolled Danny's chair to the foot of the steps and stopped. Every eye was riveted on the three boys and the wheelchair at the front of the church.

Slowly, and with a dignity beyond their years, Kevin and Eric ascended the stairs while Danny remained in his chair. Each boy grasped a candlestick and carried it back down the stairs. Reaching Danny's wheelchair, they leaned forward and offered the altar candles to their waiting friend.

Danny proudly raised the golden wand and gently lit each candle. Kevin and Eric carefully guarded the flames with cupped palms as they carried the candles back up the stairs and placed them back on the altar. Then they returned to Danny and rotated his chair to face the congregation. Slowly, they wheeled him back down the aisle.

Danny's face was a joyous thing to see. His grin blazed through the sanctuary and lit the very rafters of the church, sending a thrill through every heart. He was visibly elated and held the brass candle lighter as though it were a royal scepter. A soft glow seemed to surround the three boys as they walked to the rear of the church. I noticed it took a few minutes before the minister could trust his voice to begin the service.

I've often been proud of my sons, but seldom have I been so

touched. I had to blink a bit to see their smiling faces as they passed my pew on their way to the rear of the church. But then, my eyes weren't the only ones in the congregation blurred by tears from the pageant of love we had just witnessed.

~Marcy Goodfleisch
Chicken Soup for the Mother's Soul 2

The Greatest of These

My day began on a decidedly sour note when I saw my six-year-old wrestling with a limb of my azalea bush. By the time I got outside, he'd broken it. "Can I take this to school today?" he asked.

With a wave of my hand, I sent him off. I turned my back so he wouldn't see the tears gathering in my eyes. I loved that azalea bush. I touched the broken limb as if to say silently, "I'm sorry."

I wished I could have said that to my husband earlier, but I'd been angry. The washing machine had leaked on my brand-new linoleum. If he'd just taken the time to fix it the night before when I asked him instead of playing checkers with Jonathan. What were his priorities anyway? I was still mopping up the mess when Jonathan walked into the kitchen. "What's for breakfast, Mom?"

I opened the empty refrigerator. "Not cereal," I said, watching the sides of his mouth drop. "How about toast and jelly?" I smeared the toast with jelly and set it in front of him. Why was I so angry? I tossed my husband's dishes into the sudsy water.

It was days like this that made me want to quit. I just wanted to drive up to the mountains, hide in a cave, and never come out.

Somehow I managed to lug the wet clothes to the laundromat. I spent most of the day washing and drying clothes and thinking how love had disappeared from my life. Staring at the graffiti on the walls, I felt as wrung-out as the clothes left in the washers.

As I finished hanging up the last of my husband's shirts, I looked at the clock. 2:30. I was late. Jonathan's class let out at 2:15. I dumped the clothes in the back seat and hurriedly drove to the school.

I was out of breath by the time I knocked on the teacher's door and peered through the glass. With one finger, she motioned for me to wait. She said something to Jonathan and handed him and two other children crayons and a sheet of paper.

"What now?" I thought, as she rustled through the door and took me aside. "I want to talk to you about Jonathan," she said.

I prepared myself for the worst. Nothing would have surprised me.

"Did you know Jonathan brought flowers to school today?" she asked.

I nodded, thinking about my favorite bush and trying to hide the hurt in my eyes. I glanced at my son busily coloring a picture. His wavy hair was too long and flopped just beneath his brow. He brushed it away with the back of his hand. His eyes burst with blue as he admired his handiwork.

"Let me tell you about yesterday," the teacher insisted. "See that little girl?"

I watched the bright-eyed child laugh and point to a colorful picture taped to the wall. I nodded.

"Well, yesterday she was almost hysterical. Her mother and father are going through a nasty divorce. She told me she didn't want to live, she wished she could die. I watched that little girl bury her face in her hands and say loud enough for the class to hear, 'Nobody loves me.' I did all I could to console her, but it only seemed to make matters worse."

"I thought you wanted to talk to me about Jonathan," I said.

"I do," she said, touching the sleeve of my blouse. "Today your son walked straight over to that child. I watched him hand her some pretty pink flowers and whisper, 'I love you.'"

I felt my heart swell with pride for what my son had done. I smiled at the teacher. "Thank you," I said, reaching for Jonathan's hand, "you've made my day."

Later that evening, I began pulling weeds from around my lop-sided azalea bush. As my mind wandered back to the love Jonathan showed the little girl, a biblical verse came to me: "...now these three remain: faith, hope and love. But the greatest of these is love." While my son had put love into practice, I had only felt anger.

I heard the familiar squeak of my husband's brakes as he pulled into the drive. I snapped a small limb bristling with hot pink azaleas off the bush. I felt the seed of love that God planted in my family beginning to bloom once again in me. My husband's eyes widened in surprise as I handed him the flowers. "I love you," I said.

~Nanette Thorsen-Snipes
Chicken Soup for the Christian Family Soul

Lifted by Love

We never dreamed that Garrett would be anything other than a perfectly ordinary boy. The brown-haired, brown-eyed tornado that tore through our home seemed to have enough energy for a dozen boys! Every time we turned around, Garrett popped up, full of questions and ideas, and always on the move.

By the time he was seven, though, Garrett began to stumble and fall when he ran, and even sometimes when he was walking. His teachers noticed a change in his ability to keep up with his schoolwork, although he seemed to be as smart as ever. He got sick more easily and was always tired. We knew something was going on, but nothing could have prepared us for the shock of the doctors' diagnosis. Garrett's symptoms were due to a rare genetic syndrome called ataxia-telangiectasia (A-T), a disease that causes progressive neurological deterioration, immune deficiency and sometimes even cancer in children. There was no cure. Nothing we could do could take away this disease from our son. We dreaded the thought of standing by helplessly, watching him struggle a little more each day to speak, to walk, to do so many of the things we took for granted. Where could we turn for help? We felt alone and terrified at the obstacles we faced.

But Garrett was not alone.

Many other children were fighting the same battle—more than five hundred just in the United States. When we contacted the

National Organization to Treat A-T, we were told about a study being conducted at Children's Hospital of Philadelphia. They invited Garrett to participate in the experimental treatment at no cost to us other than the expense of our transportation. Johns Hopkins, in Baltimore, also had a research program for A-T and wanted Garrett to visit their clinical center for evaluation. This was both good news and bad. Our home in Portales, New Mexico, was a long way from Philadelphia and Baltimore, and Garrett would have to make five separate trips in a span of only a few months.

Like Garrett before his illness, I had always felt strong and independent. My husband worked hard to support us, and his income had always been adequate for our needs. Now, though, we had a challenge that exceeded anything we were prepared to face. We couldn't afford to fly our entire family to the East Coast even once! Philadelphia and Baltimore might as well have been on the moon. I called everyone—Social Security, welfare and other government organizations—trying to find out how we could get help with flights, meals, car rental and all the other prohibitive costs.

As many times as my husband and I worked through our budget, we couldn't squeeze out even a fraction of the money we needed. Our minds and hearts felt numb with the heartbreaking disappointment. We tried to pray, but our faith seemed to have grown as weak and frail as Garrett's thin little legs.

Again, God reminded us that we were not alone.

"Let's set up a fund for Garrett," my friend Tammy suggested. "We can write a story for the local newspaper and let the rest of the community know what's going on."

"Would they really print his story? And if they do, will anybody read it?" I asked with great skepticism. It had never occurred to me that other people in our town might be willing to help Garrett. I had always thought that this burden was ours alone to bear.

"Of course they will! And you just wait and see. I think you'll be surprised how much people care. Besides, what do we have to lose?"

A few days later, the newspaper printed the story and donations began to trickle into the bank. Little by little, the people in our community sent in enough to cover every one of the expenses—for the first trip. When we were ready to leave, we went to the bank and withdrew all the money.

"Thank you, Lord," I prayed. "At least we can make one trip to Philadelphia. That's better than not going at all. We'll take this journey one step at a time."

We returned home with a little better understanding of Garrett's illness, but no idea whether we would be able to continue the treatments. When we called the bank, though, we were amazed to find that the donations had continued to come in! By the time we needed to make arrangements for the second trip, we had just enough to pay all our expenses. Once again, we withdrew the entire amount.

The third and fourth months were the same. Our bank account filled up each time we had to make a trip, like the curse of oil of the widow of Zarephath in 1 Kings 17, whose handful of flour and little jar of oil never ran dry. We were even able to make the fifth trip to visit Johns Hopkins! Like Garrett, I've learned how much I need someone to lean on, too. I know better now than ever that God is always there for me. He has also taught all of us that we can lean on the love of others; they will answer His call and be there for us just when we need them most, lifted by love.

~Pat Dodson and Candy Gruner
Chicken Soup for the Christian Soul 2

A Child's Prayer

*O God, who givest unto all their food, make us thankful and
provide for all the needy, now and evermore.*
Amen.

Christian
Kids

Stories and Songs

I will open my mouth in a parable
I will utter dark sayings of old.
Things that we have heard and known,
that our fathers told us.
We will not hide them from their children,
but tell it to the coming generations.
~Psalm 78:1-4

Hezekiah

"Hezekiah is the biggest and most ornery muskie to ever make his home in Edinboro Lake," explained Grandpa Braley as he rowed us out onto the lake. "I hooked him once, maybe two years ago—back in 1949. Got him up to the boat, but my net was too small. When I tried to grab him by the gills, he jumped, shook loose and snapped the line. On his way back into the water, he somehow managed to put this scar on the back of my hand. Guess he didn't appreciate my effort to invite him to dinner as the guest of honor. Well, Robbie, this looks like a good spot. Let's drop anchor and start some serious fishing."

Grandpa's words filled my six-year-old mind with excitement about catching a fish that big, and also with fear about catching a fish that bites. "Why do you call him Hezekiah? And if I catch him, will he bite me?" I asked.

Grandpa, being an ordained Methodist minister, explained, "The biblical Hezekiah was a king who was dying, and God gave him another fifteen years to live. That muskie also had new life given to him the day he escaped my hook. That's why I named him after the former king of Judah. The way I figure it, old Hezekiah, king of the lake, was teaching me patience. Someday, if I keep trying, we will meet again. Hope it doesn't take fifteen years, though."

Grandpa went on to assure me that he wouldn't let any fish bite me. Armed with a tin can full of night crawlers and a bright red-and-white cork bobber, I threw my line into the smooth, blue-green water. As instructed, my eyes intently watched the bobber for any sign of movement. At first, my heart was beating with excitement, but after about the first half hour, I grew weary of the bobber's stillness in the water.

"Where are all the fish?" I whined.

"Patience, Robbie, patience," reassured Grandpa. "I'll pull up the anchor and we'll drift for a while. Let's see if that changes our luck."

This was how the rest of the day went. No matter how much we drifted or moved to different parts of the lake, no fish were biting. I was extremely discouraged and had thoughts of never fishing again. Finally, by late afternoon, Grandpa started rowing us back to the dock.

On the way back, he explained to me that even the greatest of fisherman have bad days. He told me the biblical story of a fisherman named Peter, who was having several bad days in a row. Being a man of little patience, Peter became angry and headed back to shore. His thoughts were to sell his boat and give up fishing forever. As the boat approached the shoreline, Peter noticed a stranger standing on shore, watching him. The stranger saw Peter's frustration and yelled out to him, "Throw your net out one more time."

Peter yelled back to the stranger, "No way, there's no fish this close to shore."

The stranger, undaunted, insisted. "Trust me, go ahead and cast your net."

Peter thought to himself, "This guy is crazy, I'll just have to show him there are no fish here." He then begrudgingly cast his net one more time. When he brought it back up, he could not believe his eyes. The net was jammed full of fish. "Thank you!" Peter shouted to the stranger. "You taught me a lesson in patience." The stranger turned out to be a man named Jesus.

Grandpa finished the story of Peter just as we pulled up to the dock. "Tell you what, Robbie, after I tie up, go to the back of the boat and throw your line in one more time just as Peter did," he instructed. "I need to get something and should be back in about ten minutes. There may be some pan fish hanging around the dock, so be patient."

I did as he said and resumed my vigil over the red and white bobber. It might have been only ten minutes, but it seemed like an hour before he returned. I never really paid much attention to what he was doing as he set his old camera on a tripod. While engrossed in my boredom and concentration on the bobber, he snapped a picture.

Just as Grandpa finished packing his camera, I saw the bobber move slightly. I awoke suddenly from my boredom. It moved a second time and then a third. I felt the tug on the line as the bobber disappeared below the water's surface. My eyes lit up and my body reacted with a quick jerk on the pole. I felt the weight of the great fish on the other end of the line. It felt huge, and I screamed with excitement, "Grandpa, it's Hezekiah! Come quick!"

Grandpa stepped into the boat and instructed me on the proper way to land a fish. As I pulled the mighty fish to the surface, Grandpa looked at me with a straight face and said in all seriousness, "Robbie, that is the biggest sunfish I've ever seen."

I was as proud as I could be of that sunfish, showing it off to Mom, Dad and everyone else back at the cottage. Grandpa taught me how to clean it and Grandma fried it up special for my supper. After eating, Grandpa told everyone of our adventures and how I hooked "Little Hezekiah" using my newfound fisherman's skills.

~Robert Bruce Riefstahl
Chicken Soup for the Fisherman's Soul

And the Answer Is...

A teacher affects eternity;
he can never tell where his influence stops.
~Henry Brooks Adams

When my sons were growing up, I enrolled them in vacation Bible school and I always signed up to teach. As they outgrew Bible school, I transferred my teaching skills to adult literacy programs. But when I heard the plea that more VBS teachers were needed, I called in and added my name to the roster. I certainly had the experience, and besides, it would be fun to be with children again. After I was assigned a class of eleven three-year-olds, I attended the appropriate workshops. I spent a week making elaborate lesson plans and constructing the visual props provided by the leader's book, incorporating the church's "Climbing Faith Mountain" theme.

The night before vacation Bible school began, I prayed, "Dear God, thank you for the opportunity to teach these little ones about you. With this prayer, I'm ready."

Well, I thought I was ready.

It had been many years since I'd stood in front of a group of little ones, so imagine my surprise to rediscover that they ran everywhere, leaping and laughing, brightly colored sandals slap-slapping against summer-tanned heels. With our combined efforts, my teen helper and I managed to corral their energies and herd them to the story mat.

We sat in a lopsided circle, busy hands folded and nestled in laps. Our first story-lesson up Faith Mountain was one of obedience. I told of God's request for Abraham to move his family and livestock to a new place. We stood and I led my group from one side of the room to the other, "baaing" and "mooing" in imitation of Abraham's sheep and cows as we trudged along.

I thought concrete examples would reinforce what I'd taught them, and mentally patted myself on the back.

We settled back into our circle. "Abraham had the faith to obey God's word," I said as I ended our story.

At the close of the morning, I asked, "Who had the faith to move his family and livestock?"

"God!" eleven cheerful voices shouted.

I smiled and shook my head no. "Abraham."

"Abraham," parroted the serious, elfin chorus.

Our story for the next day, "Joseph and His Many-Colored Coat," was about trust. I explained that when Joseph was taken from his family and found himself in prison, God still watched after and protected him.

At the end of the second morning, I gathered my charges and asked, "Who trusted and prayed for his safety and protection while he was away from his father and brothers?"

"God!" they sang loudly.

Again I shook my head. "Repeat after me," I said. "Joseph."

"Joseph." They were just a little out of unison.

Day three brought us a story-lesson of strength. "God told Joshua to lead the Israelites around the walls of Jericho and blow their trumpets, and the walls came tumbling down." We marched like little infantrymen around and around the mat. We stopped, opened our mouths wide and shouted out trumpetlike sounds, and then collapsed into a large heap onto the floor. Bodies rolled and legs kicked in jubilation.

I righted myself and studied each sweaty face. "Who was strong enough to make the walls of Jericho fall down?"

"God!" They shrieked and raised miniature fists above their heads.

I stood and retrieved the picture of the trembling walls. My finger singled out a man with a trumpet. "Joshua!" I said loudly.

Urchin faces lifted upward. "Joshua!"

For Thursday, I built an elaborate pallet, complete with a blanket and a little boy puppet, to help tell the story of Samuel. Squeals erupted and hands clapped as they watched the boy spring up and down to answer God's voice booming out Samuel's name.

"Samuel was a good listener." I narrowed my eyes and took in each stare. "God wants us all to be good listeners."

We ended yet another morning. I swallowed hard and ventured, "Who was a good listener this morning?"

"God!" Their voices bounced off the walls of the room.

My heart sank. "Sam-u-el," I said, enunciating each syllable.

Eleven pouty mouths formed the name "Sam-u-el."

On the final morning of vacation Bible school, I doubted that I'd taught my group anything as we assembled for our last story-lesson.

"God loves and cares for us so much that He sent His son Jesus to teach us about that love. And even though Jesus went to heaven, He'll be back one day." I paused and finished with a smile. "In the meantime, remember, God is the answer to our questions in life."

What? What was that I'd said? "God" is the answer? Hmmm. Maybe my three-year-olds hadn't been giving me the wrong answers all week after all.... Maybe I'd been asking the wrong questions.

I began anew. "Who did Abraham obey when he was asked to move?"

"God!" they yelled.

"Who did Joseph trust when he was in prison?"

"God!"

"Who gave Joshua the strength to make the walls of Jericho fall down?"

"God!"

"And who spoke to Samuel?"

"God!"

Finally, I said, "Jesus is the Son of—"

"God!" we said together.

The three-year-olds knew all along the response that the seasoned teacher had forgotten. Who is the answer to all our questions? "God!"

~Janice Alonso
Chicken Soup for the Christian Soul 2

A Mother Sings

Jill paused halfway down our front steps. She turned and said, "Mom, will you sing to me? Will you hold me and sing like you used to when I was a little girl?" Her husband and her two little stepdaughters stopped and looked back.

I always sang to my kids when they were young. Jill and her older brother shared a bedroom, and I knelt between them, holding one's hand and stroking the blond head of the other. I sang and crooned through "Dona Dona" and "Kumbaya." I swayed in rhythm to "Swing Low, Sweet Chariot." I never missed a verse of "Hush, Little Baby." I made up songs, too, a habit that drove my husband crazy. On nights when I was out, the kids begged, "Sing 'The Horse Broke the Fence,' Daddy," or "No, we want 'The Big Wheel' song." And they didn't mean "Proud Mary," which he might have managed, although he really couldn't carry a tune even when he knew the words.

But the kids and I always finished with "All Things Bright and Beautiful," as I watched their active bodies quiet and their eyes grow dreamy as they imagined the purple-headed mountains and ripe fruit in the garden of the old hymn. By the time I warbled my way through the refrain for the last time, one of them had usually twitched and fallen asleep.

As Jill grew from child to adult, it became apparent that she had inherited her father's trouble carrying a melody. She cuddles with her girls every night and she reads to them, but she just can't sing to them.

Recently, I babysat for our granddaughters. After I tucked them into our king-size bed, I sang "Dona Dona," "Kumbaya," and all the others. Hannah, the six-year-old, lay still as a stone, gazing at the ceiling. Four-year-old Brianna came forward onto her hands and knees, staring into my eyes from so close that her features blurred. In the dim light coming through the open door, I saw her lips parted, glistening. Trance-like, she held perfectly still, listening as if she wanted to inhale the songs directly from my mouth.

It was a few days later that Jill asked me to once again sing to her. She said, "The girls talked about your singing, Mom, and it brought back all the wonderful memories. I remember my cool pillow and your hand on my hair. I remember my nightgown with the sunbonnet dolls on it and the pink ice cream cone quilt you made. Sometimes I would wake up when you kissed me one last time."

That's when she turned and asked, "Mom, will you sing to me, again?"

Her husband stood beneath the street lamp with a child balanced on each hip. Her father and brothers stood behind me, illuminated by the porch light. She's very tall, this girl of mine. Standing on the step below me, she still had to stoop to put her head against my chest. I wrapped my fingers in her long hair, and she wound her arms around my waist.

"What shall I sing, Jill?" I asked.

"You know, Mom," she said, looking up and smiling.

"'All Things Bright and Beautiful'?"

"Of course." She snuggled closer. "All the verses."

I kissed the top of her head and began to sing.

Swallowing a lump in my throat and stroking her back, I continued through the verses. Off-key, she joined in.

She began to cry, and so did I, but the words still flowed from my mouth as my mind drifted back over the years. I remembered her birth, how ecstatic I was to have a daughter—what an easy child she was. I remembered how she loved to please others—and still does. This girl who married young and took on the daunting task of raising another woman's children is no longer under my wing. She's a young woman now, and I can't tuck the ice cream cone quilt around her shoulders each night. I can't protect her from pain, from hurt and from mature responsibility. I can't make growing up any easier for her.

Jill's tears soaked through my T-shirt that night and mine dropped onto her bowed head. She clung tightly and then looked up into my face.

"The purple-headed mountains. Don't forget the purple-headed mountains," she whispered, staring at me through the dim light, just as Brianna had a few nights earlier, drinking in the words, the memories, the song. Drinking in my love.

My voice cracked, and I could sing no more. We stood locked together on the stairs. I know the enormity of the task she's taken on is sometimes almost more than she can handle. I know how hard she's working to create a home.

Cradling her in maternal love, allowing her to remember falling asleep to a mother's singing, was the best I could offer my daughter this night. Jill squeezed me tightly and then turned toward her husband and her stepdaughters. Her dad hugged me as we watched her settle the girls into the back seat of their car—and then I heard the hymn again. I strained my ears, listening. Jill was still humming the refrain. Then Brianna's thin, little child's voice burbled from the open car window as they pulled away from the curb: "All things wise and wonderful, the Lord God made them all."

~Peggy Vincent
Chicken Soup to Inspire a Woman's Soul

Jesus Loves Me

Give what you have. To some it may be better than you dare think.
~Henry Wadsworth Longfellow

One day, a beautiful but very troubled little girl came through the door of my day nursery. From the very beginning, I became captivated by this child who had so little but needed so much. I was heartbroken that a four-year-old could suffer such heartache and pain. She was born in prison after her mom had used marijuana, crack and cocaine her entire pregnancy. The little girl was nonverbal and had very little control. I knew her progress would be a mighty battle.

Whenever somebody approached her, she became violent for long periods and ended up in a fetal position on the floor crying out. I found myself praying for her day in and day out.

As months rolled on, I began to bond with this child that no one wanted. She and I worked very hard, taking one step forward and four steps back. Daily, we sat in the big rocking chair in my office, swaying back and forth, back and forth. During our rocking time, I sang "Jesus Loves Me." She always settled down and became very still at the melody. Though she never spoke, peace seemed to fill her face as she listened to the song.

One day after a very long battle, I held my special girl to again calm her fears and pain. In silence we rocked back and forth and back and forth, back and forth. Then she looked at me with tear-filled eyes and spoke a complete sentence for the first time, "Sing to me about that Man who loves me."

Blinking back tears, I knew the battle had been won.

~Alicia Hill
Chicken Soup for the Caregiver's Soul

12

Hidden Wings

Angels shine from without because
their spirits are lit from within by the light of God.
~ The Angels' Little Instruction Book
by Eileen Elias Freeman

Daddy wasn't just an ordinary man. He was my daddy, a special kind of person who could charm the whiskers off a cat with a back rub or cajole the birds right out of a tree with a handful of seed. In my mind, he could do anything, from delivering moonshine to resurrecting a doll from decay.

I always knew when Daddy had been reading the Bible because he would burst forth in song, belting out the lyrics with gusto as he melded two songs — "When They Ring Those Golden Bells for You and Me" and "Oh Lordy, I'll Fly Away" together into one harmonious array. He sang those two songs until tears streamed down his cheeks. With a powerful shout of "Hallelujah!" he'd slap his knee and say, "Praise the Lord for hidden wings."

One morning, while Daddy was at work, I found a crippled cardinal lying in our backyard near our old concrete duck pond. Its wing was broken, and one foot was withered and drawn close to its beautiful red breastplate. I ran to the house screaming for Mother to get a bandage to wrap the wing and cried pitifully as I looked at the glorious bird writhing in such painful distress. Mother took the bird and carefully wrapped the wing in an old dishtowel. Placing the bird gently inside a cigar box, she said, "We'll just have to wait and see if the bird wants to mend its wing." I was five years old and didn't understand Mother's profound wisdom. I wanted so desperately to see the bird fly again. I said, "Just wait till Daddy gets home; he can fix it!"

That evening, when Daddy came home from a long day's work on the railroad, I met him as he came through our front gate. "Daddy, Daddy, you gotta fix 'im!" Daddy was grungy with caked-on, greasy soot from wrestling with massive steel wheels and rails and was exhausted from miles of walking. Somehow he managed to delay his rest to soothe my fears.

Daddy lifted the bird and said, "Honey, he's already been fixed. His hidden wings have taken him high into the heavens. Jesus has a special place just for him. You just weren't able to see the wings unfolding, but the little bird released a hidden spirit and soared high into the sky." I stood there in silence as Daddy explained, "Everybody has hidden wings. You just can't see them right now. The wings only unfurl when Jesus rings his golden bell."

I stood there in complete confusion when Daddy reached over and touched me on the back. "This is the place where the wings are lying, right here, between the shoulders. It's very close to the heart, and when it's time to go see Jesus, the love you have in your heart awakens the spirit. The spirit is the wings. One of these days, when you are older, you will understand what I have told you." Although I did not understand, I was content with his explanation.

As I grew older and watched my parents age gracefully, Daddy's words resounded with a thunderous roar. It was not until my mother passed away that I fully understood the magnitude of hidden wings or the wisdom of two wonderful souls. When Mother died, a peaceful grace consumed her frail little body. The years faded from her face to reveal a beautiful glow, almost stating "perfection has arrived." It was as though I could feel her spirit swirl around me, dancing with excitement. She was at peace and, strange as it might seem, so was I.

Several years later, Daddy went to a nursing home. Dementia and diabetes had taken hold of him, and he needed around-the-clock care, which I could not provide. I visited him every day, and we shared many stories of his childhood and one particular story about hidden wings. Early one Sunday morning, as I approached Daddy's room, the nurse told me that he was not responding and warned me what to expect when I went inside. As I neared his bed, I heard the strangest thing. Down the hallway, inside a dining room, a quartet broke forth in gospel songs, transposing one with another. The harmony was divine and surely sent by God. The joyous sounds drifted closer and closer until it draped the two of us with solid words: "When they ring those golden bells for you and me, I'll fly away, oh glory, I'll fly away in the morning, when I die, hallelujah, by and by, I'll fly away."

As I looked at Daddy, a single tear dropped from his steel gray eyes. Then, as day turned into night, Daddy was gone. I knew immediately what Daddy had told me was true. His hidden wings had unfurled, and his spirit soared into the heavens. When I finally left his room that day, I slapped my knee and said, "Hallelujah, praise the Lord for hidden wings."

~Joyce L. Rapier
Chicken Soup for the Father & Daughter Soul

A Child's Prayer

Thank you, Father, for bread and meat.
Thank you for the friends we meet.
Thank you for our Moms and Dads.
Thank you for the love we have.
Thank you for our work and play.
Thank you for another day.
In Jesus' name.
Amen.

Christian Kids

Favorite Kid Quotes

*One of the virtues of being very young is that
you don't let the facts get in the way of your imagination.*
~Sam Levenson

13

Who's Going to Stop Me?

Six-year-old Angie and her four-year-old brother, Joel, were sitting together in church. Joel giggled, sang and talked out loud. Finally, his big sister had had enough. "You're not supposed to talk out loud in church."

"Why? Who's going to stop me?" Joel asked.

Angie pointed to the back of the church and said, "See those two men standing by the door? They're hushers."

~Richard Lederer
Chicken Soup for the Christian Family Soul

14

Gold, Common Sense and Fur

Above all else: go out with a sense of humor.
It is needed armor. Joy in one's heart and some laughter on one's lips
is a sign that the person down deep has a pretty good grasp of life.
~Hugh Sidey

My husband and I had been happily (most of the time) married for five years but hadn't been blessed with a baby. I decided to do some serious praying and promised God that if he would give us a child, I would be a perfect mother, love it with all my heart and raise it with his word as my guide.

God answered my prayers and blessed us with a son. The next year God blessed us with another son. The following year, he blessed us with yet another son. The year after that we were blessed with a daughter.

My husband thought we'd been blessed right into poverty. We now had four children, and the oldest was only four years old.

I learned never to ask God for anything unless I meant it. As a minister once told me, "If you pray for rain, make sure you carry an umbrella."

I began reading a few verses of the Bible to the children each day as they lay in their cribs. I was off to a good start. God had entrusted me with four children and I didn't want to disappoint him.

I tried to be patient the day the children smashed two dozen eggs on the kitchen floor searching for baby chicks. I tried to be understanding when they started a hotel for homeless frogs in the spare bedroom, although it took me nearly two hours to catch all twenty-three frogs.

When my daughter poured ketchup all over herself and rolled up in a blanket to see how it felt to be a hot dog, I tried to see the humor rather than the mess.

In spite of changing over twenty-five thousand diapers, never eating a hot meal and never sleeping for more than thirty minutes at a time, I still thank God daily for my children.

While I couldn't keep my promise to be a perfect mother—I didn't even come close—I did keep my promise to raise them in the Word of God.

I knew I was missing the mark just a little when I told my daughter we were going to church to worship God, and she wanted to bring a bar of soap along to "wash up" Jesus, too.

Something was lost in the translation when I explained that God gave us everlasting life, and my son thought it was generous of God to give us his "last wife."

My proudest moment came during the children's Christmas pageant. My daughter was playing Mary, two of my sons were shepherds and my youngest son was a wise man. This was their moment to shine.

My five-year-old shepherd had practiced his line, "We found the babe wrapped in swaddling clothes." But he was nervous and said, "The baby was wrapped in wrinkled clothes."

My four-year-old "Mary" said, "That's not 'wrinkled clothes,' silly. That's dirty, rotten clothes."

A wrestling match broke out between Mary and the shepherd and was stopped by an angel, who bent her halo and lost her left wing.

I slouched a little lower in my seat when Mary dropped the

doll representing Baby Jesus, and it bounced down the aisle crying, "Mama-mama." Mary grabbed the doll, wrapped it back up and held it tightly as the wise men arrived.

My other son stepped forward wearing a bathrobe and a paper crown, knelt at the manger and announced, "We are the three wise men, and we are bringing gifts of gold, common sense and fur."

The congregation dissolved into laughter, and the pageant got a standing ovation.

"I've never enjoyed a Christmas program as much as this one," Father Brian laughed, wiping tears from his eyes. "For the rest of my life, I'll never hear the Christmas story without thinking of gold, common sense and fur."

"My children are my pride and my joy and my greatest blessing," I said as I dug through my purse for an aspirin.

~Linda Stafford
Chicken Soup for the Soul Christmas Treasury

Finger Play

F our-year-old Kayla nestled on Opa's lap while he read their favorite Dr. Seuss book—again. As she fought sleep, her dimpled fingers plucked idly at the roadmap of veins ribbing the backs of her grandpa's hands. First one, then another, she pulled each dark blue vein into a ridge and watched it melt back down.

Suddenly, she leaned forward for a closer look. Opa paused to watch as she inspected his weathered skin and compared it to her own baby-plump pink hand, touching first one, then the other. Satisfied at last, Kayla looked up.

"I think God must've practiced on you first, Opa," she said. "'Cause he did much better making me!"

~Carol McAdoo Rehme
Chicken Soup for the Grandparent's Soul

Be Slow to Anchor

Children are the bridge to heaven.
~Persian Proverb

Shortly after my daughter Nicole was born, father-daughter fishing trips became a regular occurrence. We would most often fish from my little aluminum boat at a small, shallow lake near our house. By age three, Nicole had an uncanny ability to sit in our boat for long periods, certain that a fish would bite at any moment.

Our family has also always been actively involved with our local church. One Sunday when we went to pick up our daughter from her Sunday school class, the teacher asked if we could meet with her a moment after all the parents had picked up their children.

Every parent knows that instant of dread associated with wondering what your three-year-old may have said to someone. We mustered up our courage and waited.

Finally, alone with her teacher, the truth came out. The week's memory verse was James 1:19, "Be slow to anger." When the teacher asked the children if anyone could explain what that passage meant, Nicole's hand shot up immediately.

"It means that when you go fishing, you crawl to the front of the boat and put the front anger down very slowly," Nicole said. "Then you crawl to the back of the boat and put the back anger down very slowly. That way, you don't make a splash and scare the fish away."

~Dan DeVries
Chicken Soup for the Father & Daughter Soul

Do You Disciple?

After teaching a lesson to my kindergarten class on Jesus and his disciples, I was feeling quite proud. It was a model lesson, an A, and included a game, a song and a story.

At the conclusion of the lesson, I opened the discussion to questions. With pride, I looked out at my students' wildly waving arms. My lesson was obviously a success. Teaching seemed so rewarding. I would now let them shower me with this new knowledge that I had so skillfully imparted to them.

I called on Brittney to respond. Since her arm was waving more frantically than the rest, surely her observation would be that much more brilliant. "Brittney, what do you have to say about Jesus and his disciples?" I asked eagerly.

"Well," she began, with true kindergarten confidence, "I just wanted you to know that I know a lot about disciples 'cause at my house we disciple everything. We have a special disciple can for plastic, a special disciple can for glass, and a special disciple can for paper. My mom says it's how we save the earth."

I paused, took a deep breath and said, "Let's get ready for lunch."

~Christine Pisera Naman
A 5th Portion of Chicken Soup for the Soul

You Better Watch Out!

If you listen carefully to children you will have plenty about which to laugh.
~Steve Allen

The holidays were fast approaching. Many of the homes in our neighborhood were decorated with lights, snowmen and reindeer. It was a real treat to drive around with my two-year-old daughter and hear the oohs and ahhs as she took it all in.

Kendall was a very precocious child, talking early and with great expression and drama. As she was very apt to repeat excerpts from every adult conversation she overheard, it became obvious that we needed to watch what was said around her.

It was a shock to me one day as Kendall dropped her toy and said "Jesus Christ." My first instinct was to reprimand her, then I realized she was just repeating words she had heard me say in frustration.

"You can't say that, Kendall. It's not nice."

"You say it, Mom. What do I get to say?"

"Mommy shouldn't say it either, so let's say 'darn it' instead," I suggested.

That seemed to pacify her and the holidays were now rid of any unexpected and embarrassing outbursts of swearing in front of family or friends.

A few days later, my mother called and asked if I would bring Kendall over for lunch so she could show off her granddaughter to her friends. On the way to my mom's house, we passed a beautiful manger scene on the center divider of the road. Never having seen anything like it, Kendall asked what it was. She was fascinated and seemed to enjoy the story when I explained it to her.

When we reached Grandma's, she couldn't wait to get in the house and tell everyone what she had just seen. The door opened and she ran in. Out of breath and excited, she told everyone how she had just seen Joseph, Mary and the Baby "Darn it" in the manger.

~Kristine Byron
Chicken Soup for the Soul Christmas Treasury

The Debut

Children are likely to live up to what you believe of them.
~Lady Bird Johnson

"Mom, where's the roll of butcher paper?" JoAnn asked as she rummaged in the kitchen drawer for scissors and tape. Off she trotted down the hall, clasping the items.

Gathered for our family Christmas party, all three generations had finished eating. Now, the little cousins eagerly left parents and grandparents behind to begin preparations for the annual nativity pageant. Sequestered in the far recesses of the house, the youngsters plotted behind closed doors.

Grateful for peace and quiet, we adults basked in the festive glow of the fire, nibbled remnants of our delicious dinner and continued chatting. We felt no need to hurry our budding geniuses, tickled that they found delight in planning this project together.

An occasional burst of dialogue erupted through the open door as first one then another child was dispatched on a crucial errand. A jar of craft paint, then a wide paintbrush disappeared into their inner sanctum. Intense forays commenced throughout the house as armloads of towels, bathrobes, scarves, bed sheets, belts and jewelry joined their stash. Giggles and whispers intensified as their conspiracy continued.

We knew the project must be coming together when they mounted an intense search for bobby pins, large safety pins, paper clips, even clothespins—anything to hold costumes and props in place. Everyone's anticipation heightened as the cast and crew finished their preparations.

When the designated spokesperson called for our attention, a hush fell over the room.

Two stagehands wrestled a long, butcher-paper poster and, with copious lengths of tape, secured it to the wall. Emblazoned in bright paint it read: "Bethlehem Memorial Hospital."

The makeshift stage became a busy reception area of the hospital. One bossy cousin greeted newcomers, summoned aides and kept employees scurrying. Instead of halos, "nurse-angels" wore folded-paper caps with red painted crosses. They assessed each case, wielding their make-believe stethoscopes and thermometers before sending patients off to imaginary treatments.

Mary, endowed with a plump throw pillow, entered, leaning on Joseph's sturdy arm for support. Rejected by the insensitive innkeeper, they found a warm welcome at Bethlehem Memorial where one escort whisked Mary off to delivery and another led Joseph to the waiting room.

Joseph paced; he wrung his hands; he nodded off while shuffling through old magazines. He begged for the latest news on Mary's condition. At proper intervals, a nurse appeared with an encouraging, "It won't be long now."

After our young thespians had milked the scene dry, unseen hands shoved the last performer onto the stage.

There stood Connie Beth, the youngest nurse-angel in the troupe. Her scrap of angel robe in disarray, her nurse cap askew, she inched toward Joseph. Having outgrown her role as babe-in-the-manger, this year — oh, joy — she had a speaking part.

Suddenly aware of her audience, Connie Beth froze. She ducked her head, lowered her eyes and studied the floor. Her tongue probed the inside of her cheek and lower lip. A tiny finger crept toward her mouth. The toe of her little tennis shoe bore into the carpet fibers.

Would stage fright be her undoing?

Offstage, a loud whisper shattered the silence. "Tell Joseph about the baby!"

Connie's head lifted. Her countenance brightened. Resolve replaced fear.

She hesitated, searching for the right words. Taking a deep breath, she stood before Joseph and quietly delivered her joyous message:

"It's a girl!"

~Mary Kerr Danielson
Chicken Soup for the Soul The Book of Christmas Virtues

Step, Step, Roar

The most wasted of all days is one without laughter.
~e.e. cummings

A little boy walked down the aisle at a wedding. As he made his way to the front, he would take two steps, then stop and turn to the crowd, alternating between the bride's side and the groom's side. While facing the crowd, he would put his hands up like claws and roar. And so it went—step, step, ROAR, step, step, ROAR—all the way down the aisle.

As you can imagine, the crowd was near tears from laughing so hard by the time he reached the pulpit. The little boy, however, was getting more and more distressed from all the laughing, and he was near tears by the time he reached the pulpit.

When asked what he was doing, the child sniffed back his tears and said, "I was being the ring bear."

~Richard Lederer
Chicken Soup for the Christian Family Soul

The Moses Connection

Mirth is God's medicine. Everybody ought to bathe in it.
~Henry Ward Beecher

W hen my children were in kindergarten and first grade, my husband and I owned and operated a family-type restaurant in a beach resort town.

Every weekend it was hectic, as vacationers descended upon the town to enjoy their "fun in the sun," go out for an evening meal and enjoy the amusements and activities along the boardwalk.

During the busy times, my mother would come down from the city by train to babysit my children, allowing me to work.

My mother's petite stature and pure white hair made her look quite a bit older than her chronological age.

But needless to say she was a wonder with the children.

Grandma Sissy, as my two sons called her, would arrive after work on Friday evening and leave Sunday evening.

Every Sunday morning, before our business opened, we'd all head to church.

More times then not, because of the summer crowds, we'd have to sit in two pews, usually one behind the other.

One morning in particular, when my husband, my five-year-old son and I sat in the row directly behind her and our other son, we noticed Andy seemed unusually fascinated with her hair.

He kept caressing it.

Finally, after a few minutes he turned to us and asked in a loud voice, "Is Grandma Sissy Moses?"

Before I could respond in any way, several nearby parishioners smiled; a few even giggled.

Totally unaware of the stir he caused, our son continued. "I bet she is," he declared. "She's got the same long, white hair." He gently patted it once again.

I smiled and whispered, "No, she's not Moses."

"Well," he continued. "Grandma looks just like the picture in Sunday School."

More smiles from those unsuspecting listeners. Andy grew silent.

I assumed my answer satisfied his curiosity.

Several minutes passed then we heard, "Grandma, are you Moses' mother?"

No one in close proximity, including Grandma Sissy, could hold in the laughter.

I quickly tried to explain the timeline, but Andy wouldn't have it.

He didn't give up.

He countered with, "Well, is she his grandmother?"

By now, laughter being highly contagious in the most unlikely of places, had spread to more folks than needed.

It could have been called a small commotion.

I noticed the priest stretching his head above the congregation trying to locate and identify the disruption and could see several people on the other side of the aisle looking in our direction.

Within a few seconds one of the ushers whisked past us and made his way to the pulpit.

"Oh boy," I thought, "we're going to be asked to leave." But to my surprise, the priest smiled and addressed his audience.

"I've just been informed that one of our very young parishioners believes his grandmother is related to Moses. Will our special guest please rise and satisfy our curiosity?"

Grandma Sissy stood.

The entire assemblage broke into laughter and applauded.

"See, I was right," said Andy. "Everyone else thinks so, too."

~Helen Colella
Chicken Soup for the Grandparent's Soul

A Child's Prayer

O welcome, little Christmas Guest,
Dear Jesus, from above;
Upon Thy face, so pure and mild,
We see God's smile of love.
Amen.

Christian Kids

This I Pray

*Prayers are heard in heaven in proportion to our faith.
Little faith gets very great mercies,
but great faith still greater.*
~Spurgeon

22

The Native

When the world says, "Give up,"
Hope whispers, "Try it one more time."
~Author Unknown

"Grandpa and I are going fishing," my father called on his way out the door.

I jumped up from the cabin floor and grabbed my red plastic fishing pole. "Can I come too?"

"I'll take you tomorrow, sweetheart." He headed out the door.

I trudged to the kitchen where my mother and grandmother were washing dishes. "It's not fair. I want to go fishing."

"When Daddy takes you fishing, he has to spend all his time making sure you don't drown," my mother said. "Let him fish with Grandpa today. He'll take you tomorrow."

"I won't fall in. I'm not a baby."

"Lisa, you're only six years old."

"Why don't you catch toads?" my grandmother asked.

I scowled and said, "I already did that."

"Then go fish behind the cabin." She held out a cup of night crawlers she retrieved from the refrigerator.

The creek my father and grandfather fished, across the road from our cabin in the Allegheny National Forest, was deep and wide, more like a river. Behind our cabin, a tiny stream ran under the road and into the bigger creek.

"But I want to fish in the big creek with Daddy and Grandpa."

"It's the little creek or nothing," my grandmother said.

As I left the kitchen, my mother said in a low voice, "Mom, there aren't any fish in that creek."

"I know that," my grandmother said. "But she doesn't."

I ignored them. My grandmother didn't know everything. I'd show her.

An hour later, I wondered if my grandmother knew more than I'd thought. My first night crawler still dangled on the hook. All I'd caught were crayfish.

Just as I decided to go hunt more toads, my line jerked really hard. I yanked the pole to set the hook like my father had taught me. The hook flew out of the water, empty. Something had taken my bait, and it wasn't a crayfish.

I lost two more worms without a glimpse of what took them. I threaded another worm onto my hook and cast into the little pool in the stream.

After a long time, the line jerked again. I wrenched the pole back and cranked the reel, hands shaking. Whatever it was, it was still on the line and fighting.

I wound the reel furiously until my sinker rose from the water. Right behind came a fish, flopping and twisting at the end of my line, belly gleaming silver. Before I could swing the pole over solid ground, the fish jerked and disappeared with a splash. I'd lost it. Determined, I jabbed the hook through another piece of worm and dropped my line.

My mother called, but I didn't answer. That fish could bite again at any moment.

She crashed through the brush. "Lisa Ann, I know you heard me. Come change your clothes."

"Shhh," I whispered. "There's a big fish in here. How am I supposed to catch it with you making so much noise?"

She narrowed her eyes and whispered back, "It's time to go to Mass."

I argued, but my mother said if there was a fish in that creek, it would still be there when I got back from church.

My father and grandfather were back; they hadn't caught anything.

"I almost did," I said, "but I lost it."

My grandfather raised his eyebrows. "In that little creek? Must have been a minnow."

"Nuh-uh. A big fish. I'm going to catch it."

He laughed. "That's a fish story if I ever heard one."

All through Saturday evening Mass, I prayed to catch that fish. My mother always told me not to pray for selfish things, like a new bike. I was only supposed to ask God to do something important, like make sick people well.

My mother would think praying to catch a fish was wrong, but I was sure God understood. This wasn't just about a fish. First I'd been treated like a baby, and then I'd been laughed at. I needed to catch that fish.

When we returned to the cabin, I refused to eat supper. My mother said I had to be back by dark, and that wasn't far off. "I'll eat later," I promised, running out the door.

For the longest time, I sat on a rock next to the creek and waited for a bite. Dusk fell. Maybe the fish had swum farther down the creek. I'd never catch him, and no one would ever believe he existed.

Finally he nibbled. In my excitement, I yanked too soon, and the line came up empty. I fumbled in the dark for bait.

I felt another tug and counted to three. When I jerked the rod, the weight and force of the fish dragged against it.

I reeled and he fought, just like last time. But this time, instead of lifting him straight up out of the water, I ran up the bank of the creek, rod over my shoulder.

The fish — my fish — skimmed out of the water and up the bank behind me. Only when I was well away from the creek did I lift him from the ground.

I didn't know how to take a fish off a hook. My dad always did that. So I set off for the cabin with the fish still flopping on the line.

My father looked up from a magazine when I walked through the door. "Holy cow, you caught a fish."

My grandfather's mouth dropped open. "I don't believe it. That's a brook trout—a native."

I grinned. "I told you it was really big."

"We'd better make sure it's legal," my father said.

My heart sank. The fish looked huge to me. Now it might not even be big enough to keep. My accomplishment seemed to dwindle with the size of the fish.

My father got his tackle box with inch marks on the lid. I stood behind him and my grandfather, craning for a peek while they measured.

Seven inches, I prayed. Let it be seven inches.

"Six and three-quarters," my father said.

My grandfather bent over the tackle box. "Tail's kind of curled up. Flatten it out."

I waited in silence, barely breathing. For all my insistence about not being a baby, I felt like crying.

My grandfather turned, fish in his hands. "Seven inches," he said, with a wink. "I'll cook it for your dinner."

He did, and to this day I've never eaten a better meal.

~Lisa Wood Curry
Chicken Soup for the Fisherman's Soul

23

Grandma's Prayers

I know no blessing so small as to be responsibly expected without prayer,
nor any so great but may be attained by it.
~Robert South

I t was a very hot July evening in Illinois, and our family was enjoying ice cream on the porch together. I was only eight years old, and my father was teasing me when I jumped backwards off the railing and caught my leg on the porch step. The deep cut required stitches and a trip to the hospital.

My doctor was out boating, and since it was 1947 and there were no cell phones or other means of communication, we had a three-hour wait in the emergency room. Finally, he arrived and began stitching with my mother's help. With my leg fully bandaged, I was sent home to recover. By Friday, something was terribly wrong. My temperature climbed to 103, and a quick call to the doctor revealed I had gangrene. On Sunday morning I had my second dose of antibiotics, but by afternoon I had a violent reaction, leaving me with a very high fever, delirious and completely covered with hives.

The doctor met us at his office and, after a brief exam, looked very grim. Taking my parents into the other room I heard him say there was nothing more he could do and no other drugs available for him to use. He further informed them that I had not received enough penicillin to fight the gangrene that had already eaten away the stitches, leaving a gaping hole in my leg. The only way to save my life was to amputate my leg, and he immediately scheduled surgery for the following morning.

Needless to say, all of us were in shock. No one wanted to face this. My father was especially devastated and called for the church members to come over and pray. Even though I was burning up with a fever, in pain, itching and delirious, I cried out, "I just want Grandma to come and anoint me with oil and pray for me! I know if she prays everything will be just fine."

Grandma and Grandpa Ozee lived just around the corner from us, and I spent many hours at their house. Grandma lived what she believed, and I had absolute confidence that her prayer on my behalf would certainly touch the heart of God. Whenever I visited her at 9:30 in the morning, I always found her sitting in her rocking chair with her Bible in her lap. At 10:30, I knew she would be on her knees in prayer. I often sat quietly as she shared the Bible with me. I watched as she prepared meals for the transients who rode the box-cars into our town and somehow knew their way to her door. While she cooked, they were required to read a chapter in the Bible before they could eat. While they were eating, she would gently present the salvation message and they always left with a prayer and a New Testament. I have no idea what happened to any of them, but I am confident many left knowing they had met a very special lady who not only gave them physical food but "living water" and hope for a better life.

I knew Grandma prayed for everything from a sick parakeet to the terminally ill. I remember being amused when some of the ladies from the church came to her house complaining about the church problems and the preacher. Very few words had been spoken when Grandma had them on their knees and praying for the preacher and all the problems involved. She had great faith and believed God answered prayers. She taught me the Lord was faithful and interested in even the smallest details of life.

Grandma never missed an opportunity to take any situation and turn it into a learning session. I vividly remember the time we visited the old, rickety, smelly outhouse at Great-Grandma's farm. There, in that most unlikely place, was one beautiful flower blooming through a crack in the floor. Grandma quickly explained that no matter how bad the situation or how dark and dismal things might look, there was always hope. Just as the flower could bloom in the most difficult circumstances, so could we, because God was faithful and could make something beautiful from the ashes of our lives.

That is why I was calling for my grandma in my hour of need. Soon she appeared at my door with the bottle of anointing oil in her hands. I had no doubt God would hear her simple prayer for my healing and grant her request for a miracle to save my leg. When Grandma finished praying, I knew I had been healed, and I fell into a beautiful, peaceful sleep, not at all worried about tomorrow. I had a deep abiding peace that my life would be spared and I would always walk on two legs.

The next morning at the doctor's office, my parents anxiously waited while the doctor unwrapped the bandage. All eyes were on him as he stood in obvious amazement. Slowly he shook his head and said, "I have seen a miracle. There is no way the small dose of penicillin could have done this. There had to be a power higher than me working on this leg."

The surgery was cancelled, my leg re-bandaged, and I went home to recover without need for further antibiotics.

Today, I still have the ugly scar to remind me of this very traumatic time in my life. But I also still have two legs, which reminds me of God's healing power, a praying grandma, and that flowers bloom in the most difficult circumstances.

~Sharon Ozee Siweck
Chicken Soup for the Grandma's Soul

24

The Egg

*God enters by a private door
into each individual.*
~Ralph Waldo Emerson

It was a tense day around our home. That morning, when my daughters, Becky and Lisa, returned from an overnight outing with their Sunday school class, they discovered that the egg their pair of pigeons had been sitting on was missing. A quick check around the outside of the cage had revealed pieces of the egg—someone had broken it and tried to hide it.

It didn't take a detective to guess that the culprit was four-year-old Hailey. The pigeons had fascinated her. She hadn't realized that the egg had been a developing baby bird. To her it was just a smaller version of what I cracked and cooked every day.

That night, Hailey approached her sister Becky. "I'm sorry, Becky," she said. "I prayed to God tonight and asked Him to bring you another egg. I told Him I wouldn't touch it this time."

"Yeah, right," Becky quietly responded as she turned and headed to her room. She was not ready to forgive.

In a few moments Becky was back. "Momma, you're not going to believe this." She was speaking to me but staring at Hailey. "There's an egg in the cage. It wasn't there before." She couldn't say aloud the thought that was racing through her mind.

But Hailey did. "Becky, I told you. I prayed to God, and God laid an egg."

~Dorothy M. Hill
Chicken Soup for the Christian Woman's Soul

25

A Child's Prayer

"**D**on't you remember me, Nurse?"

When people ask me if I remember them, I get a sinking feeling in my stomach. This was no exception. I was new to that particular school district, but I'd been all over Amsterdam doing school nursing as well as public health and infant childcare. How was I to remember all those mothers over the years?

I must have shown my embarrassment at not recognizing this mother. She chuckled before she said: "I don't blame you, Nurse, for it was so long ago that we met. You were still a student nurse working in the barracks with the diphtheria patients, and you nursed my son, Henk, then only five years old."

"Yes, oh yes. I remember my little Henky." He'd been such a lovable little boy, but so very sick when he came from the holiday camp. He'd been homesick and sad, being so far away from home.

My training school hospital was close to the seaside and we often treated children from these camps. That was before the war. Yes, I remembered Henky, and even his mother... only too well.

His files had said that he was Roman Catholic, so that night I prayed with him before and after supper and again just before I tucked him in for the night. I slept in the barracks, too, and my bedroom window looked out on the children in the glass cubicles. He was only one of ten patients, one I never forgot. His throat was very sore; therefore, I didn't think too much of it that he didn't pray with me or say the responses. Nevertheless, I kept on praying with him for several days. One day, he began to talk. But even though he folded his little hands and closed his eyes devoutly when I told him that we were going to pray, he never prayed with me.

One day I asked him: "Come on, Henky, pray with me; you know how, don't you?"

His big blue eyes looked up at me earnestly, and he only shrugged. I thought then that he'd forgotten about prayer, since he was in strange surroundings and it was not a Christian camp. One had to keep reminding the children; otherwise they would forget to pray, I'd thought.

From then on, Henky prayed with me—haltingly at first. But soon he was most eager to pray. Before long he was leading me in the Lord's Prayer and soon he was proud to say all the prayers by himself.

Travel was expensive, and it was difficult for the parents to visit. One day his mother came for a visit. She could not come in and had to talk to Henky through the window on the veranda. They shouted back and forth most cheerfully, and I smiled to myself when I heard Henky boast about his prayers. He was indeed a religious boy, never forgetting his prayers—even at naptime. It was always a moving moment when I saw his little hands folded and his eyes closed as he knelt beside his bed. I hoped his mother would stay to see him at his prayers.

Suddenly an angry knocking at the door startled me. I, too, was in quarantine, so I could only talk to the visitors from a distance. It was Henky's mother. Her eyes flashed as she snapped: "Who told you to teach Henky to pray?"

It was obvious that she objected to prayer—and strongly. "But he is Christian," I said lamely. "It is on his files."

She snorted angrily: "That's his father, of course. He filled in the forms and he had to write that down even though he never goes to church or prays."

I wanted to comfort her and said timidly: "A little prayer never did any harm."

"No, of course not," she agreed hesitantly. Then with a rueful smile she added: "That'll put him to shame when Henky comes home with prayers of his own." She shrugged and said almost sadly: "It won't last though; Henky's too small to keep it up. And no one will encourage him — certainly not his father. As for me...." She turned around in mid-sentence and stomped off.

She hadn't told me to stop praying, and so Henky and I cheerfully went on praying and singing the religious songs. My parents prayed and sang for every reason or season. It was part of our life. Henky loved to sing and pray, and soon he knew my whole repertoire.

When his parents came to take him home, he cried — much to their amazement. Yes, I remembered Henky.

All that flashed through my mind as I looked at the woman before me. Eleven years had gone by. I had often thought of Henky, but only as the five-year-old.

"How is Henky?" I asked eagerly.

His mother laughed. "You should see him. Thin and tall — a marvelous boy. Everybody loves him. He always talks about you."

She put a hand on my arm and said earnestly: "You did something quite wonderful when you gave Henk religion."

I wanted to protest that I had done very little in the six weeks he was with me. But she was so excited, she gave me no time to speak. She had come to see me to tell her story and was bursting to share it.

I listened in amazement as she continued. "You know, I never expected Henky's prayers to last. But he kept up and taught his little sisters to pray as well. He wouldn't eat or go to sleep without his prayers. By that time, my husband felt that he should go to a Christian school and the girls as well. Soon we both joined the children when they prayed.

"Then the war came, and we needed prayer to give sense to our lives and our suffering. We prayed and sang together as Henky taught us day after day.

"Needless to say, we all joined the church and were strengthened in our most difficult times. God has been good to us. He must have sent Henky your way to get us all into his stable. Henky's prayers went a long way."

~Lini R. Grol
Chicken Soup for the Christian Family Soul

A Piece of Chalk

Life can only be understood backward but it must be lived forward.
~Soren Kierkegaard

In our home it was natural to fear our father. Even our mother was afraid of him. As children, my sister and I thought every family was like that. Every family had an unpredictable dad who was impossible to please and a praying mama who was there to protect the children. We thought God planned it that way.

We were good children. Mama was always telling us we were, even if Daddy couldn't see it. Part of this was because we dared not do anything. We were quiet, timid children who rarely spoke, especially never when Daddy was home. People thought God had blessed Mama with the sweetest girls. She was always so proud.

Then came the day we found something new and fun to do. It wouldn't upset anyone; we'd never take the risk of doing that. We discovered we could draw pictures with chalk on our wooden front door, and it would rub right off. We could have lots of fun, so we set to work drawing and making lots of pretty pictures all over it. We had a great time. It surprised us to see how talented we were. We decided to finish our masterpiece, knowing Mama would just love it. She would want all her friends to come and see it, and maybe they would want us to do their doors, too.

The praise we expected did not come. Instead of seeing the obvious beauty in our work, all Mama could see was the time and effort she would need to clean it off. She was mad. We did not understand why, but we knew all about anger, and we were in big trouble!

Off we ran to find a place to hide. In our wooded yard it was not hard for two small children to find safety. Together, we huddled behind a tree and did not move. Soon we heard the frightened voices of Mom and our neighbors calling out to us. Still we did not budge. They were afraid we had run away or drowned in the pond out back. We were afraid of being found.

The sun set, and it began to get dark. Those around us became more anxious, and we became more frightened. Time was slipping by, and the longer we hid there, the harder it was to come out. Mom was, by now, convinced something awful had happened to us, and she resorted to calling the police. We could hear all the voices drawn together in a group. Then the search was on again, this time with strong male voices overpowering the others. If we were frightened before, now we were terrified!

As we clung together in the dark, we became aware of yet another voice, one we instantly recognized with horror: our daddy. But there was something strangely different about it. In it we heard something we had never heard before: fear, agony and despair. We couldn't put a name to it then, but that's what it was. Then came his prayers, tears and prayers intermingled together.

Was that our daddy on his knees pleading with God? Our daddy with tears running down his face, promising God that he would give his life to him if he would safely return his girls?

Nothing in our lives had prepared us for this kind of shock. Neither of us remembers making a decision to come out. We were drawn to him like a magnet, our fears dissolving into the forest. We don't know yet if we actually took steps or if God somehow moved us out and into Daddy's arms. What we do remember are those strong, loving arms holding us and crying, hugging us like we were precious.

Things were different after that. We had a new daddy. It was like the old one was buried that day in the forest. God had taken him and replaced him with another, one who loved us and was ever thankful for us.

Mama always told us that God was a God of miracles. I guess she was right. He changed our whole family with a piece of chalk.

~Holly Smeltzer
Chicken Soup for the Father & Daughter Soul

A Child's Prayer

We thank the Lord
For meat and drink
Through Jesus Christ.
Amen.

Christian Kids

Family Time

The best minute you spend is the one you invest in your family.
~Ken Blanchard

27

Reptiles Reconciled

There is nothing in the world so much like prayer as music is.
~William P. Merrill

I will never forget the Christmas of my seventh year. I was going to sing several carols with my classmates in the Christmas pageant at school. We had been practicing for about a month. A week before the pageant, my mother's family had their Christmas celebration. Mother had been bragging about how I was to sing at school and I was cajoled into singing one of the carols for the Coulter clan gathered there.

Telling my aunt which carol to play, I sang out as sweetly and sincerely as only a seven-year-old can... "Hark! Old Harold's angel sings, glory to the newborn King. Peace on earth so mercy smiles, 'cause God and reptiles reconciled...."

That is as far as I got because my aunt could no longer play the piano, she was laughing so hard. My uncle laughed so hard he spilled his drink on his lap and when he tried to mop it up, he lost his balance and slid out of his chair.

I was mortified. I had no idea why everyone was laughing at me. I burst into tears and ran upstairs to my bedroom crying. I really was surprised when my oldest and most straitlaced aunt came into my room. (I had always been a little afraid of her.) She tenderly took me in her arms and with loving words told me not to cry. Everyone was laughing because of the wonderful new words I had sung for that Christmas carol. And even though everyone else had learned it a different way, mine was so much better.

She kissed me and then washed my face and told me to come downstairs with her because there was a surprise waiting for me. Hand in hand we took the stairs down to the living room. Just as we got there the music began to play and the whole Coulter clan began to sing my own words. As I stood listening to them sing my misconstrued version of "Hark! the Herald Angels Sing," I felt more loved than I ever had in my life.

My lips were still trembling as I stepped forward and began to sing. As my extended family sang carol after carol and arms slipped around each other in a warm familial glow, I realized Christmas wasn't about festive decorations or the Christmas tree or even the gifts under it. Christmas was about love given freely and with joy.

As one of my older cousins gave me a squeeze and a smile, I was sure Hark, old Harold's angel, was singing with us, and I had gotten the words right after all.

~Linda C. Raybern
Chicken Soup for the Soul Christmas Treasury

The Commandment

*Pretty much all the honest truth telling there is in the world today
is done by children.*
~Oliver Wendell Holmes

A Sunday school teacher was discussing the Ten Commandments with her five- and six-year-olds. After explaining the commandment to "honor thy father and thy mother," she asked, "Is there a commandment that teaches us how to treat our brothers and sisters?" Without missing a beat, one little boy, the oldest in his family, answered, "Thou shall not kill."

~Richard Lederer
Chicken Soup for the Christian Family Soul

Three Days Old

There's no other love like the love for a brother.
There's no other love like the love from a brother.
~Astrid Alauda

The first time I held my little brother, Michael, he was only three days old. I was nine. It was the morning after he and my mom came home from the hospital. I woke up because I heard him crying from within my parents' bedroom. We lived in a pretty small apartment, and I could hear my parents awake and moving around in the kitchen. So, why didn't they hear him crying? I thought. I lay in bed waiting for someone to go to him. I decided that as soon as someone did, I would rush out of my bedroom to meet the baby. But Michael kept crying. Then I sensed an opportunity... should I go to him? Quickly, before anyone else could hear him, I crept toward my parents' room.

I had only seen him once before, at the hospital, when I looked through a big glass window into a nursery with a lot of babies lying in tiny plastic cribs. When my dad pointed to him and said, "Congratulations, new big sister, that's your new baby brother!" I secretly felt terribly disappointed. Michael was the ugliest baby in the whole place! His face was all red and blotchy, his nose was mashed down to one side, the top of his hairless, pointy head seemed kind of orange, and compared to the other newborns, he looked like a blimp! I imagined the kids in the neighborhood teasing me for having such an ugly brother. Well, I had thought to myself at the time, I still love him and at least he's mine. I've waited so, so long for him.

Now that I was inside my parents' room, I was nervous and excited as I did a fast tiptoe over to Michael. This was our chance to be alone with one another. To really meet for the first time. There in the crib, which used to be mine, lay the most beautiful baby in the world. (In my opinion, anyway.) Yes, it was the same baby from the hospital, all right. But he looked much better! He was still practically bald, but now there were little indications of reddish-blond hair. His skin looked smooth and soft. He had these big, blue eyes that so resembled marbles, I wondered if they actually were. I just stared at him for a second. Was he real?

Carefully, I picked him up. I made sure to place one hand under his head for support. I held him close to me, closer than I had ever held anyone before.

"Hi," I whispered, "...hi." I wondered if he could understand hi.

I was in love — love that I knew would never go away. Not the mushy kind of love like girl-boy love. Not like the way you love a friend. And not like loving a mother or father, either. It was special. I had been waiting for years to share it, because I had been an only child. I had always been lonely, especially when it rained and I had to play at home by myself. I felt empty when I watched my friends get hugs from their little sisters and brothers when we all arrived home from school. My parents were fun, loving and kind. Yet, I sensed a blank space in our family. An extra picture frame with no photo. Something missing. I felt it. And it made me feel alone. Finally, after all these years of waiting, I didn't have to feel that way anymore. "How come you took so long to get here?" I breathed.

I was finally a sister. Better yet, I was Mikey's big sister. And he was my little brother. My own brother. He was so small — so dependent on me — yet, I needed him, too. I whispered more secrets to him. I told him I would love him no matter what. Good or bad, together or apart, I would always have love for him in my heart for the rest of my life. I wished with all my soul that he could understand me, even though I knew he couldn't — he was only three days old. Still, I wanted to tell him how lucky I felt. After nine years of growing up without him, I was old enough to realize something that most kids took for granted when their own brothers or sisters were born. Having a sibling in one's life is a gift straight from God.

I had friends, but my cousin had always told me, "Friends will come and go; family is forever." At the time, it seemed to be a weird thing to say. Holding Mikey now, I understood that special bond. Nothing could ever come between us. And, this very morning, I was given a chance to tell him that in private. I was smiling and sniffling all at the same time.

Mikey rested his little bald, orange head on my shoulder. He wasn't crying at all now. He closed his marbley eyes and fell fast asleep in my nine-year-old arms. Maybe, deep down, he had understood me after all.

~Jill Helene Fettner
Chicken Soup for the Preteen Soul 2

30

Peaceful Coexistence and the Bogeyman

Father!—
to God himself we cannot give a holier name.
~William Wordsworth

When we were five years old, our parents, Gladden and Carmen, read bedtime stories to my twin brother Norman and me. Together we recited our prayers and were kissed goodnight. After this comforting ritual, I would snuggle down in my cozy bottom bunk bed with Norman on the top bunk, and we'd drift off to sleep.

Then suddenly, "OOOOOOOOOH! It's the bogeyman, and I'm going to get you!"

The booming, eerie voice terrified me. It sounded like Norman, but my fears always stopped me from getting out of bed to verify this suspicion.

Sometimes I would challenge the bogeyman and yell, "I know it's you, Norman!" But then the bed would shake and the wailing became even louder and more frightening.

My terror reached a point of no return. One night I tearfully called for Daddy to come and rescue me. I expected Norman to be punished on the spot, but that was not my father's style. He was a teacher, a man of faith, nonviolent reconciliation and consensus. He usually discussed issues with us and, more often than not, got us to work out our own problems.

So my father came in and I tearfully poured out my tale of woe. The top bunk was very quiet. I think Norman was awaiting his fate, but my father merely patted me on my shoulder and left the room. Both Norman and I were too stunned to speak or move. I was painfully disappointed not to be rescued and have the guilty severely punished.

A short time later my father returned with a small picture in his hand. He taped it to the underside of the top bunk where I could see it. It was a picture of Jesus as a Shepherd holding a baby lamb. Daddy knelt down beside my bed and whispered, "You can give your fears to God, and He will protect you and always be with you. You needn't be afraid of the bogeyman or that the upper bunk will shake and fall and crush you." Then he kissed me and turned off the light.

The next night the usual bedtime ritual was followed, and I had my eyes on my Shepherd and the lamb. When the lights went out, the bogeyman was out in force. "OOOOOOOOOH! It's the bogeyman, and I'm going to get you!"

With a quivering voice I announced, "God will protect me."

~Sylvia Boaz Leighton
Chicken Soup for the Christian Soul 2

31

You Are
on Speaker Phone

I think every military wife will tell you that one of the hardest things is being a "Daddy substitute" when Daddy is gone.

In our house, my husband's special time with our three-year-old is bath time. For thirty minutes a day, one on one, they sing "Old MacDonald" at the top of their lungs, practice the ABCs and discuss their days between laughs and splashes. Next, Braeden runs down the hall to his bedroom with Daddy close behind, puts on his favorite Superman pajamas and carefully adjusts his cape. After "flying" through the house to clean up the toys, my husband calls out, "Time to pick out a book."

These moments are my favorite.

We settle together on Braeden's bed and read a carefully chosen story: me, my husband, our son and our newborn daughter. We pray as a family, thanking God for one another, and, of course, for baseball and football! As we say good night, we sing his favorite song, "The Great Big Book of Everything," kiss all three of his stuffed animals, cover him with his two favorite "blankies" and begin the debate of who loves whom more. That is when we receive our reward, and our precious little boy says the magic words. "I love you, Mom and Dad."

When Daddy leaves, the bedtime routine is suddenly turned

upside down. Our "key player" is absent from the game. Thanks to modern technology, we have a fix for it. While Braeden is in the tub, we talk about what Daddy is doing. PJs go on, toys are picked up and then I say, "You pick out a book, and I'll call Daddy."

We all get into bed together: me, our son, our daughter and the telephone.

"You are on speaker phone," I tell my husband. I read the story, and we pray as a family, thanking God for each other, for the day and for Daddy's safe and speedy return. We sing the beloved Disney song, I do all the kisses and then we debate over who loves whom more. Before we end the call, my husband yells out, "I love you, bud." And we are rewarded with our son's reply.

"I love you, Mom and Dad."

~Angela Keane
Chicken Soup for the Military Wife's Soul

32

Innovation 101

So often time it happens,
we all live our life in chains,
and we never even know we have the key.
~The Eagles, "Already Gone"

When I heard the back screen door bang, I gathered up the stack of unpaid bills I was staring at and tucked them back in the manila folder. My ten-year-old daughter Tiffany rushed in and plunked her backpack down on the table beside me.

"Sorry I forgot and slammed the door again, Mom, but wait till you hear this. We had an assembly and a film about world hunger at school today."

She reached into the cookie jar as I opened the fridge to pour her a glass of milk.

"Do you know that, with a hundred dollars, we can help feed a family of six for a whole year?" she continued with her mouth still full of cookie.

This kind of enthusiasm wasn't typical of my steady-as-she-goes oldest daughter. Something had clearly ignited her imagination.

"So, can we give a hundred dollars, Mom?" she asked, pushing straggly brown bangs out of wide blue eyes.

I opened my mouth to say what I was thinking, what I'd heard throughout my childhood, probably what my parents heard throughout theirs: "We can't afford it." Then something, like an invisible hand on my shoulder, miraculously stopped me.

Suddenly, my thoughts drifted back to words I'd read an hour before. I'd been researching materials for a workshop that I was preparing on the topic of innovation. Mired in background information and possible approaches to take, my mind became a blur. My eyes and spirit grew weary. I took a break and sat down with a cup of Earl Grey tea and a book on prosperity, one I liked to turn to when I needed inspiration. The book reminded me that habits of thinking become beliefs that are more limiting than any force in the world. Like the short chain and stake placed around the ankle of a baby elephant in the circus, by the time it reaches adulthood and could easily break the chain and go free, the elephant has stopped trying. It reminded me of how I stopped asking my parents for things as a kid.

I believe that desire is healthy; indulgence is not. I didn't have the means to indulge my children with many extras, but their minds were another matter. I wanted to lavishly encourage them to use their intelligence and passion to reach for the best life has to offer.

Moving the folder out of sight to the chair on the other side of me, I sat down next to Tiffany, thinking, I want to support her dreams; I need new words.

"That's an interesting idea, Tif. I wonder what it would take for us to be able to do that."

Her visionary ten-year-old mind and generous heart went to work on the problem immediately. "How much can we give?" she asked.

I thought back to the argument my new husband Ted and I had the night before. Our bank account was overdrawn—again. I'm a worrier by nature; a saver, not a spender. Our new home had stretched our finances as tight as a rubber band.

Tiffany recognized the look on my face before I realized it was there. The years when I was a single mother had bonded us to the point where I could hide little from my wise daughter.

"Okay, how much do we spend on groceries for the five of us—everything, including juice, snacks, meals out and Ted's glass of wine?"

"Our budget is $150 a week. That usually covers it," I said, feeling the role reversal.

The next night at dinner, a rare silence fell over the table as Tiffany unveiled her plan. She'd enlisted the help of her seven-year-old sister Anna and nine-year-old stepbrother Mike.

She began slowly, "Mahatma Gandhi said, 'Live simply that others may simply live.'"

Tiffany explained that by reducing our grocery bill from $150 to $50 for a week, we'd be able to donate $100 to help feed a family in need.

By the end of the meal we'd each signed handwritten contracts prepared by Tiffany, Anna and Mike. We agreed, in writing, to consume no more than $10 each in groceries for the coming week. I insisted we look at the Canada Food Guide to make sure we made healthy choices.

None of us will ever forget that $10 week. We were quite a sight at the Grant Park Safeway in Winnipeg. Two elderly women spoke in hushed tones after Anna wheeled her cart up next to mine as I reached for a dozen eggs. "Mom, don't get eggs. Go thirds on a jar of peanut butter with Tiffy and me."

I half expected someone from Family Services to be waiting for me when we left the store. At the checkout, the five of us lined up like ducks in a row with our carts of carefully planned purchases, each clutching a $10 bill.

I hoped to lose a few pounds that week as a bonus. It didn't happen. None of us lost an ounce. The image that's etched most clearly in my mind is our dining room table at the end of the week, piled high with all the food we'd purchased, but not eaten. Like Jesus' tale of the loaves and fishes, we started out blessing a little and ended up with way more than we needed.

I learned more from my ten-year-old about innovation that day than from all my management experience and research. Tiffany's fresh idea, propelled by a heartfelt vision and passionate commitment, was a powerful creative force—an unchained elephant.

I also learned that whether managing my household food budget or an organization, a vital leadership task is removing fear-based road-blocks and limiting beliefs. Worn-out words, thoughts and actions must give way in order to offer new ideas a path to run on.

I treasure the gift I was given to stop autopilot words like, "We can't afford it," and ask the right question to fan the flames of creativity that gave our family life-enriching new possibilities.

When one of us wants something that may seem impossible, I've come to love the question, "That's an interesting idea. I wonder what it would take to be able to do that?"

~Joanne Klassen
Chicken Soup for the Soul Stories for Better World

Just One Wish

ox River gave life to the country town of Colby Point, for the road and the river ran alongside one another. Colby Point was really the name of a road that crept between the hills and valleys of McHenry, Illinois. Homes were scattered here and there—mostly summer homes and retirement homes. At the very end of the road three houses all faced one another. Three sisters—all single, all seniors—lived in one of the homes. Across the way, their widowed first cousin lived in a yellow house. Next to her lived their brother, Bill, and his wife, Cleo.

Cleo had multiple sclerosis, so the pair had moved to Colby Point seeking a quiet, relaxed life. Little did they know when they relocated to this serene area that they would end up rearing their granddaughter, Margie. Before long, the once-quiet neighborhood became active with the sounds of a child.

Margie always looked forward to the arrival of Christmas, and this year was no different as winter began to settle like a warm blanket around Colby Point. Everyone was in a flurry, for at the church Margie and her family attended, the congregation was preparing to share their Christmas wishes with each other. Since Cleo couldn't make it to church, and Bill didn't like to leave her alone for too long, he was in the habit of dropping Margie off at church early on Sunday mornings; the aunts would bring her home.

As Margie sat in church that morning, she rehearsed in her mind over and over what she would say. She wasn't afraid, for she knew what an important wish this was. The service seemed to drag on and on. Finally the pastor uttered the words Margie had been anticipating all morning, "This is a special time of year when everyone around the world celebrates peace and goodwill toward our fellow man. This year, here at St. John's, we want to hear your Christmas wishes. We cannot fill everyone's wish, but we would like to try and fill a few. As I call your name, please come forward and tell us about your Christmas wish."

One after another, the church members shared their wishes, large and small. Margie was the last and the youngest to speak. As she looked out at the congregation, she spoke confidently, "I would like for my grandma to have church. She cannot walk, and she and my grandpa have to stay at home. They miss coming so much. So that is what I wish for. And please don't tell them, for it needs to be a surprise."

Riding home with her aunts, Margie could tell they were speaking in low tones about her wish. She hoped that they would keep her secret. As the next Sunday came around, Margie was getting ready for church when Grandma asked, "Why are you so fidgety? You haven't sat still all morning."

"I just know that something wonderful is going to happen today!"

"Of course it will," said her grandma with a chuckle. "It's almost Christmas, you know."

Grandpa was getting on his coat when he happened to look out the front window. He saw some cars coming down the dirt road one after another. Now at this time of year there wasn't too much traffic, so this was really amazing. Margie pushed her grandma to the window so that she could see all the cars. Pretty soon the cars were parked all up and down the road as far as a person could see.

Grandpa looked at Grandma, and they both looked at Margie. Grandpa asked, "Just what did you wish for, Margie?"

"I wished that you and Grandma could have church. And I just knew that it would come true. Look! There's the pastor, and everyone from church is coming up the walk."

The congregation arrived with coffee and cookies and cups and gifts. They sang Christmas carols and listened to the pastor speak on giving to others the gifts that God gives. Later that night, Margie slipped out the back door and walked outside to look up at the stars. "Thank you," she whispered, "thank you for giving me my wish."

That was just one of the many wishes granted for Margie as she grew up. Her childhood overflowed with the love of her grandparents, four great aunts and many wise, caring neighbors. Margie was truly a blessed little girl.

I should know—I was that little girl.

~Margaret E. Mack
Chicken Soup for the Golden Soul

34

Where's My Little Sister?

In the cookies of life, sisters are the chocolate chips.
~Author Unknown

For months, we looked forward to the new baby sister. Even though we were not positive that she was a little girl, in all of our hearts, there was no doubt. My husband Roy, twin sons Brad and Chad, and I prepared a pink room filled with dolls and lace. Because the boys were at the ripe old age of four, they were able to help out a great deal. We made her future arrival a family affair, filled with fantasies of a precious little angel who would make our home complete.

The day finally arrived. My husband rushed me to the hospital, while my in-laws got the boys ready to go meet their little sister, the newest member of our family. The labor went quickly, and before I knew it, my husband and I were in the delivery room.

With the piercing of a scream, Becky came into the world. She was just as beautiful as we had imagined. After the nurse cleaned her up, she placed her in my arms. Her crying turned into a cooing hum, as her little eyes met mine. Tears flowed down my husband's face as he welcomed her into the world.

"Go get the boys," I shouted. "They are a part of this, too." With that, my husband rushed out the delivery room door, while the nurse pushed Becky and me into the hallway. In a few brief moments, the doors from the waiting room swung open. Roy came back in carrying a twin in each arm. I saw the perfect picture of my three men with huge smiles on their faces.

"Brad and Chad, this is Becky," Roy proudly announced, while the nurse watched.

"Hi Becky," Brad said, as he reached down toward his little sister.

I noticed Chad as he began wiping tears away from his eyes, looking all around.

"What's wrong, Chad?" I asked.

With his little lip quivering he asked, "Where's my little sister?"

"Becky is your sister too, Chad," I replied.

"Becky is Brad's sister. Candy was supposed to be mine," Chad said to the nurse. "We both wanted a sister."

After a few minutes of trying to console him, my in-laws took the boys back home. As they left, Chad continued to look around for his missing baby.

For several months their bedtime prayers ended in this manner: "Jesus, thank you for our little sister. Please give us another little sister."

Becky was a colicky baby and spent almost every night up screaming at the top of her lungs. After about three months of sleepless nights, I heard the boys as their prayer slightly changed. In unison they said, "Jesus, thank you for our little sister, but we don't need another one."

~Nancy B. Gibbs
Chicken Soup for the Sister's Soul

35

Caregiver's Handbook

Every time you smile at someone,
it is an action of love, a gift to that person, a beautiful thing.
~Mother Teresa

I heard the sounds of car doors opening and shutting and nine-year-old Ellen's eager hop-skippity. In the flick of an eyelash she stood at the door, arms stretched wide. "Grandma, I've been missing you!" The radiance of that smile made me forget the punishing weight of relentless July heat.

Her arms locked around my waist, her head pressed against my chest.

I looked down. "New shoes?"

She nodded. "Fast ones," she said, then announced, "I came to give Grandpa a big hug."

Red flags whipped from my caregiver's antennae. For the bezillionth time in the past three years, my frustration level shot off the chart. I needed a caregiving how-to book where I could run my finger down the table of contents, point to a key word, flip to that page, and read the answer. Should I let her see him?

I drew Ellen closer and gazed over her to meet my son's eyes. She'd seen her grandpa two days ago, but....

"He's much worse," I mouthed. "Seeing him might frighten her."

My son's gaze held steady. "She'll be all right, Mom. She needs to hug him."

I felt compelled to protect her. Would she store up nightmare images that frightened away memories of his healthy years?

And I felt just as compelled to protect my husband. Yesterday's words from our hospice nurse still echoed sharply inside me. "He needs to relax and let go," she'd advised. "Distractions now will disrupt the dying process."

How could I take responsibility for even a single minute's extra suffering? Yet how could I deny either of them a last hug? I teetered on the edge of denial and consent.

Where was that caregiver's handbook?

My son's arm circled my shoulders. "She'll be okay, Mom, I know."

My emotional teetering steadied. I nodded at Ellen, whose face glowed with expectation. "He's sleeping," I said, "but he'll wake when he knows you're there."

Tip-toeing into the bedroom, she gazed at the still, slight form beneath the covers. In seconds she was on the bed beside him, arms gentle around his neck. He turned to her with a sun-and-stars smile that matched hers. "Hello, Ellen. How's my buddy?"

"I love you, Papa," she said.

"I love you, too."

She snuggled beside him, stroking his face. "I have new sneakers."

"They'll help you run faster," he said. His eyelids grew heavy.

My son signaled Ellen and with a farewell pat on Grandpa's shoulder, she climbed down.

"Did I help him feel better, Grandma?"

"Yes, you did. Much better." I watched as he rolled again to the place where his body rested more at ease.

Leaving him, the three of us moved to the cool shade of the deck for ice cream bars.

"I wish he could get well," Ellen said. "But I'm glad I made him smile."

"Yes, and he gave you the best smile ever."

Last week she'd asked when he would get better. I'd tried to explain that he couldn't get well, that his body had used up all its strength. The cancer, I told her, was taking his body, but it could never take away who he really is—his sparkling smile, the light in his eyes, his love for her.

Looking back on the countless teams of caregivers—the teams shifting and changing with each new twist and turn, every team giving their all to his care—I saw that Ellen herself had been a constant. For the entire three years of his illness, her steel thread of caregiving never wavered. She brought a kind of caregiving no one else could offer, partly through the innocence of childhood. There was more, though. She and her grandfather had always shared a special bond, but his illness had deepened their connection.

Since infancy Ellen herself had been in and out of clinics, emergency rooms, and hospitals but the summer her Grandpa underwent major surgery, she seemed to set aside her own fear of hospitals. During the month of his stay, she often rode the elevator to his fourth floor room and blended into the sterile atmosphere with the nurses and doctors bustling in and out, the beeping monitors, the medicinal smells, the tubes and needles attached to his body. With a clinical interest, she inspected each object, asking how it would help Grandpa get better, the way she'd gotten better.

He explained, "I'm trying to be brave, just like you, Ellen."

How do you tell a child about dying? How do you tell her that soon Grandpa won't be with us?

How I yearned for that caregiver's book.

As she ate her ice cream bar she said, "I'll miss him, Grandma. It makes me sad." After a moment her brown eyes grew round. "Will he be an angel soon?"

"Yes, he'll be an angel watching over us even when we can't see him. And he'll stay in our hearts always."

My son knew his little girl. She had needed to see her Grandpa one more time.

I thought about how as a teenager I'd felt hurt and left out when my parents kept me from seeing my dying grandmother. Now I'd nearly repeated history, trying to protect my own granddaughter.

Did her visit disrupt his dying process? Maybe. But her farewell touch gave a loving grandfather a last moment's earthly treasure. He, in turn, gave the gift of that moment back to her, to our son, and to me.

Ellen didn't need a caregiver's handbook. She opened her heart and followed it.

~Beverly Haley
Chicken Soup for the Caregiver's Soul

The Good Night Kiss

God always answers our prayers,
but sometimes the answer is no.
~Author Unknown

our feet. Just forty-eight inches. But it might as well have been the Grand Canyon for all the difficulty my mother had in crossing that gap—the space between my little sister's bed and mine. Each night I watched from my bed as my mother tucked in my little sister to go to sleep. I patiently waited for her to walk over to tuck me in and give me a good night kiss. But she never did. I suppose she must have done so when I was younger, but I couldn't remember it. I was seven now, a big girl—apparently too big for bedtime rituals. Why or when my mother stopped, I couldn't remember. All I knew was that she tucked my little sister in each night, walked past my bed to the door, and, before she turned out the light, turned and said, "Good night."

At school the Sisters said that whatever you ask God for at your First Holy Communion you will surely get. We were supposed to think very carefully about this, but I didn't have to think too long to know what I was going to pray for. This was the perfect time to ask Jesus to make my mother tuck me in and kiss me good night.

The day of my First Communion drew to a close. That night, as I hung up my communion dress and got ready for bed, butterflies danced in my stomach. I knew in my heart that I was about to get the best gift of the day. When I climbed into bed, I pulled the blankets up around me, but not all the way up. I wanted to leave some for my mother to pull up. The nightly ritual began. My mother put my sister to bed, tucking the blankets around her and kissing her good night. She stood up. She walked past my bed to the doorway. She started to say, "Good night," but then she stopped. I held my breath. This was the moment. "This was a beautiful day," she said softly. And then she said good night and turned off the light.

I quietly cried myself to sleep.

Day after day, I waited for that prayer to be answered, but it never was. My mother's actions taught me that sometimes God answers "no," and though I never knew why my mother couldn't cross that small space to kiss me good night, I eventually came to accept it.

Deep down, though, I never forgot. When I grew up and became a mother myself, I vowed that my children would always know that they were loved. Hugs and kisses were freely given in our home.

In the evening, after tucking the children in their beds upstairs, I usually went back downstairs and dozed off on the couch in the living room. My husband worked the night shift, and as a young mother, I felt safer sleeping downstairs. One night—it must have been after midnight—I was wakened by the sound of footsteps coming down the stairs. At first the footsteps were loud, and then they suddenly stopped. Whoever it was had seen me.

Finally! Now I would find out just which of my children was raiding the cookie jar during the night. No more waking to be greeted by crumbs all over the kitchen table and blank, innocent looks, in response to my accusations. Tonight the culprit would be caught!

I didn't move, pretending to be asleep, and waited for the footsteps to resume. When they did, they were ever so gentle on each step so as not to wake me. But they were not coming down toward me anymore. They were retreating back upstairs to the bedroom. I heard a little scurrying above, then quiet footsteps again, almost imperceptible, slowly tiptoeing back down the stairs.

The steps softly came close to me, then stopped. They did not continue on into the kitchen. Smart child, this one, I thought, wants to make sure I'm really asleep. Well, I was up to the challenge. I didn't move a hair's breadth. I continued to breathe deeply as if I were fast asleep. I wasn't about to play my hand too soon. I was going to catch this cookie thief in the act. I was already preparing my lecture.

Suddenly, I felt a heaviness settle on me. I didn't move even though it caught me off guard. What was it? Then I realized that this child was putting a blanket over me. Ever so carefully, so as not to wake me, the child covered my feet, then my arms, and finally, with the utmost care, my back. Little hands briefly touched the back of my neck and then the child bent down and, soft as a feather, gave me a loving good night kiss.

The footsteps retreated—not to the kitchen, but back upstairs. As I cautiously looked to see who it was who had covered me, I was glad that my youngest daughter, Patricia, didn't look back from the staircase. She would have seen her mother with tears streaming down her face.

God did give me what I asked for at my First Holy Communion. Maybe he took a little while, and maybe he didn't answer my prayer in the way I expected, but I was satisfied. Even though my mother hadn't known how to cross that gaping four-foot space to kiss me good night, somehow my children had learned how.

~Georgette Symonds
Chicken Soup for Every Mom's Soul

The Hymnbook

He didn't tell me how to live;
he lived, and let me watch him do it.
~Clarence Budington Kelland

I watched intently as my little brother was caught in the act. He sat in the corner of the living room, a pen in one hand and my father's hymnbook in the other. As my father walked into the room, my brother cowered slightly; he sensed that he had done something wrong. From a distance, I saw that he had opened my father's brand new book and scribbled across the length and breadth of the entire first page with a pen. Now, staring at my father fearfully, he and I both waited for his punishment.

My father picked up his prized hymnal, looked at it carefully, and then sat down without saying a word. Books were precious to him; he was a clergyman and the holder of several degrees. For him, books were knowledge, and yet, he loved his children. What he did in the next few minutes was remarkable. Instead of punishing my brother, instead of scolding or yelling or reprimanding, he sat down, took the pen from my brother's hand and then wrote in the book himself, alongside the scribbles John had made: "John's word 1959, age two. How many times have I looked into your beautiful face and into your warm, alert eyes looking up at me and thanked God for the one who has now scribbled in my new hymnal? You have made the book sacred as have your brothers and sister to so much of my life." Wow, I thought. This is punishment?

From time to time I take a book down—not just a cheesy paperback but a real book that I know I will have for many years to come—and I give it to one of my children to scribble or write their names in. And as I look at their artwork, I think about my father, and how he taught me about what really matters in life: people, not objects; tolerance, not judgment; love which is at the very heart of a family. I think about these things, and I smile. And I whisper, "Thank you, Dad."

~Arthur Bowler
Chicken Soup for the Christian Family Soul

A Child's Prayer

Precious Babe of Bethlehem,
Gift of love to sinful men,
Thou, our Savior, Lord, and King—
May we all Thy praises sing!
Amen.

Christian Kids

The People We Know in Heaven

Our death is not an end if we can live on in our children and the younger generation. For they are us, our bodies are only wilted leaves on the tree of life.
~Albert Einstein

38

Dial H for Heaven

Out of the mouths of babes and sucklings has thou ordained strength.
~Psalm 8:2

After my fourth child was born, distance and deteriorating health prevented my mother and daughter from knowing one another very well.

In the beginning, Grandma could make the flight from New Jersey to Colorado for a visit, but as time passed, the high altitude became detrimental to her well-being and she was forced to stop her trips.

So began a mailbox/telephone relationship for the two of them. Amy sent her special pictures to her grandmother and learned to dial the long distance phone number. With some assistance, she phoned her grandma two or three times a week to chat, however brief it may have been. When Amy learned her letters, she also wrote short notes.

For a year, the pair enjoyed their unusual friendship. When Amy's grandmother died, she asked a lot of questions. Several stood out.

"Where is Grandma? Why doesn't she call? Isn't there a phone where she is? Why can't I call her?"

Of course I tried to explain death and its permanency as gently as possible and ended with, "Grandma went to heaven."

It was hard to know if my little girl understood, but I felt I did my best.

One day, while folding laundry, Amy asked, "How do you spell heaven?"

Her tiny fingers struggled, and it did take her a while, but she wrote it down, letter by letter, as I told her.

She thanked me and scooted off.

Shortly after, while putting the clothes away, I found her in the bedroom crying.

Sitting next to her on the bed, I asked, "What's wrong? Why the tears?"

Picking up the phone she said, "Watch." I did.

Between her sobs she dialed: H E A V E N.

"There's no one there. Listen." She handed me the phone. "I even did her area code, like you taught me."

I hung up the phone, wrapped my arms around my daughter and explained the best I could, again.

"There are no phones in heaven?" Amy asked. "Then how do I talk to Grandma?"

The only answer I knew to give was, "In your prayers."

"You mean like I do when I talk to God?"

I nodded.

"You mean Grandma is with God?"

I nodded again.

Amy wiped her wet cheeks, replacing them with a smile.

"That'll work," she said.

~Helen Colella
Chicken Soup for the Grandparent's Soul

39

Nellie

To love another person is to see the face of God.
~Victor Hugo

Nellie was only two years old, the only child of a single mother whose boyfriend had walked out when he found out she was pregnant. Not an unusual story in an inner city—but Nellie was unusual. She wrapped your heart around her little finger the moment you met her. Her eyes, huge ovals and black as shiny metal, looked out of a pale, round face. I was told her hair was once dark and curly, but when we met she was bald from chemotherapy.

Nellie had leukemia. During her six months in the hospital, doctors had tried one chemotherapy regimen after another, trying to save her life. I was Nellie's primary nurse at a time when primary nursing was not the norm. We all felt Nellie needed someone constant in her life. Her mother, unable to cope with Nellie's devastating illness, rarely visited. Whenever a care conference was scheduled to discuss the next mode of treatment, Nellie's mother came to be included in decisions. She wanted to make sure everything possible was being done for her daughter. But she just couldn't visit. I always thought she had already said goodbye.

When I first met Nellie, she had just started the fifth round of chemotherapy. Her face and body were swollen from steroids. She had a BROVIAC line in her chest for medications and IV fluids; she had severe stomatitis and was unable to take anything orally; her perirectal area was red and raw from constant diarrhea. Yet she had the most beautiful smile I had ever seen, reaching all the way to her eyes. I wondered when she had decided that pain was just a part of everyday life and decided to smile anyway.

Two things made Nellie happy: being rocked while I sang soft lullabies, and going bye-bye in the red wagon. With a fireman's cap on her head, a face mask on to protect her from anyone else's germs, and the red light flashing on the wagon's front end, we walked around and around the unit saying "hi" to all the "'ick babies." Nellie had a problem with her S's.

And she had a faith in God only a child could have. "Unless you become as little children…" Nellie bowed her head each time she said his name. She called him "'oly God." H's were a problem, too. When I would finish doing her morning bath and dressing her in a soft fuzzy sleeper, she would snuggle into my lap and ask me about "'oly God."

"Is his 'ouse big?" she would ask with wonder in her voice. "How big is it?" Then, "Tell me again about the 'treets of gold." She remembered all the children's Bible stories her mother had read to her.

One morning she surprised me with the simplicity of her trust. "Pretty soon I go to 'oly God's house."

"Everyone will go to Holy God's house someday," I replied, trying to deny the truth that she had already accepted.

"I know that," she said with all the assurance of a two-year-old who understands the mysteries of the universe, "but I'm going firstest."

"How do you know that?" I asked, choking back tears.

"'Oly God. He told me," she said matter-of-factly.

When the fifth series of chemotherapy drugs failed to have the desired effect, the doctors coordinated a care conference. Nellie's mother was coming and the plan was to get permission to try a new set of experimental drugs, not yet approved for use in pediatric patients. I was surprised at my angry response. "When are we going to say that's enough? It's time to let Nellie go." I couldn't believe this was me speaking. I never thought there would come a time when I would think it was not only okay, but the only right thing to do, to stop treatment on a child. I was more pro-life than the Pope, yet in the deepest part of my spirit I knew someone needed to fight for Nellie's right to die.

My worry was needless. When I returned to work the next night, Nellie was off all drugs. The plan was to keep her as comfortable as possible. She was my only patient that night. In the past twenty-four hours, her already swollen body had become even more edematous. I'm not sure why, but for the first time, Nellie didn't want to be held or rocked. I sat alongside her crib and stroked her puffy face. The short stubble of hair on her head was scratchy under my fingers. Nellie lay awake the first part of the night. I never left her side.

Somewhere around three in the morning, she turned and said, "You hold Nellie now. Nellie going bye-bye."

"The wagons are put away for the night, Nellie," I said, clinging to my denial.

"You hold Nellie now," she repeated. "Nellie going bye-bye."

Gently, I lifted her fragile body from the crib and cradled her in my arms. I held her on my chest with her head resting on my shoulder, her warm breath on my neck. We rocked back and forth, back and forth, as I stroked her and sang, "Jesus loves the little children."

After several minutes, Nellie lifted her head, using all the strength she had left and said, "He's here," then lay her head back down on my shoulder. I could no longer feel her soft breath on my neck. I'm not sure exactly how long I held and rocked her as the tears ran down my cheeks. Finally, I put on the call light to let someone know that Nellie had gone bye-bye with 'oly God.

~Joan Filbin
Chicken Soup for the Nurse's Soul

Grace

God is closest to those with broken hearts.
~Jewish Saying

My husband, seven-year-old son, Colin, and I sat down to breakfast on a Saturday morning in the spring. It seemed a typical start to a weekend, eating our cold cereal interspersed with discussion of chores to be done and the upcoming soccer game. However, my husband and I knew that this was to be a memorable meal. I began the discussion with my common phrase, "Colin, we've got something to tell you."

"I know, I know," he replied. "You love me!"

My husband and I chuckled. "Of course we do, but there's something else we want to tell you," my husband began. "You know how you've been praying for a baby brother or sister?" Colin's eyes began to grow wide in disbelief.

I continued. "Well, we just found out from the doctor... I'm pregnant!"

Colin's jaw dropped, he got out of his chair, and began jumping up and down next to the table. A barrage of questions followed. "Will it be a boy or a girl? When will it be born? Where will it sleep?"

The months passed by, my belly growing noticeably bigger. Colin would often sit next to me on the couch as we watched a television show, his hand on my belly, ready to feel his baby brother or sister kick. Sometimes he would follow a good night hug with a "belly kiss" for his baby sibling.

Colin would also imagine what life would be like. "Mom, if it's a boy," he said one day as we were driving home from school, "I could teach him how to play soccer, like Uncle Pete taught Uncle Matt. We could wrestle too!" He obviously was setting his sights on a brother.

The day finally came when we'd find out if Colin could look forward to having a sports buddy or a teatime buddy. (Despite my efforts at promoting gender equality, he emphatically claimed, "Girls are just not as good at sports as boys.") It was a hot June day in Colorado, and Colin was outside playing with his neighborhood friends when we arrived home from having the ultrasound. Colin came bursting into the kitchen, not giving us a minute to savor the moment. "Well, what is it? Is it a boy or a girl?"

I looked deep into his eyes, wondering how he'd react. "It's a — girl!" His eyes darkened for a millisecond and I sensed a glimmer of disappointment. "Oh." He paused, then smiled. "I'm going to have a baby sister!" He then ran out of the house to share the news with his friends.

But all was not right with his baby sister. In the weeks that followed, we shared other news with him — she had Down syndrome. We chose not to share the more painful news that our baby, Grace Ann, had developed fluid in her lung and brain cavities. While she might live to term, it was more likely, given the amount of fluid, that she would die in utero. For the next two months, we lived in a state of uncertainty. We were praying for a miracle, and at the same time, wondered what life would be like for our baby if she did live to term. Meanwhile, Colin was modifying his dreams of the future. He talked about how Grace might need to come to his room at night to feel protected from a loud thunderstorm. We smiled as he was beginning to assume a "big brother" identity, yet we also grieved, wondering whether he'd get the chance to assume the role.

At seven months, every mother's worst nightmare came true: Grace stopped kicking. The ultrasound confirmed my worst fear — a still body and no heartbeat. An induction delivery was scheduled for the following week. We agonized over when and how to tell our son that his baby sister had died. We decided to err on the side of caution by telling him after the delivery. He knew there were some complications, as I was going to the hospital before the due date. In his mind though, this just meant that he'd get to see his baby sister sooner.

The next day he came to the hospital. He was very quiet as we explained what had happened. He then left the hospital room with his dad and went for a snack in the lounge. Colin asked many questions and wanted to see pictures of Grace. As children often do, he shared his first impression when he saw the photo. "I don't mean to be mean, but she looks kinda weird!"

The days that followed were a blur of mourning mixed with a sense of purpose—that we honor our baby girl with a funeral and involve her big brother in the event. Colin seemed poised and confident in his black suit as he wheeled her casket from the altar to the limousine and carried her tiny casket to the gravesite. It was his moment, his brief chance to guide his baby sister, although not in a way that we ever imagined.

After the funeral we tried to maintain Colin's routines. Each night, as we had every night, we sat together on his bed and said our "thank you" prayer. Colin sometimes interrupted with questions. "What's it like in heaven?" "Can Dad cut the word 'Grace' in the backyard grass with the lawn mower so I can see her name from my bedroom window?" "Why can't we bury her body in the backyard since she's part of our family?"

After a few nights, it seemed Colin was finished asking questions. Perhaps like us, he was gradually beginning to accept the situation.

But one night, after ending his prayer with the usual, "God bless Colin, God bless Daddy, God bless Mommy, God bless Grace," Colin stopped. "Wait!" he said. "Why are we saying 'God bless Grace?' Why are we praying for her when she's already in heaven? We should say 'Grace bless us.'"

And so we do. Every night we end our prayer with "Grace bless us." We know she's guiding her parents. She's guiding her big brother, even if he thinks girls can't play sports as well as boys!

~Margaret Berg
Chicken Soup for the Christian Soul 2

Black and White

O ne day, while driving in the car with my seven-year-old daughter, we began talking. Somehow, the conversation turned into a discussion about my childhood. She was amazed when I told her that television in my day had no remote control and that the picture on the tube was only in black and white, no colors. She thought about it for a short time and asked me if I was in black and white then, too. I assured her that was not the case and went on to tell her that many changes and new things had happened in the world during my lifetime. I further explained that we could not imagine how the world might change during her lifetime.

When I told her I would probably not live to see all the things that would happen in the world while she was alive, she fell silent, digesting what I had told her. She thought for a moment and said, "Don't worry, Dad. When it's done, I will come to heaven and tell you all about it."

~Al D. Luebbers
Chicken Soup for the Father & Daughter Soul

Don't Forget to Wait for Me

I remember my dad so well: the way he laughed, the way he smiled, the corny jokes he used to tell and that goofy look he put on his face to cheer me up. When I was growing up, my dad was in the Navy, first sailing, and then later working in the office. I remember how his office was covered in cards that I had made him.

After my father retired from the Navy, I got to know him much better. We did more things together, we talked more often and he'd always, always listen to everything I had to say. I never guessed that those good times would come to such an abrupt end.

On April 21st, my dad sat down with me and told me something that changed my life forever. He had terminal lung cancer. When he told me, I felt hot and cold all over at the same time. I couldn't move. I couldn't breathe. I couldn't make a sound. I just sat there, and we both began to cry.

Months went by with regular hospital visits, chemotherapy and radiation. My father looked better, but then started to get worse with each passing day. I watched him, that strong, amazing, fearless man that I once knew, become weak, sick and tired. As the weeks went on, he could no longer eat, and he was worse than ever before. My mother had planned to bring him home to visit, but as December came, he became too sick to come home.

December 11th came. My birthday. We brought a cake to his

room and he tried to sing happy birthday for me, then he called me over to his bed and kissed my forehead. I tried to believe that everything would be all right. That everything would go back to normal.

Two days later, I spent the night with my dad. I sat by his bed and watched him sleep, and he looked so peaceful. It was really hard for me to see him the way he was though, with IVs in his hands, and tubes all over. I cried myself to sleep every night after that.

On the night of December 20th, I spent the night at my mum's friend's house. I lay awake that night, thinking about the next morning and, for some reason, fearing it. Maybe I knew or maybe I had a sense that something was going to happen. The next morning, she took me to the hospital and my mum was there. I sat down on a chair in the lounge, and I overheard my mother talking to her friend, "The nurses say that today is the day."

I felt exactly like I had eight months ago, a surge of hot and cold filling my body. My grandparents were at the hospital too; my tiny grandmother was shaking, and my grandfather was talking to a nurse. I didn't cry, though. There were other patients in the room, and I didn't want to upset them.

I went to see my dad. He looked so sick, so thin, but I held back my tears. I didn't want him to see me crying. I walked over to his bed and I bent down and hugged him. He whispered into my ear, "I love you," and kissed my forehead. I hugged my dad, kissed his cheek and whispered, "I love you, too, Daddy."

I stayed with him in that room until the nurses told me that I should get something to eat. My two sisters, my brother and my sister's boyfriend were waiting for me, so that we could all go out to lunch together. We went across the road, and we were halfway through our lunch when my sister's cell phone rang. I dreaded this phone call. My sister, in tears, mumbled something to the caller and hung up. "It's time."

We quickly paid the check and ran across the street. There were cars coming, but we didn't care. We wanted to see our father. When we got there, my grandma was standing in the hall crying. She told us that he was gone. It was too late. My sister collapsed on the floor and couldn't get back up. I ran into my dad's room and saw his lifeless body, just lying there, motionless. My mum was beside him, holding his hand and crying. I didn't know what to do; I was so confused. I just started crying and ran up to him. I hugged him and said, "Daddy, come back, come back," but he didn't.

We had a service for him on December 27th. My mum had put an announcement in the paper about his death, giving details about the service. There were so many people there. Most of them didn't talk; they just sat there and cried. My godfather and my aunt both gave speeches, and both burst into tears when they finished.

To this day, almost six months after my father's death, I think about all those people crying for one man, for my father. I think a lot about different things. I think about how he isn't suffering anymore and how he is up in heaven with his grandparents smiling down at me. I think about how he won't be there for my graduation, and how he won't be able to walk me down the aisle at my wedding, but I also think about how he'll always be here for me—not in body, but in spirit—and how he'll forever be in my heart.

If I could say one thing to him right now, and he would be able to hear it, it would be this... Daddy, don't forget to wait for me.

~Heather McPherson
Chicken Soup for the Preteen Soul

43

The Great Fish Story

One summer afternoon, my grandpa and I were out in his boat fishing when I ran out of line on my fishing pole. Grandpa felt sorry for me, so he handed me his best, luckiest fishing pole to use.

On my second cast, the pole slipped out of my hands and went flying into the lake. I tried to grab it before it sank into the dark water, but I was too late. I jumped into the water after it, but it went down, down, down.

I climbed back into the boat feeling totally defeated. Then Grandpa came up with a plan to try to snag the line with our other two poles, by casting them down to grab the sunken line with one of the hooks. We tried about five times, but we had no luck. I felt so bad. It was Grandpa's favorite pole, and now it was lost forever.

Grandpa, not willing to give up yet, said, "Okay, Max, this will be our last time." Just then, my grandma, who had died two months earlier, popped into my mind. Maybe Grandma could help. So I prayed, "Grandma, please help Grandpa and me find his fishing pole," over and over while I watched Grandpa hook his special silver lure onto the line.

When he was done fixing the lure into place, he threw it into the lake and dragged it around on the bottom. I kept praying to Grandma as I watched the line circle around the lake. When Grandpa reeled the line in, he had caught the sunken line in the middle! He pulled and pulled on one end of the line and then, out of the depths of the lake came his favorite fishing pole! I couldn't believe it! As he pulled, he noticed a tug and a strain on the line. It took some strength to bring it in. Suddenly, we heard a splash and there, on the end of the line was a beautiful fourteen-inch bass!

Grandpa and I laughed our heads off, while I thanked Grandma over and over in my head. I decided to tell Grandpa how I had been praying to Grandma as he searched for the pole. "Yep," he said, "I bet she did do this for us. That would be just like her."

When we told people what had happened, they said that it was "the fish story of all fish stories."

Two weeks after that incredible fishing trip, my grandpa died. I lost my amazing and wonderful grandma and grandpa within three months. It was so hard for my family to give them up.

Now I often ask both of them to help me with lots of different things. And you know what? After that amazing moment out on the lake, I know that they haven't really left me, and they definitely hear me.

~Max Alexander
Chicken Soup for the Preteen Soul 2

44

Tammy and the Diamond Dress

Many people will walk in and out of your life.
But only true friends will leave footprints in your heart.
~Eleanor Roosevelt

Sitting on the flowered print couch, I paged through the Kissees' family album: there was nine-year-old Tammy, ten-year-old Tammy, eleven-year-old Tammy. Then I looked across the room at twelve-year-old Tammy playing checkers with her father. Her long blond hair was gone; the radiation had left only a wisp of fuzz on her head. Her fair complexion was now a chalky gray. The skeleton-like limbs made her appear weak and breakable.

Tammy caught a side glimpse of me staring, and she figured out pretty quickly that I had to be comparing her to the robust girl sitting astride the black horse in the picture. She smiled at me as if to say, "It's okay. I'll be that girl again someday."

My four-year-old daughter Kimberly leaned over Tammy's shoulder to watch her next move on the game board. "I think you should jump the black checker with the red one, Tammy." Tammy laughed, touching her dark curls with envy. "I am the black checker."

We met the Kissee family a year earlier when they began attending our small country church, soon after Tammy had been diagnosed with liver cancer. They joined the congregation, and we all began to pray daily for a healing miracle.

There was something so ethereal about Tammy. Kimberly couldn't resist her and became her shadow. Often Tammy felt weary from treatment, but she somehow managed to add strength to her patience in dealing with this admiring fan. Tammy had two older brothers, so she treated Kimberly as a welcomed younger sister. With their heads together, one nearly bald and the other thick with lustrous curls, they paged through the children's Bible.

One day, as I sewed, Kimberly said, "I need a diamond dress to wear for special occasions, like to parties and weddings and funerals." I flinched at her last word. Tammy laughed and seemed to understand something I could not grasp.

"Why funerals?" I could not meet Tammy's eyes.

"Because when people die they go home to heaven. I really need a dress for that celebration!"

Monday morning, Kimberly and I sorted through stacks and rows of fabric in the basement of an old Ben Franklin store.

"Here it is!" she exclaimed, holding up some purple cloth with a colorful jelly bean print on it. "Diamonds!"

"Honey, those are jelly beans."

"No, they are diamonds, beautiful colored diamonds."

I looked at the material for a long time, trying to see what Kimberly saw, but finally gave up. I asked for two yards to be cut, picked out matching thread and paid my money. All week I struggled with making my daughter's diamond dress. To make it fancier, I sewed on a lace collar and dotted it with rhinestones. Kimberly was happy with the result; she saw diamonds, I saw jelly beans.

Christmas was festive at church with a wonderful program and platters of carefully prepared food. Tammy admitted she felt awkward around girls her own age, as they didn't quite know how to act toward the girl who looked so different from them. So she remained by her little four-year-old friend and was a wonderful help in serving the food.

I thought I detected a little color crawling back into Tammy's wan cheeks. Surely she would recover and be just fine. I said another silent prayer for the hundredth, the thousandth, the millionth time.

I watched Tammy out of the corner of my eye all evening. She checked plates and cups, making sure everyone had enough to eat and drink, and served more when needed. She seated the elderly in the most comfortable chairs. I saw her push back the constant fatigue she experienced in order to help turn the pages for the pianist's music. At last, she sat with the children gathered about her feet, leading them in Christmas songs, listening intently to their stories. She was a young girl who was not self-absorbed in makeup and boyfriends. She was a young girl absorbed in helping others.

Two days after Christmas, we received a call from Tammy's parents. She had been rushed to the hospital. Walking into her room, I noticed how small she looked among the bed sheets. Her mother rubbed her forehead and smiled into the blue eyes that were heavy with sleep. My husband and I stood by her bed, along with her parents and brothers. Although we had prayed for healing, God performed His own miracle and just before midnight took Tammy home to live with Him in heaven.

The members of the church dreaded the funeral of one so young. We seem to understand and accept better the death of someone elderly who has lived a long and full life. This young life slipping away from us, however, made our own mortality seem more brittle. And there were the nagging questions: Had we failed Tammy in not believing hard enough, in not praying long enough?

I held my four-year-old daughter's hand as we walked up to the old oak casket. Tammy appeared as if she had gotten ready for church and then simply laid down for a quick rest among her favorite toys. I squeezed Kimberly's hand tighter. If she got too close to the casket, would death snatch her too? Sensing my fears, Mr. Kissee picked Kimberly up into his arms so she could clearly see Tammy's face.

"She is at peace now. See, no more pain on her face," he told her.

Kimberly looked into the pain-filled father's eyes and then nodded seriously, turning her attention back to her friend.

"Thanks for helping me be quiet in church," my daughter whispered to her. "See, I wore my diamond dress for you today. You knew how important it was. I am so happy that you can see heaven. Save me a seat next to you."

During the service, Tammy's parents sat close together holding hands, their grieving sons on either side. The pastor spoke, "This is not the end but the beginning for Tammy. Let her beginning be a new beginning for us as well. Let's finish what she has started, and may it be a work in progress."

It was true. Tammy left us with so much. She set her own needs aside to help others. She cheerfully illustrated to my impressionable daughter, to children yet to be shaped, and to adults set in their ways, how to be of service to others when pain and tiredness are your greatest enemies.

That night I tucked my own little daughter into her bed, thinking that Tammy would never be tucked into hers again. Kim looked at me with concern. Her tiny finger brushed away one of my tears.

"Mommy, when I close my eyes I can see Tammy. She has her long blond hair back and wears a beautiful dress with stones all over it. I think her diamond dress is even prettier than mine," Kimberly whispered while pointing to her jelly-bean dress hanging in the closet.

I closed my eyes too. Yes, I can imagine Tammy with her long hair and pink, glowing complexion. I think she is probably wearing her own diamond dress as she gallops through the streets of heaven.

~Robin Lee Shope
Chicken Soup for the Christian Woman's Soul

45

The Swing

*While we are mourning the loss of our friend,
others are rejoicing to meet him behind the veil.*
~John Taylor

Meg, Katie and I sat rocking on the swing on Meg's front porch. Because Katie had the longest legs, it was her job to keep us moving with a gentle push every now and then. Today, our swinging was sporadic. Katie was caught up in Meg's description of the heart surgery she would undergo in two days.

"The doctors say now is the best time," Meg explained. "I've grown all I'm going to, I'm healthy and they don't want to wait any longer. The walls of my aorta are weakening every day."

Katie and I listened quietly. We'd always known that one day Meg would have heart surgery, but we weren't prepared for it to happen this summer. We were having too much fun.

Katie and I had always known Meg was different. She often complained about the way her eyes protruded from her head and about the extra-thick glasses she wore. We teased her about her slightly bucked front teeth, lovingly calling her "Bugs" after Bugs Bunny. But we never teased her about her heart condition. Meg's family had known from her birth that one day she would require an operation. Now, the day had come.

Meg went shopping with her mom the next day, so Katie and I didn't see her until late. We sat on the porch swing, each of us lost in our own thoughts. When Meg's dad called her in, I hugged her tightly. "I'll be praying for you," I said.

"Thanks," she replied with a smile. "Pray for the doctors, too." We all laughed. Meg's remark had broken the tension.

I didn't sleep very well that night, so it was late when I got up the next morning. I went outside for some fresh air and looked down the row of houses to Meg's. I saw her dad and brother with their arms around each other.

They're home early, I thought. I went in the house just as the phone rang. It was Katie.

"Teresa, I have terrible news."

I could tell she was crying. My heart sank.

"Meg died," Katie said flatly. "When the doctors touched her aorta, it was so weakened, it just dissolved. She died on the operating table."

I was in shock. "Katie, I'll talk to you later," I said, and hung up the phone. As I headed for my room, I passed my mom in the hall.

"Any news on Meg?" she asked.

I shook my head, still too stunned to tell anyone the news. I didn't want to believe it. I shut my door and lay down on my bed.

It can't be true, I told myself. Meg can't be dead. Katie heard wrong. It was some other girl who died. Meg will call and tell me everything's okay.

As the hours stretched on, I knew Katie was right — but I couldn't admit it. I heard Katie's mom call mine to tell her the news. When my mom knocked on my door, I told her to go away. "I want to be alone," I pleaded.

On the way to the funeral home, I kept telling myself that Meg was okay. But when I walked into the room with my parents and saw Meg lying there, reality hit. My friend was dead. I walked over to the casket and looked at Meg's peaceful face. She looked like she could jump up any minute and ask why everyone was so sad, but she didn't. Meg was dead.

I cried hot, angry tears. I couldn't understand why Meg had died, and I was mad at God for allowing it to happen. I thought, The

ﾪ is full of horrible people. Why didn't you take one of them? ﾪy did you have to take the sweetest, kindest person I know?

God didn't give me any easy answers. At Meg's funeral, her pastor read John 3:16: "For God so loved the world that he gave his only begotten son, that whoever believes in him shall not perish, but have eternal life."

I knew Meg was a Christian, and I was comforted by the fact that she was promised eternal life. As the days passed, I drew on God's promises for those who believe in him. Jesus told his disciples that he was going to prepare a place for them in heaven. I knew that included a mansion for Meg. I missed Meg terribly, but I could feel my anger lessening.

One evening several weeks later, Katie and I were walking when we found ourselves heading for Meg's front porch. We sat on the swing, both uncomfortably aware of the space between us.

"I miss Meg," Katie said as she gave a push.

"Me, too," I replied placing my hand on the empty seat. "But you know," I told Katie with a smile, "Bugs will have perfect teeth in heaven."

Katie laughed. "You're right, and she can't complain about her eyes or her thick glasses anymore!"

"And no heart defect...."

The front door opened and Meg's mom came out. "I thought I heard someone," she said. "I was hoping you girls would stop by. Please keep using the porch swing. Meg's dad put it up for the three of you, and we hate to see it empty."

"We'll be back," we promised.

"No heart defect," Katie said with wonder, as our swinging resumed.

We scooted together, closing the space that had separated us. "Do you suppose there are porch swings in heaven?" Katie asked.

"I'm sure of it," I said firmly. "And I'm sure Meg will be saving us a place on one when we get there."

~Teresa Cleary
Chicken Soup for the Girlfriend's Soul

46

How Many Grapes Does It Take?

How wonderful it is that nobody need wait a single moment
before starting to improve the world.
~Anne Frank

Melissa lived in a trailer park, miles from my campus, in one of a dozen turquoise units wedged between a bowling alley and the turnpike. Beer cans and abandoned clothing speckled the lawn outside #9—a scene not unfamiliar to your average college student, if this were the aftermath of a frat party. But those rusted training wheels? That Barbie lying face down in the mud?

"Mol," I said. "What are we doing here?"

Molly nosed the car up to the only patch of ground not littered with anything and replied, in that deliberate way that only a best friend can, "We're making a difference. Remember?"

Three weeks before, propelled by the fervor of the liberal arts curriculum, I had charged back to my dorm room with all the righteousness of Robin Hood. "I'm signing us up for 'Big Brothers Big Sisters,'" I told Molly. "What's an $85,000 education worth if we don't use it to make a difference?"

Molly smiled at me, the same smile she always wears because she knows me so well she can read my mind: Who do we think we are—with our J. Crew barn jackets and our name-brand educations?

do we think we are, showing up on this family's doorstep and napping their daughter?

Fearing the awkward moment of face-to-face economic disparity, we knocked on the door. Much to our relief, the parents didn't answer. Melissa did, in all her kindergarten splendor. Tiny and stick-limbed, she peered up at us and wrinkled her nose like a rabbit. Sniff. Sniff. Could these big girls be trusted?

Behind her stood two older children, each with Melissa's shaggy blond hair and blue eyes. They hung back as she gave us a tour of the trailer.

"Here is the TV. Here is the beanbag chair. Here is the picture I drawed in art."

Melissa's parents, quiet in chairs, watched her flit about. They smiled with the amused detachment of any parent watching a child take the spotlight.

"Here is me when I was a little baby. Here is my twin baby, Mark, that died."

Molly and I leaned in closer to see the photos clearly: one baby dressed in pink, one in blue.

"Missy," the mother said softly, beckoning with her finger. Melissa walked over to her mother and leaned in to hear the secret. Missy regarded us solemnly. "Mama said he's in heaven with the other angels."

There was a shuffling silence from the agnostics in the room. Molly and I tried to fill the air. We offered unbidden assurances: seat-belts fastened, the four food groups, home by eight.

Then the older sister piped up, "How come Missy gets extra sisters and we don't?"

"Yeah," chimed the brother. "How come she gets a dinner at college?"

From his chair at the opposite end of the room, the father spoke for the first time. His voice was deep and strong. "Tonight is Missy's night."

Melissa grabbed one of my hands, one of Molly's and started bouncing. "Katie... Dusty, I'll eat for you," she announced.

Walking to the car, Melissa still held onto our hands. She managed to turn around and wave, with her foot, to Katie and Dusty who had their noses pressed against the windows.

"They wanted to come," said Melissa as we tucked her into the back seat of the car.

"Next time, kiddo. Tonight's your own special night," we told her. Melissa spent the drive to campus bouncing in the back seat: Tonight's my special night, my special night, my special night.

In our cafeteria, Melissa was about the same size as the dining hall tray she was carrying. Since she insisted on carrying it herself, she was oblivious to the throng of students towering over her, thundering past her. She only saw the food.

"Can I eat... anything?" she asked.

"Sure," we told her. "Pizza, pasta, cereal, soup, salad...."

Melissa turned in circles for a few minutes, open-mouthed, until we guided her over to the salad bar in the middle of the Commons where she rested her tray along the slide and thought for a minute.

She pointed to items in a metal tin. "What are them things?"

"Grapes. Green grapes."

Over Melissa's head, I mouthed to Molly: She's never had grapes?

"They good?" Melissa asked.

"Delicious," we told her, relieved she didn't go straight for the ice cream machine.

I lifted Melissa up so she could reach the grapes with a pair of salad tongs. She piled enough on her plate to feed a large colony of fruit flies. "Whoooa, cowgirl," I said.

That was all she wanted. Grapes. From the staggering display of food in our dining hall, all that Missy wanted was grapes. She thought they were "the most prettiest," "the most yummiest" thing she had ever encountered in her life. She wanted to eat them every day of the week for every meal.

We finally had to tell Melissa, ever so gently, that too many grapes would equal one very big stomachache, and that now would be a very good time to stop. The look on her face was priceless.

"But I ain't never gonna eat grapes again. I gotta eat enough for everyone."

"Missy," I affirmed, "there will always be enough grapes."

All three of us walked back to the salad bar and started filling plastic cups with grapes—one for each member of Melissa's family, one for her for tomorrow, one for Molly and one for me. We promised there would be grapes the next time we brought her to dinner, and the next, and the next.

Our drive home was a quiet one. Melissa sat very still in the back seat, careful not to spill her bounty, smiling down at the cups with reverence.

We drove out onto the turnpike, past the bowling alley, through the trailer park and up onto the only patch of ground not littered with anything, before Melissa spoke.

"Guys," she said, "are there grapes in heaven?"

Molly reached over and squeezed my hand, silently saying this question was all mine.

"At every meal, baby," I told her. "At every meal."

~Natasha Friend
Chicken Soup for the Volunteer's Soul

A Child's Prayer

Now the light has gone away;
Savior, listen while I pray.
Asking Thee to watch and keep
And to send me quiet sleep.
Jesus, Savior, wash away
All that has been wrong to-day;
Help me every day to be
Good and gentle, more like Thee.
Let my near and dear ones be
Always near and dear to Thee.
O bring me and all I love
To Thy happy home above.
Amen.

Chapter 7

Christian Kids

Giving

Let no man despise thy youth;
but be thou an example to them that believe,
in word, in manner of life, in love, in faith, in purity.
~1 Timothy 4:12

The Drummer Boy

The manner and thought of giving is worth more than the gift.
~Pierre Corneille, Le Menteur

I couldn't have been more excited. The pastor and his wife were coming for dinner! I had a few favorite people in the world — and one of them was Pastor Shick. No matter where I saw him, he would always open up his big arms and give me a bear hug.

When my parents told me that he was coming for dinner, I jumped up and down with as much excitement as a seven-year-old could show. Then I realized I didn't have a present for him, and it was a week before Christmas.

Kneeling down near the wrapped gifts under the tree, I burrowed around the mountain of presents, hoping my mom or dad had left him one. Nothing was labeled Pastor Shick. Just as I was getting up, an ornament caught my eye; it was a hand-painted wooden drummer boy, about three inches tall. I thought to myself, Pastor Shick's son, James, had played his drum during church last night while a teenager sang, "The Little Drummer Boy." The pastor must like that song to have his son play it at Christmastime.

Hurrying, I yanked the wooden figure off the tree, grabbed some wrapping paper and ran to my mom's bedroom. Quickly, I covered the ornament with the colorful paper and began encircling the small package with Mom's entire roll of cellophane tape.

Soon the pastor and his wife arrived. We sat down at the dining room table, and I began eating meatballs and spaghetti while the adults talked. The meal was so delicious and the conversation so interesting that I almost forgot about my gift until dessert.

Reaching under my chair, I grabbed my secret surprise. "Here," I tossed the mummy-taped gift over the table with no introduction. "Merry Christmas!"

My parents' faces went pale. They had no idea what I had given him.

The pastor reached for the gift with a smile. "How sweet of you, Michele." For several minutes he tried to unfurl the tape, then he turned to my father, saying, "I think I might need a pair of scissors. Would you have some handy?"

My father rose and grabbed a pair from a drawer.

With a few cuts and a hard pull, the minister discovered what I had bundled: the wooden drummer boy. It was very small and looked a bit worse from the tape.

"My goodness!" the minister gasped. "This is really something, young lady."

"It reminded me of last night when James played the drum," I smiled. "I love 'The Little Drummer Boy' song!"

After we finished our ice cream, the pastor gave me another warm hug, and he and his wife left. I wasn't too sure if he had really liked my gift, but I was still glad that I had remembered him in a special way.

The moment Pastor Shick was out the door, my father turned to me and questioned, "Why did you give him that old ornament?"

"I thought he'd like it," I sputtered.

"Next time, ask before you take something off the tree," my father warned. "If you wanted to give him an ornament, you should have given him one of these big, fancy glass or crystal ones."

"Oh." Now I felt my gift wasn't good enough and my eyes fell to the floor. "Sorry."

The next Sunday, I was almost too embarrassed to go to church. I thought that my dad was probably right. I should have given him a larger ornament, one with fancy colors that glistened or twinkled with lights. After all, Pastor Shick was a very important person.

We sat in the first pew as usual, but I couldn't even look up. When it came time for the sermon, I began fidgeting in my seat, kicking my feet.

"I want to tell you all of a wonderful Christmas gift that was given to me this past week," the pastor said, holding up the familiar drummer-boy ornament. "It's one that shows that even a seven-year-old knows the true reason why we give to one another at Christmastime. Out of all of the presents I received this year, this one means the most to me. And let me tell you why.... For those who didn't attend the Christmas concert service, my son played his snare drum for 'The Little Drummer Boy' song. Yesterday, my son left to go back to college. Now I will keep this on my desk, reminding me that wherever he is, he is my drummer boy."

The congregation clapped.

He continued, "Over the years, I prayed to God that my family would impact your lives and that we'd make beautiful memories together. And now I know that my son's music meant something to a special little girl, as much as it meant to my family. I would like to thank her from the bottom of my heart." His eyes got teary. "She reminded me that it isn't the gift that is most important, but the love that prompted it."

After the service I went up to the pastor and received my big Sunday hug. He thanked me again for the precious ornament. Those surrounding us realized I was the girl who'd given the drummer boy gift and smiled at me knowingly.

"After I gave it to you, I was worried if you'd like it because it was so small," I finally stammered.

"Well, you're small, and I love you," the pastor said.

"But it's not fancy; it doesn't have lots of sparkles."

"Well, Jesus didn't have fancy things when he walked on Earth, but I love Him very much, too."

To this day, each Christmas when I hear "The Little Drummer Boy," I remember Pastor Shick's family fondly. That ornament was so tiny, but the meaning became larger than life to me. I learned at seven years old that it's not the gifts themselves that are important; it's making someone happy, and being willing to show love by sharing, that represent the true spirit of giving.

~Michele Wallace Campanelli
Chicken Soup for the Soul Christmas Treasury for Kids

48

Buying Something for Herself

Whoever welcomes children in my name welcomes me.
~Mark 9:37

Our granddaughter Tanisha jumped down from the giant yellow school bus and ran up the sidewalk, backpack swinging, waving something in her hand. I opened the door and in she flew.

"Papa! Grandma!" she yelled excitedly. "I didn't know you were coming to visit."

Papa picked her up and swung her around. "What's this in your hand?" he asked.

"It's my report card," she replied, handing it to him.

Papa turned to me and said, "Look at this, Grandma, it's all As!"

"Wow! That's wonderful," I replied, giving her a hug.

"All As deserve something special. What would you like me to buy you?" Papa asked.

"I don't know, Papa."

Digging into his pocket, he produced a five-dollar bill.

"Here you go. You can buy something for yourself. How about that?"

"Thanks, Papa!" she squealed.

"That's from your Grandma, too," he said as he gave me a look that asked if it was okay.

Tanisha turned to me and echoed, "Thanks, Grandma."

"You're welcome, Sweetheart. We are very proud of you. Spend it wisely," I added.

As I watched her bound from the room with her treasure, I thought of how we miss this bright-eyed, curly-headed little grand-daughter of ours. Tanisha had lived the first few years of her life with us in sunny California, while her parents spent their mandatory time at sea with the Navy. Now, she is with her mommy and daddy as well as her little brother and sister. They live in military housing in Washington, D.C. At seven, she is already in the second grade and getting so tall we hardly recognize her.

As with most grandparents who visit grandchildren only a few times a year, we try our best to spoil them when we actually see these precious little cherubs! The five dollars for the report card was just part of the spoiling. We did not think about this being more money than she had ever had. We did not realize what an awesome respon-sibility this was going to be for a seven-year-old little girl.

While on outings during our week's visit, we asked if there was anything she saw that she wanted to buy with her money. She searched the shelves for the perfect item. She sighed and scrunched up her nose and thought hard as she looked carefully, but she could not find one thing she wanted to buy with her newfound wealth. She said she wanted to save it for something very special.

"When you see it, you'll know it," I said. "Don't worry about it."

After a week of books and movies, ice cream and Playland at McDonald's, it was time for Papa and me to return home. We did so with long faces and sad eyes. We were going to miss the fun Tanisha and our other two little grandchildren brought into our lives during our stay. But work beckoned our vacation to an end.

Once home and back to the daily routine, Papa and I forgot about the report card reward we had left with our eldest granddaugh-ter. It was not until months later that I remembered our gift and asked her, "By the way, what did you buy with that five dollars Papa and I gave you for getting all As on your report card? I hope it was something special."

"Oh, it was," she said. "But I didn't buy anything."

Confused, I asked, "What do you mean?"

"I spent it. I just didn't buy anything. I put it in the collection plate at church."

"Oh," I said with a proud lump in my throat. "That was very nice of you."

"There was a special collection at church for poor people. I figured their kids needed it more than me. So when they passed around the plate, I dropped it in," she said, as if it was no big deal.

"How thoughtful of you." Tears rolled down my cheeks as I thought of her unselfishness. "I'm proud of you all over again," I continued. "I love you very much."

"I love you, too, Grandma. Can I talk to Papa?" she asked.

Papa looked at me with worry. He whispered, "Why are you crying?"

I pushed the phone into his hands and said, "Here, she wants to talk to you."

We had wanted our granddaughter to buy something special for herself. In the end, that's exactly what she did. She bought something for herself that we could never have given her. She bought the gift of giving to others, of doing something for someone in need.

Without knowing it, she bought us gifts as well. She bought us the knowledge that we had not failed her during her formative years when she lived with us—and a special pride in calling her granddaughter!

~Karen Brandt
Chicken Soup for the Grandparent's Soul

Lights for Lena

Cherish your human connections:
your relationships with friends and family.
~Barbara Bush

I t had been the perfect winter night to view Christmas lights. "Hurry, kids!" I shouted upstairs to my children. "Daddy's already outside warming the van." Within minutes I heard excited voices. "Mommy! Mommy!" my six-year-old daughter Abigail shouted, sliding on her behind down the carpeted stairs. "Is the hot chocolate ready?"

"It's in the van," I told her, smiling as my two-year-old son Simeon tugged at my shirt. We were all wearing our pajamas. After all, this was a Christmas tradition! Each year at Christmastime, we'd get into our sleepwear, pack a bag full of munchies and head to our van to go looking at decorations on neighboring houses. We had just stepped out of the door when Abigail surprised me by asking, "Mama, can you give me more money for doing my chores? I want to buy you, Daddy and Simeon the best gifts for Christmas!"

"The best gifts are those that come from the heart," I grinned, recalling how she had drawn me a picture of a rainbow the previous day after learning I hadn't been feeling well.

"You mean that instead of buying people things at the stores, that there's other ways to give them gifts?"

"Yep," I answered, securing her seat belt. "All people have to do is look into their hearts, and they'll find many good gifts to give."

Settled into the van, we opened the bag of goodies, and the kids cheered as we passed house after house decorated with snowmen, Santa and his reindeer and nativity scenes, glowing brightly in Christmas lights.

Suddenly, it began snowing lightly just as we rounded the corner of a street that led into the neighborhood that my husband Jeff and I had lived in years before. The headlights flashed onto the first brick home of the street. The house appeared disturbingly dark compared to the bright lights displayed by its neighbors.

"The people who live there must not like Christmas," Abigail noted from the back seat.

"Actually, honey," my husband said, stopping the van briefly along the curb, "they used to have the best decorated house in the neighborhood." Jeff clasped my hand, and I sighed, remembering Lena and her husband and how they used to take such joy in decorating their home for Christmas. "It's for the children," they'd say. "We like to imagine them in the back seat of their parents' cars, their little faces full of Christmas magic as they look at our home."

"Why don't they decorate it anymore?" Abigail asked, bringing my attention to the present.

"Well," I began, remembering the dark days when Lena's husband had been hospitalized, "her husband died a few years ago, and Lena's very old. She only has one child, and he's a soldier living far away."

"Tell me what she's like," Abigail said, and for the next few minutes Jeff and I filled her in on the kind things Lena used to do.

"And every Sunday after church, she'd make homemade cookies and invite us over. She's an incredible person," Jeff concluded.

"Can we visit her now?" asked Abigail.

Simeon met Abigail's question with enthusiastic agreement, and I shared our children's excitement. Both Jeff and I looked down at our attire.

"I knew this would happen one day," he said, rubbing his forehead. "First I let you talk me into wearing pajamas in the van, and now you're going to want me to actually go visiting, right?"

I kissed his cheek and an hour later, after leaving Lena's home,

Abigail and Simeon clutched the crocheted tree ornaments she'd graciously given them.

"I wish I had a gift for her," Abigail said, waving at the elderly woman standing in her doorway.

The next morning, my children gave me strict orders not to come upstairs. They said something about it being a secret mission for Christmas. After rummaging through drawers, closets and toy chests, they came down the stairs wearing toy construction hats, snow boots and Simeon's play tool belts.

"What is all this?" I laughed. "Are you going to fix things around here?"

"Nope," Abigail smiled brightly. "We're going to give a gift to Lena. Since she's too old and doesn't have anyone to do it for her, we're going to decorate her house for Christmas!"

Her words brought tears to my eyes. "That's a wonderful idea," I said, calling their father. "But I think you'll need Daddy and me to help. Is it okay if we're part of your secret mission?"

"Sure!" they replied. Hours later, we stood with Lena, who couldn't have been happier, on the sidewalk in front of her now brightly glowing house. The lights we had found in her basement were shining with pride over snow-capped arches and windows. Candy canes lined the sidewalk and welcomed passersby to the nativity scene that Abigail and Simeon had positioned on the snow covered lawn. A car cruising along slowed its speed to view the lights. Two children peeked from the back window, their faces full of excitement. Lena watched them, her eyes aglow.

It had been a day full of hard work, but it was worth every second to see the joy on Lena's face. Suddenly, she disappeared inside her home and returned carrying a tray of freshly baked cookies.

Abigail reached her hand inside my coat pocket and clutched my fingers.

"You were right, Mom," she sighed, her dark eyes content.

"About what, sweetie?"

She leaned her head against my arm and replied, "The best gifts are those from the heart." I kissed the top of her head, so proud of her for using her own heart to think of this, and then I turned to my husband. Our eyes met and he smiled.

"Looks like decorating Lena's house can be added to our list of Christmas traditions," he announced. The kids heartily agreed.

~Karen L. Garrison
Chicken Soup for the Soul Christmas Treasury for Kids

I Baptize You...

In praising and loving a child,
we love and praise not that which is,
but that which we hope for.
~Goethe

Years ago I attended a Catholic nursing school, but no one in our class was Catholic. This posed a problem with some of the church doctrines. In our first year, the entire class almost missed being "capped" because we refused to do a procedure: baptize a fetus or person after death. Since we were all Baptist or Pentecostal, this was contrary to our religious beliefs.

As president of the class, I took the brunt of the lecture from Sister James Cecilia. "Miss Sanefsky, you knew this was a Catholic school when you applied. You should also have known that you would have to adhere to our teachings." I wasn't convinced, but I wanted my cap as much as my twenty-three other classmates did, so we compromised. We agreed to learn it if we could be assured we would never have to take part in this procedure.

Years went by. I married Harley and moved to Ohio where I worked in a small eighty-bed hospital. There were many Catholics employed there, so I never worried about having to perform last rites or baptisms until one stormy night.

The rain came down in buckets and lightning flashed as I worked second shift in the nursery. A woman came in and delivered two months prematurely, giving birth to a baby weighing two pounds and

MOTOVUN-ISTRA

Hi Jeanne — Just about
the time you think the
postcard tour is over, in
little Italy they do Bled
in RADOVLJICA-bee
museum from beautiful
JalisBled — and spent
while Earl bit fell off
likes OK — did to get
pictures — Janet miss U 😊

Molimo ne pisati ispod ove crte • Do not write below this line • Bitte nicht unterhalb dieser Linie schreiben • Ne pas écrire au dessous de cette ligne • Non scrivere al di sotto di questa riga

Tisak MORE • Rijeka • 051-624-464 • 051-624-177

CROATIA

PLITV

SVERCA SORBERG
'556 DUNKIRK RD
TMR, QC H3R-3K3
CANADA

Republika HRVATSKA

4.60

2012

WOHP

Hrvatska golubka (Hemaris croatica)

3 859892 311018

one ounce. We knew this little person had little chance of surviving. Our nursery was primitive. We had no neonatologists; only incubators, oxygen and prayer.

As the tempest raged, we worked to clear this little guy's lungs. All we knew to do to keep him alive was to keep the incubator at 98 degrees.

I took him to see his mother and her first words were, "I want him baptized." When I phoned her priest to come, he told me he had no transportation on this stormy night. He would be there first thing in the morning.

This gave us cause to panic. We knew this baby had a slim chance of surviving the night. I went back to the mother and let her know what the priest had said. She was devastated as she repeated the doctor's prediction that her baby might not be alive in the morning. Desperately, she begged me to baptize him. I paged my Catholic supervisor. She was off. I called all over the hospital. Not one single Catholic was on duty. It was falling to me. I prayed, "Oh no, God, you know how I feel about this. I can't do it."

After talking to the mother once more and seeing her desperation, I conceded. I would baptize him "conditionally" as I was taught years before. I explained that I was not Catholic and how my faith viewed infant baptism. I told her I would do it if she really wanted me to, or we could pray that the baby live until the priest came in the morning. Adamantly, she insisted she wanted it done right then. So I proceeded to the nursery and the task I felt unprepared to do.

I prayed as I got a sterile medicine cup, sterile water and sterile cotton balls. Gently, I lifted this precious baby's head in the palm of my hand. With my other hand, I poured the sterile water over his head. "Joseph Sanchez, I baptize you, conditionally, in the name of the Father, the Son and the Holy Spirit." With tears running down my face, I wiped this angelic little head with the sterile cotton, changed the wet towel beneath him and took him back to his mother.

Overwhelmed, she cradled this tiny gift of God in her arms. I knew then I had done the right thing. I brought peace to this young mother so she could give him back to God, if that was in the scheme of things.

The story doesn't end there. Over the months that followed, this baby became "Little Joe" to us in the nursery. Each day we prayed he would live through our shift, then we gave the responsibility to the next.

One afternoon, I was met in our staffing room with, "Little Joe had a bad day, and he may not live through the night." I prayed, "Please Lord, don't take him on my watch." I made rounds on all the babies in the nursery and came to the incubator. The temperature gauge read 80 degrees. The temperature had to be at a constant 98 degrees or he would die! I went around to the back of the incubator, and I found the electrical plug lying on the floor. I quickly plugged it back in, called the doctor and then my pastor. I asked him to pray. We worked frantically to bring Joey's temperature back up, placing warm towels on his body. Prayers went up to heaven for him. He lived through the night.

I was off for three days. When I came back, he was gone. He had reached five pounds and was sent home at three months of age. After having cared for him all those months, I was crushed I didn't get to say goodbye.

The Bible says, "Some plant, some water and then some harvest." I prayed that this little boy would grow and be nurtured in the love of God for he was indeed a miracle baby.

But the story doesn't end there, either. Years went by and then one night, my husband, Harley, came home from a men's church dinner. "Wait 'til you see what I have for you." In his hand was a picture of a young boy. On the back was this message:

Dear Ms. Houseman,

My name is Joseph Sanchez. I am fourteen years old and weigh 140 pounds. Thank you for taking care of me when I was born.

Little Joe.

God puts us in places to do special things, and we may not always agree, but we better be obedient.

~Beverly Houseman
Chicken Soup for the Nurse's Soul

Helping Lauren

It would be safe to say that I was definitely not looking forward to my first Christmas after moving to southern Georgia, away from the comforts of my home, friends and family back in Baltimore. Of course, I was looking forward to the presents, but in spite of the joys of the season, I approached Christmas skeptically. I missed the cold weather, the steaming mugs of hot cocoa, my best friends' annual Christmas party, our front hall with its gleaming tree and, most of all, Christmas at Grandma's house.

Our family would tramp into her warm kitchen, all six of us, after a long two-hour drive. The delicious aroma of cookies baking and the turkey roasting in the oven always made my mouth water. Grandma would bustle in with her apron covered in flour, smile and give us each a hug. She would cluck about how cold it was getting, pat us on the head and send us kids off to play. My three sisters and I would wait eagerly for our cousins to arrive. When they finally came, we would all rush down to the basement to discuss Christmas presents in secret.

Every Christmas, for as long as I can remember, that's what we did. But now that my family had moved, that Christmas tradition was gone. It was depressing, really; Christmas this year would be different. Yet I learned, with the help of a five-year-old girl named Lauren, that I'm not so unlucky after all.

School was finally out for the holidays, and we were going

Christmas shopping—not for us, not even for friends, but for a little girl named Lauren. Lauren was a poverty-stricken five-year-old, and my family and our friends were buying Christmas presents for her that her family could not afford.

I walked into Target wondering what kind of toys a five-year-old little girl would like. But as I gazed down at the list her mother had sent us through Lauren's school, I realized that it didn't have a single toy on it. Lauren had asked Santa for socks, underwear, clothes and shoes—necessities that I had always taken for granted. I can remember many occasions being disappointed by certain presents. I would eagerly grab a box labeled, "To Maddy from Santa" and rip off the shining paper to find... clothes. I would toss it aside. It never dawned on me that some people really don't have these luxuries. Lauren wanted as gifts the things that most kids her age would classify as a waste of wrapping paper.

My sisters and I delighted in picking out little outfits for her and choosing pajamas that had to be warm because, as my sister pointed out, "They probably don't have heat."

The real shock came, however, when we went to deliver the packages. We arrived early, at seven o'clock, to spare the little girl's mother possible embarrassment. The whole street was asleep; not even a dog barked as we approached. We drove past the dark windows of abandoned shops, tumbledown houses and trailers. Many of the houses did not have street numbers, and it was difficult to find Lauren's. Her tiny, rusty trailer sat in what seemed to be a random plot of land. They didn't have a driveway, not even a mailbox. Their ancient, dilapidated van was parked in the middle of the muddy yard among trash and broken furniture. The yard was so small that we could barely fit our car into it. The rickety wooden steps leading up to the door looked as if they would collapse under the weight of our bags, and the windows were taped over with black trash bags. Our bright red and green presents stood out against the dark, gloomy landscape.

My mother cautiously picked her way across the grassless yard and approached the steps. Slowly, she laid the bags down and knocked. She returned to the car and was about to drive away when the rusty trailer door slammed open. A woman stepped out, looking angry and confused.

"This is for Lauren," my mother explained through the car window, smiling. The lady appeared not to have heard and continued staring blankly at my mother. She hadn't noticed the bright bags at her feet. I quickly reached over and shut off the ignition. My mother got out and once again explained, "We've left something for Lauren—it's for Christmas." The lady's dark eyes softened, and she smiled. She seemed too stunned for words. Offering a simple, "Merry Christmas," we drove off, leaving the woman still standing in her doorway, smiling.

That Christmas, as I sat looking at my brightly wrapped presents, the shining tree and my happy family, I remembered Lauren. I hoped that she was having just as wonderful a Christmas with her family. I felt like we had helped to keep a little girl's belief in Christmas alive.

Without realizing it, little Lauren helped me learn how truly lucky I was. She taught me a lot about giving and love, and the true meaning of Christmas. That Christmas truly was a memorable holiday. Wherever Lauren is, I hope she felt the same way.

~Maddy Lincoln
Chicken Soup for the Soul Christmas Treasury for Kids

52

Happy Heart Day

A happy heart is the best service we can give God.
~Maria Chapian

Wednesday was Valentine's Day—the day of the girls' Bible club meeting. As the club's sponsor, I planned to make "heart day" special. I baked chocolate cupcakes and decorated them with candy hearts. The girls would trade homemade valentines. During craft time, we'd sew calico hearts on pink cloth to make a wall hanging.

I wanted to do more, however. Preteen girls can be critical of their friends. Valentine's Day was my chance to help them see the good in each other. I decided the girls would trade valentines of a different sort. Not lacy cards with printed verses, but spoken valentines—words of appreciation from their hearts.

When I got to class I had second thoughts. While the regular girls chatted and laughed together, a new girl, Julie, sat hunched at the end of the table. Should I scrap my Valentine idea? What positive words could Julie say to girls she didn't know?

I had further doubts when I noticed Brandy in class. Three months earlier, a dog had attacked her and tore her left cheek, leaving a large, jagged, red scar on her flawless complexion. The wound had healed, but the scar ate at Brandy's confidence. She often covered her left cheek with her hand. She tended to turn her face and look sideways when speaking to people. Usually a confident girl, I now saw confusion in her eyes at times. Should I risk someone making a thoughtless remark about Brandy's scar?

Despite my doubts, I decided to go ahead.

"Valentine's Day is a time to show love and appreciation for our friends," I told the girls. "I want you to think of something you appreciate about the girl next to you and tell her. It will be a spoken valentine. I'll begin."

I turned to Brenda. "I appreciate your faithful attendance in Girls' Club, Brenda. You work to memorize the Bible verses and you have a great attitude."

Brenda thought a moment. She looked at the girl next to her. "You are real friendly and have a nice smile."

Without hesitation, Justine turned to Julie, the new girl. "You seem like a nice person, someone I'd like to have for my friend."

The girls' remarks were sincere. The valentine idea was working.

It was Julie's turn. What will she say to Brandy, a girl she hadn't met until today?

Julie turned to Brandy with a glowing smile and said, "You're so pretty!"

"Oh!" Brandy gasped. She began to raise her hand to cover her scarred cheek. Instead, she dropped her hand to her side. Brandy's eyes shone. She straightened in her chair. Smiling, she turned to give the girl beside her a valentine.

Did Julie see the scar? No doubt she did. But God allowed her to see more. Her valentine assured Brandy that true friends see beyond scars and flaws. With the heart, they see the heart.

~Jewell Johnson
Chicken Soup for the Christian Woman's Soul

53

Presence and Accounted For

The best of all gifts around any Christmas tree:
the presence of a happy family all wrapped up in each other.
~Burton Hillis

Every gift had been wrapped, each recipe prepared, and all the ornaments hung. I had seen to every detail; I knew I hadn't overlooked a thing. And now, with my three anxious children tucked in bed at last, I leaned back in my favorite recliner—satisfied—to survey our perfect, shimmering tree.

I admired the gay packages arranged meticulously underneath. Thanks to my early planning and a little extra money this year, Christmas was going to be wonderful. I couldn't wait to see my children's faces when they tore into their presents the next morning, discovering all of the new clothes and great toys I had bought for them.

I began a mental accounting of the treasures tucked inside each package: the Dallas Cowboys jacket for Brandon, the Fisher-Price castle for Jared, the Victorian dollhouse for Brittany...

Basking in the glow of twinkling lights and my own thoughts, I barely noticed Jared sneak into the room. My normal reaction would be to jump up and rush him back to bed. Languidly curious this time, I chose to sit still and watch, hoping he wouldn't notice my presence.

I needn't have worried.

Jared was a five-year-old with a mission. The glimmering tree illuminated his small figure as he made his way straight to the nativity beneath it. Sinking to his knees, he held out a paper and whispered, "See, Jesus, I drew this picture for you."

Not wanting to miss a word, I held my breath and leaned forward.

"On the left side, that's me." Jared's finger traced a path across the page. "On the right side, that's you." He pointed. "In the middle is my heart." He smiled sweetly. "I'm giving it to you."

With tenderness, Jared placed the picture beneath the tree.

"Merry Christmas, Jesus," he said and scurried back to bed.

My throat tightened, and my eyes filled. All the sparkling decorations and all the shiny wrappings in the room suddenly dulled in comparison to Jared's innocent crayon drawing. It took my small child's gift of love to remind me that only Jesus can make Christmas wonderful this year. And he always does.

~Vickie Ryan Koehler
Chicken Soup for the Soul The Book of Christmas Virtues

54

The Easter Egg Christmas

aster was just a week away when the radio announcements began. Each day, as the holiday approached, my five-year-old daughter Ashley and I would hear updates about the Easter egg hunts coming up at local parks in our area.

With the first mention of the events, Ashley began pleading with me to take her to one of the big egg hunts the coming weekend. I knew in my heart that sometimes events like these could set kids up for disappointment. With so many kids scrambling for only so many eggs, the odds of her not finding any at all were very real. Still, I did not want to be the reason why she might feel let down, so I smiled at her and agreed to take her, all the while hoping that she would be able to find at least one egg.

Saturday came and we drove to the hunt that Ashley had decided would be best. The parking lot was jammed with cars loaded with children. Frustrated by all the chaos, I considered leaving and just going home again when Ashley jumped out of the car with basket in hand, eager to begin hunting. She was not discouraged in the least by the crowds.

After I parked the car, I joined Ashley and as we began walking toward the event area, we heard an announcement on the loudspeaker. The Easter Bunny had hidden hundreds of eggs early that morning, and each and every one contained a surprise inside.

Ashley's eyes lit up as she imagined what treasure she might find inside the special eggs.

I glanced across the field that was roped off for the hunt and was easily able to see several eggs lying out in the open area. To make sure that the hunt was fair for kids of all ages, the field was roped off in sections and each section had an age limit. Ashley signed in and was directed to the proper line for her age group. When the whistle blew and the rope was dropped, the children ran into the field searching quickly for all the eggs they could find. After the hunt was officially over, each child began his journey back across the field.

Disappointment showed on the faces of the children who didn't find any eggs. Huge smiles were on those who did. I searched the crowd for Ashley, growing concerned that she might be in the group of children who didn't find anything. I hoped that her heart had not been broken.

Just then, I spotted her in the distance running toward me with her basket. To my relief, she was smiling. Once she reached me, I counted three eggs lying in her basket. She plopped down on the grass and reached for one, which she quickly twisted open.

The egg contained a certificate for a Happy Meal™ compliments of McDonald's. That made her day right there, regardless of what else might be in the other two eggs. We decided we'd go there for lunch.

The second egg rattled when she shook it. The mystery was quickly solved when several golden tokens to Chuck E. Cheese fell from the plastic egg. Ashley looked up at me with pleading eyes and asked if we could go there and play for a while after we ate at McDonald's. I agreed as she reached for the last egg.

I didn't think that anything would top what she had found in the first two eggs until we saw it with our own eyes. There, inside egg number three, was a gift certificate to Toys "R" Us for fifty dollars!

Ashley had won the grand prize!

She jumped up and down, thrilled, as I expected she would be. But I had no idea that her happiness wasn't simply because she had won a toy-shopping spree until we got in the car.

"Mommy, can we stop by the mall on the way home?" Ashley asked.

I assumed that she wanted to spend her gift certificate, and I agreed. As I buckled her into her seat, I quizzed her on what toy she had in mind.

"I don't want any toys for me, Mom. I want to buy some toys for an angel," she replied.

"An angel?" I questioned. I couldn't understand what she was talking about. And then I remembered what had happened during the previous holiday season.

Last Christmas, Ashley and I had been doing our Christmas shopping in the mall. We came upon a gigantic tree in the middle of the mall with paper angels hanging from the tree branches. Each angel had the name of a child written on it. Ashley asked me what they were for. I explained that sometimes Santa can't visit every child's house on Christmas Eve, so he sends a list of kids to the Salvation Army. They put the names on angels and hang them on this special tree in the mall. That way, people can help Santa out by giving presents to one of the children whose name is on an angel. The tree is called an Angel Tree.

Ashley just stood there, looking at the tree and all the names hanging there. Distracted with thoughts of completing my Christmas shopping and thinking that I had satisfied her curiosity, I rushed her off so I could finish looking for the items I had on my Christmas list.

Later that night, as Ashley was getting ready for bed, she wanted to know what happens to the angels who no one buys presents for. "Will they get any toys?" she asked.

I explained that the Salvation Army would try and see to it that every child would have a visit from Santa on Christmas. Her concern touched me so much that I suggested we say a special prayer for every kid whose name was on the Angel Tree. So we offered a prayer that all of the Angel Tree children would get presents for Christmas. She closed her eyes and drifted off to sleep.

I had thought that was the end of it, but now, months later, I realized that she had never forgotten about the Angel Tree children.

I pulled over to the side of the road and looked into the eyes of this little girl sitting beside me. Though small in size, her compassion for others was huge. I explained to her that the Angel Tree is only in the mall at Christmas and it was now Easter. There would be no Angels to adopt at this time of year.

Ashley sat there in silence for a minute and then she looked at me.

"Mommy, can we save this money until Christmas?" she asked.

"Yes, we can," I answered. "And we will make some girl or boy very happy!"

I looked at the excitement on Ashley's face and realized that all along I had acted like Christmas was all about buying the right gifts for my family and friends, decorating our home and creating a wonderful Christmas dinner. It had taken my five-year-old daughter to make me realize that it is up to all of us to help the less fortunate, especially at Christmas. Her compassion woke me up to what the true spirit of Christmas is all about. As I pulled back onto the highway, I knew in my heart that I had developed a respect for my daughter that I would carry with me forever.

That next Christmas, Ashley and I went to the mall on the very first day that the Salvation Army put up the big, beautiful Angel Tree. We quickly picked out two Angels, one for Ashley and one for me, and with smiles on our faces we set off for an extra-special shopping trip.

That early December day, we began a Christmas tradition that all started because of an extraordinary Easter egg hunt and a little girl with a very big heart.

~Denise Peebles
Chicken Soup for the Soul Christmas Treasury

Miracle on
Mercer Street

I t was a balmy summer day of sunshine and gentle breezes. Sea
gulls screamed and fluttered overhead in the blue skies as a
group from our church boarded the ferry bound for Seattle. We
were headed for Seattle Center's opera house to see Chico Holiday
and a cast of stars perform the musical, *Miracle on Azusa Street*.

After the ferry ride, our party walked to a waterfront restaurant
for seafood.

While the rest of our family ordered fish and chips, five-year-old
Ryan wanted a hamburger and fries. He was too excited to eat more
than a few bites.

After lunch, I grasped Ryan's hand as we trudged up steep hills
toward the monorail that would zoom us to Seattle Center. Ryan
clutched a doggy bag holding the remains of his lunch. My husband
Ted and our teenagers mingled with the group ahead of us.

We heard groans as we approached the monorail. It was closed
for repairs. From there we decided to catch a city bus.

Our gang spread out as we boarded the crowded vehicle. My
friend Ann, Ryan, and I found seats near the front of the motor coach.
Ryan stared at a bedraggled stranger sitting across the aisle from us.
The unkempt man eyed Ryan's doggy bag.

"Would you like my hamburger?" Ryan asked.

The stranger nodded and mumbled "Thank you," as he reached

for the bag. His intoxicated smile revealed missing teeth. He was unshaven and his clothes were dirty.

Ryan's blue eyes watched intently as the man wolfed down the hamburger and fries. He wiped his mouth on the back of his hand and asked, "What's your name, little boy?"

"Ryan. What's yours?"

"My name's George. Thanks for the burger."

"You're welcome," Ryan said.

George directed his gaze towards me. "Where are you all going this fine day?"

I told him we were on our way to see a play at the opera house.

"Oh," he said, before proudly announcing, "I'm an American Indian."

"Really!" I said. "My friend, Ann, has Indian blood, too."

Ann engaged him in a discussion of their ancestral ties. George gave his full attention, but his responses didn't make much sense.

We reached our destination and our gang filed off the bus. My husband caught up with us and reached for Ryan's hand. George got off the bus too, and fell into step behind us. His disheveled clothing reeked of body odor and stale urine.

"How much does the play cost?" George asked. Alcohol fumes permeated his breath.

"It's free!" Ted answered.

"Can anyone go?" George asked.

"Sure," Ted said. "Would you like to go with us?"

George nodded.

Ann and I exchanged glances as we joined the throngs of well-dressed people headed for the Mercer Street opera house. The splendor of the posh lobby impressed our guest. George stuck close as we made our way through the crowd and were ushered down thick red carpet to the front of the theater.

Since we were early, we had time to kill before the play started. Ted struggled to ignore the rank odor as he conversed with George. George began confiding in Ted, educating him about the danger of life on the streets. He confessed that he had "a bit of a drinking habit."

He said he'd been burned in a fire when he was a boy and had scars over most of his body. He rolled up his shirtsleeves and showed us disfiguring scars.

Before long, the huge opera house was full. We had the best seats in the house! The lights dimmed and the play began. We were soon carried away to Azusa Street as singers and actors portrayed the story.

When the time came for intermission, George left the theater abruptly. Ted went to look for him, but couldn't find him in the crowded lobby. We were saddened to think that George left before the end of the play. Shortly before the lights dimmed, George returned to his seat. He'd washed his hands and face, and combed his hair. He seemed to have sobered up considerably. Somewhere beneath his grimy exterior lived the soul of a ruggedly handsome man.

I overheard George confide to my husband, "You know my mother has been praying for me for years, always begging God to save me."

The curtain opened as the orchestra began playing. As the story progressed towards the climax, George repeatedly brushed tears from his eyes. When the play ended with an altar call, young and old alike made their way to the front of the theater to dedicate their lives to Christ. George was at the head of the line.

We bid our new "brother in Christ" goodbye as we exited the grand opera house. George held his head a little higher as he slowly made his way down Mercer Street.

~Carol Genengels
Chicken Soup for the Christian Woman's Soul

56

Ashley's Garden

"Mommy, would you be sad if I died?" Disturbing words quickly tumbled from the mouth of four-year-old Ashley, taking her mother, Kathleen Treanor, by surprise.

"Of course, I would, Ashley. I'd miss you terribly."

"But don't be sad, Mommy. I'd be an angel watching over you."

With a wink and a promise to stay close by her side, childish giggles soon filled the air. Yes, everything was back on key, with no more talk of four-year-olds going to heaven before their time.

A few days later, Kathleen brought Ashley to Grandma LaRue's house. Grandma was a wonderful sitter, whose home overflowed with love, comfort and joy. Without a doubt, crafts and homemade cookies would soon be on their way.

After tenderly kissing Ashley goodbye, Kathleen jumped in her car and hurried off to work. She'd hardly arrived and settled comfortably in her chair, with a steaming cup of freshly brewed coffee, when she heard it. A huge blast rocked Oklahoma City, and just as quickly destroyed her world.

Confused and unsure of what happened, a coworker flipped on the television. Everyone in the office stood in reverent shock as the news began to unfold. There'd been an enormous explosion at the Murrah Federal Building. Kathleen could hardly believe her eyes. Not in my hometown, she thought. Not here! Soon, young mothers were running back and forth in a frantic search for their children. Kathleen was horrified to discover there'd been a daycare facility in the building. My God, the children, she thought, as she began to pray for the desperate families.

Within moments, her sister called with unimaginable news, unraveling the last shred of Kathleen's protective shroud of peace. Luther and LaRue Treanor had taken Ashley to their social security appointment, which was inside the Murrah building. Suddenly, the room began to spin. Surreal humming filled Kathleen's ears. Ashley was in that devastated structure—the one she was watching on the news!

It took days to discover their complete loss. But slowly, the details came forth. Her mother-in-law and father-in-law, along with Ashley, were found among the dead. Kathleen immediately slipped into a deep, dark depression, not able to comprehend how evil minds could change the destiny of so many innocent souls.

But months later, Kathleen recalled a prayer she'd uttered just days before the bombing, pleading with God for a message of hope to share with a hurting world. Then her mind raced to Ashley's words just before the explosion, "Don't be sad if I die. I'll be an angel watching over you." Suddenly, Kathleen realized she was being prepared for a mission far beyond her understanding.

In gratitude for the peace only God offers, she planted a memorial for her daughter. Today, Ashley's Garden is adorned with a graceful weeping willow, a fountain and an abundance of lively, brilliant flowers. For all who see it, the message is clear. Life goes on. Joy follows sorrow. Light rises from darkness.

Through five years of journals and endless prayers, Kathleen's dream to see her daughter's legacy shared within the pages of the book *Ashley's Garden* have finally come to pass, and her prayer for a healing ministry has reached far beyond her dreams.

When Kathleen awoke on the morning of September 11, 2001, along with the rest of the world, she froze in disbelief. America had, once again, been struck by the evil of terrorism. In that moment, she knew, her words of hope and healing would reach far beyond the borders of Oklahoma. They would now take her to New York City.

So, along with survivors and victims' families, she boarded a plane and flew toward her destiny. It was there she saw the ultimate fulfillment of prayer as she escorted grieving individuals, one by one, to Ground Zero, beginning the long, but vital, process of healing. By meeting the Oklahomans, the people of New York were able to see firsthand that time and faith heal all wounds.

No one knows what the future holds, but for now, Kathleen's on a mission, reaching out to the hurting, the wounded and to all who grieve with an inspiring message of hope born of prayer.

And back in Oklahoma, Ashley's Garden still blooms.

~Candy Chand
Chicken Soup for the Grieving Soul

57

The Easter Bunny

Real generosity is doing something nice for someone who will never find out.
~Frank A. Clark

When I was a little girl, every Sunday my family of six would put on their best clothes and go to Sunday School and then church. The kids in elementary school would all meet to sing songs, and then later divide into groups based on their ages.

One Easter Sunday, all the kids arrived with big eyes and big stories about what the Easter Bunny had brought. While all of the kids shared their stories with delight, one young boy, whom I shall call Bobby, sat sullenly. One of the teachers, noticing this, said to him, "And what did the Easter Bunny bring you?" He replied, "My mom locked the door by accident so the Easter Bunny couldn't get inside."

This sounded like a reasonable idea to all of us kids, so we kept on going with the stories. My mom knew the true story, though. Bobby's mom was a single parent, and she suspected that they just couldn't afford to buy carrots for the Easter Bunny.

After Sunday school was over, everyone went off to church. When my dad came to meet us, my mom announced that we were going home instead. At home, she explained that to make Bobby feel better, we were going to pretend to be the Easter Bunny and make a basket of our goodies for him and leave it at church. We all donated some of our candies to the basket, and headed back up to church.

There, mom unzipped his coat, hung the basket over the hanger, and zipped up the coat and attached a note.

Dear Bobby,

I'm sorry I missed your house last night. Happy Easter.

Love,
The Easter Bunny

~Beth H. Arbogast
Chicken Soup for the Christian Family Soul

A Child's Prayer

Be near me, Lord Jesus!
I ask Thee to stay
Close by me forever
And love me, I pray.
Bless all the dear children
In Thy tender care
And take us to heaven
To live with Thee there.
Amen.

Christian
Kids

Creatures Great and Small

All things bright and beautiful,
All creatures great and small,
All things wise and wonderful:
The Lord God made them all.
~Anglican Hymn

58

Mound of Dirt

The year I was in first grade I ended my prayers each evening with a plea to God to send me a dog. It was a plea that did not go unnoticed by my parents, who knelt beside me. Two weeks before my seventh birthday, which was in May, they told me that they wanted to get a load of dirt for our backyard. I didn't realize something was up until Dad parked the car in front of a ranch house in a suburban neighborhood.

"This doesn't look like a place for dirt," I said, eyeing the surroundings.

While my parents exchanged nervous glances and whispered to each other, a woman named Martha ushered us inside the house.

"I bet you are a very good student," said Martha. I didn't know what to say. I was anything but a good student. As hard as I tried to do well in school, I was failing first grade.

Sensing my discomfort, Martha asked, "Well, I guess you probably want to see the 'dirt,' don't you?"

"Yes," I answered, eager to get off the subject of school.

Martha set a large box in the middle of the living room floor. I padded up and peeked inside. Six black dachshund puppies clawed at the inside of the box, each begging for my attention. Snoozing at the bottom was the runt. I rubbed my fingers on a tuft of hair that stood up in the middle of her back.

Martha said, "That one will never be a show dog."

It didn't matter to me whether she'd ever be a show dog. Her brown eyes looked up at me with such hope. When I picked her up, she snuggled against my heart. There she stayed on the long ride home. I named her Gretchen.

As Gretchen grew, she loved to chew on bones, bury them in the backyard and chase squirrels that dared to disturb her burial mounds. Watching Gretchen's determination and persistence in protecting her bones was a learning experience for me. I saw that because Gretchen never gave up in her battle against the squirrels, they finally left her alone.

As unwavering and fierce as she was with the squirrels, she loved children, especially my neighborhood friends. If I played mud pies with Sally, Gretchen was right there with us. If Markie and Joanie wanted to walk to the corner drugstore, Gretchen begged for her leash. If the neighbor kids put on a play, Gretchen had a part. If Gretchen slipped out of the gate, all the kids in the neighborhood helped chase her down. She was not a dog to us. She was a play-mate — a friend.

Gretchen was the only friend I told about my troubles with learning. While we sat underneath my father's workbench, I told her about my failure in school, about feeling like a dummy because I couldn't read and about how the other children made fun of me. I believed Gretchen understood my problems because as the runt of the litter she had struggled from the moment of her birth. The closer we snuggled in our secret little space, the more I came to believe that maybe things weren't as bad as they seemed. Maybe there was hope for me. She seemed to understand how much I needed her. And I needed her a lot that summer before second grade. I wanted to get smart, and I figured the best way to do this was to read every day.

"Which book?" I'd ask her as she jumped up on my bed.

Gretchen, who used her nose to move anything I set on the bed, would nose toward me one of the books lying on the coverlet, and I'd read it aloud. It wasn't easy for me to read, but Gretchen was patient. Sometimes she'd sigh when I fumbled with the words. Once I made it through a rough spot, she'd nestle against me and lay her snout on my heart. It made me feel better to have her with me as I read. My fears about being a dummy melted away with her beside me.

The summer passed—book by book—until it was time to go shopping for school clothes. Since it was such a hot day, my mother felt Gretchen should stay home. Gretchen whined about being left behind. She hated it when I went someplace she couldn't go. And no amount of trying to explain to her that dogs couldn't go shopping would stop her whining. I looked back just in time to see her head pop up in the window before we drove off, but when we came back from shopping, I didn't hear her claws clicking against the hardwood floor to greet me.

My mother noticed the hall closet door ajar.

"Oh, no," she whispered upon closer inspection. On the floor we found chewed up containers of poison that Gretchen had dug out from the dark recesses of the closet. We found Gretchen behind the living room sofa. She beat her tail in slow motion as I approached. We rushed her to the vet.

"Gretchen is very sick. The vet says she is not responding to treatment," said my mother at the dinner table.

"She's going to get well," I said firmly.

"It's best we prepare ourselves for the worst," my father said.

"No," I cried. "She's going to get well. She's going to come home."

I thought about how lonely Gretchen must be. She probably thinks I don't love her anymore. She probably thinks she'll never see me again. Gretchen had always been there to comfort me when I was sad and hurt.

"I want to go and see her," I told my parents. "If she could see me, I know she'd get well."

"Wake up, Gretchen," I said, after following the vet to a back room in his office. Hearing the sound of my voice, her tail beat the bottom of the cage, again, in slow motion. The vet couldn't believe it when Gretchen stood up in her cage and whined for me to open the door to hold her. It wasn't long before she recovered and came home to stay.

Gretchen and I continued reading together for the whole following year. My reading definitely improved, but it was third grade that was the turning point of my life. That year I became the best reader in my class. My third grade teacher understood that I was a bright child who had a learning problem. She told stories about people like me who struggled successfully to learn despite obstacles.

Although I appreciate everything my teacher and parents did for me, I feel I owe so much to that little "mound of dirt" my parents bought me on my seventh birthday. Persistence and determination were only a part of the story. The runt who would never be a show dog taught me that love is a healing and nurturing soil in which a broken spirit can grow whole once more.

~Paula Gramlich
Chicken Soup for the Dog Lover's Soul

59

A Lesson on Faith

One day last summer, my five-year-old son Parker and I decided to go fishing. We picked the perfect day for it. The wind howled at forty miles per hour out of the south, the red dirt blew past, rubbing our skin raw for the eager UV rays, and clouds of mosquitoes parked on our lee side.

Parker had fished before, but hadn't yet developed the same passion for it I had. We'd go to a farm pond, hook on a dab of earthworm, throw Parker's line into the water, and in about three seconds the bobber would go under and Parker would tree-top a three-inch bluegill.

Parker considered all that a great and exciting adventure. Then he was off, throwing rocks in the water, looking for frogs, picking flowers for his mom and generally ignoring this whole process of fishing.

So on this particular day, I resolved to teach Parker a lesson. I wasn't taking him to just any farm pond, but a fisherman's haven—a place by the name of Dewayne's Pond. What's more, we were leaving the earthworms behind. I brought along a minnow bucket and on the way out of town we stopped at the bait shop and ordered two dozen shiners.

Bass bait.

And that meant bass fishing.

Yes, I had decided that Parker needed to graduate to real fishing. I knew there were enough bass in Dewayne's Pond to keep us stepping lively, and I figured Parker might even catch a couple in between me hauling several out on my plastic-worm rig.

I figured wrong. I managed to catch a couple in between all Parker hauled out. And of the twenty or so bass Parker caught that day, two weighed more than two pounds.

"Creel-worthy," I said and put them both on the stringer.

"Wow!" Parker said, "I bet Mom won't believe I caught both of those and you didn't catch any."

"She might," I ventured. "Now hush and try to catch another one."

Parker tried, but he couldn't keep his mind off the two monsters already on the stringer. I could tell, though, that something was beginning to bother him.

"Dad," he said, prodding one of the bass with the end of his fishing pole. "We're taking these home to show Mom, right?"

"Certainly," I said. Parker concentrated on his bobber for a moment.

"How are they going to stay alive?" he asked.

I anticipated his question and congratulated myself for having a ready answer.

"Well," I began, trying to be as gentle as possible, "they aren't. I mean, we're going to clean them when we get home so we can eat them, and they'll have to die then, right?"

"I guess so," Parker replied. He remained silent while he caught a couple more small ones that we threw back.

"Dad," Parker finally said in a small voice, "we'll see these fish again in heaven, won't we?"

This question blindsided me. I didn't know what to say. It wasn't the theological ramifications that stymied me; it was my young son's total faith. I had planned on teaching Parker a fishing lesson, and he turned the tables on me.

"Gee," I said, sheepishly. "I don't know what we'll see in heaven, son."

"I've got an idea," Parker announced.

"Tell it."

"Let's put them back in the pond."

"I'm with you," I said, unsnapping the stringer and letting the two fish slide free. We stood together and watched them swim lazily back into the green depths of the water.

A couple of lessons came my way that day. First, I hope that in my zeal for the outdoors, I never do anything that would diminish Parker's respect for God's creation. And second, I pray I can learn to hold my faith as dear as does my young child.

~Keith Long
Chicken Soup for the Fisherman's Soul

Mosquitoes

W hile on a campout at Cumberland Falls State Park several years ago, my son Tim and I spent the night sleeping in the back of our van.

In the middle of the night, Tim awoke scratching one of many mosquito bites and whispered, "Daddy, why did God put mosquitoes on Earth?"

I didn't have an answer, so I countered with a question, "Why do you think he did, Tim?"

He didn't respond and quickly fell back asleep.

The next morning, as we headed home, Tim suddenly exclaimed, "Daddy, I know why God put mosquitoes on Earth!"

I looked over and couldn't wait for the answer from his proud face.

"Because he didn't want them in heaven, that's why!"

~Guy Lustig
Chicken Soup for the Nature Lover's Soul

61

Blu
Parts the Veil
of Sadness

Dogs are miracles with paws.
~Attributed to Susan Ariel Rainbow Kennedy

A black-and-white border collie came to our house to stay. Her smiles brushed life's cobwebs away.

Only Blu knows of her life before she was tucked into a small space with wired walls labeled "Animal Shelter." We had been without a dog for a couple of months when Blu's telepathic message, "I need a loving family," reached the ears of our teenage daughter Christine.

At the time, our family of six had a home in the country. Our small acreage bordered the Plateau River outside Casper, Wyoming. Resident pets included an assortment of aquarium fish, laying hens and a few silky chickens that resided in the chicken coop. The 4-H bunnies nestled in their hutch. A Manx cat, dressed in dolls' clothes, often accompanied our younger daughters during their imaginary adventures. And last but not least trotted Smokey, our two-year-old Quarter Horse.

Into our Wyoming Noah's Ark came Blu. Needless to say, she was overwhelmed. To hide from the confusion of her new surroundings, Blu sought an invisible cloak in a variety of shapes. She took cover beneath the chicken coop, under the hay manger, the water trough or the loading chute—any place where she was in the shadows of the activity but could observe our day-to-day routines.

Her behavior gave us clues to the abuse that she'd endured before coming to our home. It left her cowering whenever a hand was raised to pat her or voices were too loud for her sensitive soul. Yet as the weeks dissolved into months and our calendar pages went out with the trash, Blu's demeanor changed. She progressed from following us during chores to romping out front as our leader. When someone approached her with a hand for a pat, Blu no longer cringed or slunk away. Instead, she sought affection from us. If we didn't acknowledge her when she came near, Blu would nudge our hand until she received the hug and loving words she now enjoyed.

She trotted alongside Smokey when the girls rode him bareback. Blu's herding instincts were displayed when she gathered stray chickens and drove them back to the coop. After playing tag with the cat, Blu's impish smile was reflected by anyone observing her play. At the close of day, Blu rested at the bedside of one of our daughters. Like our children, she listened with rapt attention to their bedtime stories. The beauty of her canine soul touched our lives in many ways. Then one cold evening, she showed us her remarkable capacity to love.

That year, eleven-year-old Joanne and her sister Kathy were each given a calf to raise for their 4-H projects. Morning and evening, they faithfully made sure there was fresh water in the trough and food in the bunker for their calves. When the colder weather arrived in late fall, they made straw bedding inside the calving shed.

One evening, the cold stiffness of winter hung icicles off the barn roof and wrapped a blanket of snow across the meadow. I had just put dinner in the oven when Kathy yelled from the back porch.

"Mother... hurry... Joanne's calf is hurt!"

Zipping up my jacket, I ran to the barn, where I found Joanne sitting on the snow-covered ground. Blu lay close to Joanne's side while the calf lay across her lap, legs stiff. Blue wool mittens off, Joanne's one hand cradled the calf's head, the other clamped nostrils shut while she blew puffs of air into the calf's mouth. Tears streamed down her cheeks. "She's barely breathing, Mommy." She blew again into the calf's mouth. "I found her lying here... all by herself. I don't want her to die."

"Honey, she could have been kicked by another cow. You need to understand that she may have injuries inside beyond our help."

"I know." She wiped the tears trickling down her cheek.

"Let's get her to the house where it's warm." I carried the calf. Blu followed close to Joanne.

Only the kitchen clock marked the passage of time while we worked on the calf. Blu kept her vigil just paw steps away from Joanne.

The calf's labored breathing slowed... stopped.

I hugged Joanne close. "I'm sorry, honey."

"She was too little to die. Why...?"

The sadness on her face was like a blow to my chest. I gulped for air. My mind whispered, "Oh honey, I wish I could protect you from death... but I can't." I felt so helpless.

I said, "Injuries from an accident don't always heal; sometimes the animal or person dies. And for a little while, we cry our sadness."

Kathy took her sister's hand. "I'll share my calf with you."

"That's okay... I don't want another one right now."

My vision blurred while I explained to Joanne that when an animal or person dies, it is only the end of a tangible life, that her dad and I believed life is ongoing for the soul. Before my words were out, I realized that there would be time later for us to talk about our spiritual beliefs, to help Joanne build the personal strengths that would ease her through other losses. Just now, she was an inconsolable little girl, and I didn't know how best to help.

As I watched, Blu crawled across the floor and put her head in Joanne's lap. Blu nudged her hand until fingers moved through her black-and-white fur. Slowly Joanne bent her neck and kissed the top of Blu's head. The dog raised her head and looked into Joanne's eyes. No words were needed in those quiet moments when unconditional love touched Joanne's bruised spirit. She hugged Blu and whispered, "I love you, too."

Filled with wonder, I witnessed a black-and-white border collie — who was once afraid to love — part the veil of sadness from my young daughter's heart.

~Margaret Hevel
Chicken Soup for the Dog Lover's Soul

62

Polar Wish

Dreams do come true.
~Author Unknown

I came around the corner just in time to see that my seven-year-old son, Nick, was upset. "I'll never get to see where polar bears live," he cried.

Nick's dream of seeing these magnificent animals with his own two eyes started years before, when he was just a toddler. We had gone to a neighborhood garage sale with his four-year-old sister, Jessie. Nick had found a sweet-but-old stuffed polar bear in a box of old junk selling for a quarter, and he instantly latched on to the bear. Seeing this, Jessie took out her money and proudly bought "Spot" for her little brother.

Soon, Nick had created a whole life of adventure for his new-found friend. Together, they would raid the kitchen, cover the floor with oil to slide on and play pranks on everybody in sight. But mostly, Spot's adventures consisted of traveling with Nick along to the tundra to find his parents to take care of the polar bears.

Now things were different. Nick was in the middle of chemotherapy to treat a tumor around his optic nerve. The chemo and drugs caused mood swings and depression. Because of his illness, he missed a lot of school and no longer had time with his friends. Now Spot was his constant companion as he went for his weekly treatments. My little boy had been a model patient, but that day he hit a low point and had given up on his dream.

Then, just a few days later, we attended a Children's Miracle Network fundraising reception and Nick's nurse told us that he qualified for a wish. We couldn't believe it. A representative came to our home and asked Nick what his wish would be. We all knew what he would say.

The possibility of seeing polar bears helped the months of treatment go by. The stories of Spot's adventures grew, and we all started sharing Nick's dream. By the day our trip began, Nick was healthy and he had the most important item in his bag—Spot.

From the moment we headed out, it seemed that everyone we met knew how important this trip was for Nick. People went out of their way to ensure his wish was perfect.

The kids were even allowed into the cockpit and got to wear the captain's hat. In Winnipeg, the driver gave Nick and Jessie stuffed animals. The hotel manager gave us a complete tour including a ghost story. Even the hotel cook left the children with hugs. It was already the best adventure they had ever had.

The train was going to take us to Churchill, a small town on Hudson Bay. The first morning, the chef came out to greet Nick and to invite us to meet his family who happened to be riding along. We spent the day playing Monopoly with his children and were treated to special snacks that he himself prepared. The train's engineers spent hours explaining the engine and the unusual aspects of traveling on the frozen ground. The train attendants became our best friends and explained the sights and local traditions of the towns we passed.

When we arrived, we headed out to the tundra. We saw polar bears everywhere. At one point, Nick was nose to nose with a beautiful bear who was as curious about him as he was about her. She stood on her back paws to look through the tundra buggy window, her black nose hitting the spot where Nick's face peered out. The driver quickly named her "Suzy Doorbanger," and she became our favorite polar bear.

The days were filled with activities. The driver and his family gave us a tour that included the history of Churchill. A local scientist spent part of his day telling Nick his polar bear adventures and shared with him what it would take to be a scientist. We met other travelers and together we found igloos, sleigh dogs and more bears. In town, we would run from one heated building to another. Each breath felt like our lungs were freezing, but Nick wanted to be outside all the time.

When we finally boarded the rail to come home, we thought our adventure was over. However, we were completely surprised when the train stopped at a small town late one night and an attendant named Sandy asked if we would mind a visitor. We were introduced to the mayor of Pas, Manitoba. He had gone out in the cold weather to present Nick with a special pin representing their town.

As we headed back to Winnipeg, Sandy even got off the train and started a snowball fight with Nick and Jessie. She told us that often, when returning home from trips, she would look out of the train to see her grandmother watching for her from her apartment balcony. That night as we pulled into town, all four of us were at the window looking for her grandmother.

Nick is eleven, and next year he'll be considered a cancer survivor. His room is filled with posters and school reports of polar bears, and Spot still sits on his bed. He's a bit worn and fragile now, but we'll never forget our precious garage sale gift from God—the spark for a child's dream that helped heal our family.

~April Riggs
Chicken Soup for the Traveler's Soul

63

Hope

God also bearing witness both with signs and wonders,
with various miracles,
and gifts of the Holy Spirit,
according to his will.
~Hebrews 2:4

Scott and Janice had tried for many years to have a baby, and when their son, Scotty, entered the world, our church celebrated right along with them. Soon, however, the doctors diagnosed Scotty with serious heart problems.

Rallying behind the young family, our church supported and reminded them of God's promise never to fail or forsake His children. Nine months passed, and Scotty's doctors determined that he needed open-heart surgery. His chances of surviving the operation were slim, but without it, his chances of living past his first birthday were slimmer.

Throughout his ordeal, one thing had become amazingly clear about Scotty: He absolutely loved the color yellow. Whenever he'd catch a glimpse of the bright hue anywhere, he'd squeal in delight. Even his nurses added a touch of yellow to their uniforms when caring for him.

Sadly, Scotty's operation wasn't a success, and the attempt to save his little heart failed.

His parents, grief-stricken, escaped to a friend's vacation home soon after the funeral. Weeks passed but the gaping wound left by

Scotty's absence remained unbearable. One evening at sunset, Scotty's parents walked along the beach. As they clutched each other's hands, they felt the dark realization that Scotty's tiny fingers would never again be clasped between theirs. Too heavy a cross to bear, they felt alone in their grief and prayed there on the beach for a glimmer of hope to dispel the darkness.

And then, along the water's edge, it appeared: A bright yellow bird landed between them as they walked. Neither had ever seen such a bird before. It didn't scurry or fly away but continued to scamper between them on their bare-footed journey in the sand.

The bird's comforting presence filled them with peace, the peace granted to believers in 1 Thessalonians 4:13-14: "But I would not have you be ignorant, brethren, concerning those that have fallen asleep, lest you sorrow as those that have no hope. For if we believe that Jesus died and rose again, even so God will bring with Him those who sleep in Jesus."

After they'd made it back to the beachfront house, the bird remained, seemingly studying them for a few moments, then lifted its wings and headed upward towards the sky.

While watching its graceful flight, they imagined Scotty, in the presence of God, soaring high above the clouds and making his way to that incredible yellow ball for a warm kiss upon his chubby cheek.

Hope had come to them: a yellow bird messenger fashioned by the Creator's own hands.

~Karen Majoris-Garrison
Chicken Soup for the Christian Soul 2

A Child's Prayer

My God, accept my heart this day
And make it always Thine,
That I from Thee no more may stray,
No more from Thee decline.
Anoint me with Thy heavenly grace,
Adopt me for Thine own,
That I may see Thy glorious face
And worship at Thy throne.
Let every thought and work and word
To Thee be ever given;
Then life shall be Thy service, Lord,
And death the gate of heaven.
Amen.

Christian Kids

Send Me a Sign

And many other signs truly did Jesus in the presence of his disciples,
which are not written in this book:
But these are written, that ye might believe that Jesus is the Christ,
the Son of God; and that believing ye might have life through his name.
~John 20:30-31

64

Grandma's Cloud Game

Angels sail back to God on the sea of joy.
~Adeline Cullen Ray

I worked hard picking that bouquet of dandelions from the field in back of Grandma's house. When I presented my gift to Grandma, she smiled and hugged me.

"Oh, child," she'd said, "you warm the cockles of my heart."

"You have cockles in your heart, Grandma?"

She laughed. The best part of Grandma was her laugh. It wasn't exactly the sound so much as the way it filled her whole face, and the way her belly made her white apron wiggle.

Grandma placed the dandelions in a glass jar filled with water. They stayed on her kitchen windowsill until every last one of them was as brown as the wood it was sitting on.

Grandma smelled like vanilla and coffee. I remember the first time we made cookies from scratch. I thought one of the cups of stuff she put into the bowl was "scratch." She explained, "There are two kinds of cookies; store-bought and scratch."

She had a secret recipe and it was magical because it didn't matter if we put raisins or nuts or even chocolate chips in the batter, the cookies always tasted like heaven. Grandma gave me her secret scratch recipe and I keep it in my wooden treasure box under my bed.

I also have a four-leaf clover in my box. Grandma taped it to a piece of cardboard for me. We spent two hours crawling around on our hands and knees in her backyard looking for that four-leaf clover. We held hands and danced in a circle when I finally found one.

I loved spending the night with Grandma. She taught me how to play Rummy. I always added up the points because she said I was such a good counter.

The smell of coffee was usually what woke me up in the morning. Breakfast always tasted great. Breakfast started with a big kiss on my forehead followed by orange juice. Sometimes we had eggs, but Grandma knew pancakes were my favorite. She always made more pancakes than we could eat. We crumbled the leftovers and scattered them in the backyard for the birds. I think the birds came from miles around to visit her backyard when I spent the night.

Grandma had what she called a "bottomless" candy dish. We could eat candy in the afternoon and after dinner in the evening. The next morning the candy dish was full again. It always held my favorite kind—white buttery mints. Grandma taught me to hold them on my tongue and feel them magically melt. We held contests to see who could keep their mint on their tongue the longest. Most of the time Grandma won that game.

Grandma's porch swing was my favorite place in the whole world. She sat on one side. I sat beside her and leaned against her, my feet and legs taking up the rest of the swing. I could smell Grandma's cookies in her cotton apron and coffee on her breath as she hugged her arms around me. We found pictures in the clouds as Grandma gave the swing a nudge once in a while with her foot.

Mostly, we talked. We talked about the neighbor's good corn crop. We talked about Dad's job and Mom's charity work. I told her my most important secrets and she crossed her heart she would never tell.

"Someday," she told me, "when I'm living with the angels, you look up into those clouds and say hi to your old grandma, okay?"

"Okay, Grandma, I will." I never worried about that day because I knew it would never come.

That was two months ago. Mom and Dad are in the house now, packing Grandma's belongings. I am sitting on Grandma's porch swing, giving it an occasional push with my foot. The backyard is quiet. There is no laughter. I don't know if I will ever laugh again.

Grandma is here. I feel her presence everywhere. Her kitchen still smells like vanilla and cinnamon and coffee. Maybe she's just playing our game of hide-and-seek and she's out of sight just beyond that old lilac bush she loved so much. I know better, but I sure wish that was true.

A white, fluffy cloud moves across the sky, directly overhead. I look up, remembering our "pictures in the cloud" game. The wind shuffles the cloud as I watch. I see Grandma! There she is, sure as the world! Her wings are spread wide and her white dress is falling in folds around her feet. She has a happy smile on her face!

"Hi, Grandma," I call out, "I love you!" I knew she was there! She just doesn't need this old house and all the stuff in it anymore. I see her gently wave. Smiling, I spread out on the porch swing to watch her as she floats across the sky.

~Nadine Rogers
Chicken Soup for the Preteen Soul

65

Kristina

The soul can split the sky in two and let the face of God shine through.
~Edna St. Vincent Millay

I t was a dreary day, and my dad was driving me home to my mom's. I spent the weekends with my dad since my parents' divorce. I had grown accustomed to the fact that I would visit him separately, maybe because they divorced when I was so young.

Suddenly, my dad turned to me and said, "Ashley, your cousin Kristina has been diagnosed with cancer." The words threw daggers at my heart.

"What?" I gasped. I knew what cancer could do to a person because I remembered what had happened to my Granny. She died from it.

Shortly after my dad told me about Kristina, she started going to the hospital often. Sometimes when I went to visit her, I would have to wear a mask so that I wouldn't bring in any of my germs. Although she seemed uncomfortably pale and had tubes in her skin, everyone thought she would be fine, and it would soon be over. But "a few months" turned into two long years. During that time, her strength was an inspiration to me. When we played together, we would laugh and giggle, because we were both pretty young; she was only ten years old and I was only eight.

During the summer, it seemed that a miracle happened. For a few months, the cancer was still. Kristina was home, and it seemed that she was better, although she had a tube coming out of her chest that the doctors had used for her chemotherapy. Because of that, she wasn't allowed to go swimming, but she still wanted to go to the beach with me and our little cousins. She had to wear a hat at the beach because she was bald. Her beautiful, wavy brown hair had been lost. She would play with my long blond hair and whisper, "You're so lucky to have hair like this." I didn't understand. Inside I felt lonely and confused, but Kristina seemed to be okay with what was going on, and she was really happy to be home with her family.

Kristina seemed to get better and she went back to school. She was through with her treatments, and her hair started to grow back. Then, early the next spring, she went back to the hospital for a checkup, and they found out that Kristina's cancer had spread. We were all slowly losing hope, though we continued to pray. I didn't get to visit her for a while, but then when I finally saw her again, the look of joy and laughter was gone from her eyes.

That whole summer, Kristina was in a wheelchair, and by August, she had grown thinner and thinner. I wasn't allowed to see her anymore because she was very tired all the time, and it was hard for her to breathe. Our whole family knew that she was dying. And she did, just like that. Even though we sort of expected it, it still hit everyone hard. Especially me. When I was told, I sat quietly collecting the pieces of shattered memories in my soul.

At the funeral, our family sat in the back. The room was so crowded with people who loved her. I just looked straight ahead. I wanted to mourn, but I couldn't. I would never accept her death, and I didn't know why.

Then Dad explained to me about the "Rainbow of Hope." It seems that when Kristina left us, her mom, my Aunt Kathy, had asked for one thing. She asked God for a sign that Kristina was safe with him. The very next evening a huge rainbow appeared in the sky, and my Aunt Kathy knew that she had her answer.

After the funeral, we tossed Kristina's ashes into the sea, near where we had scattered Granny's ashes. On the way home, a glittering star of all colors was shining in the sky. It was Kristina smiling down on us from heaven with peace, tenderness and love.

In Kristina's honor, Aunt Kathy and Uncle John joined an organization to help raise money for children with cancer and blood diseases. That year, my dad's whole family, and many friends, walked for Kristina in a fundraiser for the organization. We all walked proudly. Our group was called "Kristina's Krew." Every September we walk for Kristina—rain or shine.

The next year, Aunt Kathy designed a ribbon to bring awareness to people about childhood cancer. It has the rainbow on it that Kristina sent to us. Aunt Kathy went to our state government with her "Rainbow of Hope" pin, and New Jersey made it the official symbol for childhood cancer awareness in our state. The next year, Aunt Kathy started her own website called "Kristina's Rainbow of Hope."

I am at ease now with Kristina's death and have come to realize that everything happens for a reason. Because of Kristina, a lot of people will know more about the effects of childhood cancer and how they can help children in treatment. I know that would make Kristina happy.

~Ashley Kopf
Chicken Soup for the Preteen Soul 2

66

Flying a Kite

When our mortal eyes close on this world for the last time,
our angels open our spiritual eyes and
escort us personally before the face of God.
~The Angels' Little Instruction Book
by Eileen Elias Freeman

Her skin was the color of rich, hot chocolate and her brown eyes twinkled with intelligence and humor. Her name was Michelle and she spent her days in a purple wheelchair because she had been born with cerebral palsy. She rolled into my classroom—and my heart—when she was just three years old. Her courage was an inspiration to me and her spirit touched my heart.

Michelle and her mother once gave me a figurine of a beautiful black child sitting in a wheelchair. I displayed the cherished gift on a shelf in my den at home. It always reminded me of the little girl I loved so much.

When Michelle was seven, she was to undergo open heart surgery for the third time. The night before surgery, I sat in the chair beside her bed and held her hand.

"I'm tired, Bicki," she said weakly.

"Why don't you close your eyes and try to get some sleep?"

"No, not sleepy. Tired."

I thought of the tiny, imperfect heart that had to work so hard, the grand mal seizures, terrible headaches and tight, spastic muscles that made her every move difficult and painful. I was heartbroken at the wisdom of the little soul who understood the difference between sleepy and tired at such a young age.

"Will I go to heaven soon?"

I placed my hand on her forehead. "I don't know—that's up to God."

She glanced at the stars through the window of her room. "How will I get all the way up there? An airplane?"

"No, God will send a special angel to show you the way. You won't have to take your wheelchair or your leg braces or any of your medicine because you won't need any of that in heaven. You'll be able to run and play just like your brother."

Her eyes filled with hope. "Do you think I could fly a kite?"

I swallowed a tear and smiled, "I'm sure if you ask God for a kite, he would find one for you."

"Oh, I hope so, Bicki."

It was very early in the morning while I was doing my prayer time when the figurine of Michelle, for no apparent reason, fell from my bookshelf to the floor. The impact of the fall separated the figure of the girl from the wheelchair. I was devastated and vowed to have it repaired. Later that same day, Michelle's mother called to tell me that her daughter's heart had simply stopped beating and she had peacefully slipped away in the early hours before dawn.

I have since thrown the ceramic wheelchair away, and the little girl sits on the edge of the shelf with her legs dangling over the side. She's smiling toward the sky. I always think of Michelle on warm, windy days. I imagine her running through the clouds with a kite dancing above her!

~Vicki L. Kitchner
Chicken Soup for the Christian Woman's Soul

67

Mended Hearts and Angel Wings

Tears are the safety valve of the heart when too much pressure is laid on it.
~Albert Smith

I broke the angel's wing the year my grandmother died. I was ten, Nana was eighty and the angel was older than both of us put together. Nana had lived with us for as long as I could remember, and that was fine with me because she had neat stuff like tiny cases of perfume and powder and a sewing box with fancy buttons and bits of lace, and she let me play in her room whenever I wanted to. I was the youngest in my family and usually in the way or trying to tag along with somebody. Nana was special because she was the only one who actually wanted me around.

Breaking the angel's wing and Nana being sick enough to die — both seemed impossible to me. I knew how easily things could break, and I knew that people died, but I was certain something as precious to Nana as that angel could never break, and someone as precious to me as Nana could never die.

Nana's angel was a Christmas angel, a gift from her grandmother long ago. Each year when the decorations were brought down from the attic, we opened the angel's box, carefully unwrapped the tissue paper and the angel would emerge, pure and sparkling, to take her place behind the cradle in the crèche.

She never stayed where we put her though; she moved around

as if she could really fly. She sometimes landed next to the telephone, where nervous hands fingered her delicate wings while talking, or she perched on a desk to watch over an anxious teenager studying for exams. Sometimes she would alight on the windowsill by the kitchen sink where my mother scrubbed and whispered prayers for a daughter or a son or, the year Nana was sick, for her mother.

That year everyone was praying for Nana. Christmas approached but not nearly as gaily as it usually did. I unwrapped the angel by myself that year, and she wasn't the same either. Her china white gown, her crystal blue eyes and the gold ribbons around her waist still sparkled, but somehow she seemed like a fake angel, not a real one. She sat in the crèche forlorn and untouched.

Nana stayed in bed night and day and our house got quieter and quieter. One morning I brought the angel up to her. She held it in her soft wrinkled hand and stared at it for so long that I started to feel bad because it seemed to make her sad, and I thought she might cry. But she turned to me and smiled and in a whisper I could barely hear she told me to take good care of her little angel. I wondered if she meant me, but before I could ask her, she drifted off to sleep. She never spoke to me or to anyone else again.

Nana died before Christmas came that year. Everyone said I handled it well. They talked to me about death, saying how it's a part of life; they told me how good I had been to Nana and how God needed her to care for little children in heaven as she had cared for all of us. They said it was okay to miss her, and it was okay to cry. I listened and nodded, but their words made no sense to me because none of it was real. I couldn't grasp that Nana had really left me. Until I broke the angel's wing.

Christmas was over, and I was wrapping the angel gently in extra folds of tissue paper when my brother threw his new football at me, shouting, "Catch!" a second too late like he always did. The ball hit my arm, and the angel fell in slow motion down onto the kitchen floor where her wing broke away from her white china gown and shattered into pieces.

I cried then. Loud, aching sobs that I had hidden inside came tumbling out as I realized for the first time how final death is. How real and how wrong that Nana, my best and often only friend in the whole world, was gone forever.

Everyone made a big fuss over me then and sent all sorts of cards and gifts trying, I guessed, to fill the giant empty space in my heart. Time did ease the pain, but sometimes all it took was a whiff of perfume or the sight of an old white head in a church pew, and I would feel an aching tug in my heart.

I forgot about the angel until the next Christmas. As I slowly unwrapped the tissue inside her box, I began to imagine that if the angel was healed, I would be too; maybe all those tugs on my heart had been Nana sewing it back together up in heaven. Just as she had mended my torn clothes, she had been mending my broken heart with those memories and signs, telling me she wasn't gone and never would be.

I don't know who fixed the angel, and I never tried to find out, because it would have stolen the precious wonder and peace I felt when I held the mended figure in my hand. It was my first glimpse of the tremendous power of love and faith that is so much stronger than death.

Many Christmases have passed since then, and many stages of my life: from child to woman to mother to grandmother, and my belief in that power has never dimmed, but strengthened, just as surely as the angel's beauty has never dulled, but brightened.

I have seen Nana's eyes in each new baby I've held, felt her touch in each gentle embrace I've shared, and spoken to her and been answered in every prayer I've whispered. I feel her hand on mine every year as I unwrap the angel. And when I tell the story, I know that she's listening and watching and smiling with me.

~Anne S. Cook
Chicken Soup for Every Mom's Soul

Olivia

You give little when you give of your possessions.
It is when you give of yourself that you truly give.
~Kahlil Gibran

"Please drink," De Lewis coaxed, holding an eyedropper of water to the tiny infant's parched lips. The four-month-old Haitian baby was badly dehydrated and malnourished. She also had pneumonia and a raging stomach virus.

Cuddling the listless infant in her arms, De remembered a seven-year-old girl from North Carolina who once told her mom and dad, "When I grow up, I want to go to a poor country and help care for sick children." Well, here she was in Haiti, where the conditions were ten times worse than she ever dreamed possible. What De never once dreamed, however, was that her very first day in Haiti she would fall hopelessly, helplessly, head-over-heels in love with a sick baby girl named Olivia.

After her divorce in 1994, De had moved to Anchorage, Alaska, where there was a call for her skills as a pediatric physical therapist. She joined a local church, and in September of 1995, De left her patients in a colleague's able care and volunteered for three months of mission work in a Haitian orphanage.

De cried when she reached Port-au-Prince and saw thousands of hungry Haitians teeming in the streets, smoldering piles of garbage everywhere and not a tree in sight. The walled orphanage seemed like a tranquil oasis. Still, there was never enough food or money to buy medicines for the dozens of sick children who lived there.

Olivia was to be the very first Haitian infant De held in her arms.

"A bread vendor found her abandoned in the street only hours after she was born," the orphanage director explained. "She's very sick. We've done all we can with our limited resources."

De couldn't put Olivia down. The moment their eyes locked she'd felt an inexplicable bond with this tiny baby who was so weak she could hardly move her head.

Over the next several days, De pitched right in and helped change diapers and administer medicines to the orphanage children. But whenever she had a spare moment, she always hurried to Olivia's side. De carried the infant to see the doctor every morning, and every night she slept holding Olivia in her arms. "Why, of all these sick children, do I love this baby so much?" she wondered, but De knew it was a question only God could answer.

De's itinerary called for her to spend just a few days in Port-au-Prince before moving on to another orphanage in the remote Haitian countryside. Because of Olivia she delayed her departure for several weeks, and then one night she told the orphanage director, "I'm not going at all unless I can take Olivia with me."

Tears spilled down the director's cheeks. "You really love that baby, don't you?"

"Yes, I do," De replied.

At the smaller, remote orphanage, De used an old towel to make a sling and carried Olivia snuggled against her chest wherever she went. On those rare occasions when she did put her down, even for a moment, Olivia flailed her arms and cried until De picked her up again. "You're getting so strong and healthy," De marveled when she heard Olivia's lusty cries.

When the other children called her "Olivia's Mama," De began dreaming of adopting Olivia and taking her home to Alaska. She tried to initiate adoption proceedings, but was thwarted at every turn.

Rocking Olivia in her arms, she lamented, "Maybe it's not meant to be."

De extended her stay in Haiti until the beginning of February to be with Olivia, but finally she knew it was time to return to the many sick children in Alaska who also needed her care. Before she left, she carried Olivia back to the main orphanage in Port-au-Prince and implored newly-arriving missionaries, "Please take special care of Olivia, and show her to anyone who comes looking for a sweet baby to adopt. If I can't adopt her, I want more than anything for her to find a loving home."

De sat up the whole night before she left, cuddling Olivia. "Will I ever see you again?" she wondered. "Please God, keep this precious child healthy and safe."

Back in Anchorage, De ran up huge phone bills calling the orphanage every other day to ask about Olivia. "She's doing wonderfully," reported the orphanage workers who all knew how much De worried about Olivia.

Then, one morning at 4:00 A.M., De awoke shouting, "Olivia!"

Somehow she knew she had to call right away.

It was four hours later in Haiti. The woman who answered the phone was a stranger to De. When De asked about Olivia the woman said, "Oh, that poor baby is so sad. Ever since her American mama left, she just cries and cries."

"I'm Olivia's mama!" she sobbed into the phone. "Tell my baby I'm coming back for her. Tell her if they won't let me adopt her, I'll move to Haiti to live."

De called the adoption agency only to receive more devastating news. A family from British Columbia had already expressed interest in adopting Olivia.

De felt torn in two. More than anything she wanted to adopt Olivia herself. "But what if that isn't what God intended?" she asked her own mother over the phone. "What if God only meant for me to take good care of Olivia until the family she was meant to be with could find her?"

De prayed for a sign from God, and that Sunday she got one.

It was Mother's Day, and during the service the pastor presented heart pins to all of the congregation's moms. Then he walked straight to De and handed her a pin, too. "This is for Olivia's mother," he announced.

De burst into tears. She knew exactly what she had to do.

Soon she was back in Port-au-Prince. At the orphanage, all of the children gathered around cheering, "Mama Olivia! Olivia's mother is here!"

Inside, De barely recognized little Olivia. She had nearly stopped eating, and her hair had turned red from lack of protein.

De sobbed over the tiny crib. "Olivia, it's me—your mama." Slowly, Olivia opened her brown eyes. And then she smiled.

De lifted Olivia into her arms and hugged her. "First, I'm going to get you well again," she vowed. "Then I'm going to take you home with me to Alaska."

This time the red tape practically cut itself. Olivia's adoption was quickly approved, and in less than six weeks De was back in Alaska with her brand-new daughter.

Today, Olivia is a happy, healthy little girl who loves hiking and camping with her mom in the scenic Alaskan wilderness. In their cozy home, she carries her toys and picture books to De and snuggles in her arms while her mama reads to her. Wherever De goes, Olivia is sure to be close behind. Her wide brown eyes follow De's every movement as if to say, "I lost you once. I'm never going to lose you again."

It's a sentiment her mama shares with all her heart.

~Heather Black
Chicken Soup for the Nurse's Soul

A Child's Prayer

Tender Jesus, meek and mild,
Look on me, a little child;
Help me, if it is Thy will,
To recover from all ill.
Amen.

Christian Kids

God's Angels

Angel of God, my guardian dear,
to whom God's love commits me here;
Watch over me throughout the night,
keep me safe within your sight.
~Traditional Guardian Angel Prayer

69

Pushed by an Angel

God could not be everywhere, so he created mothers.
~Jewish Proverb

Mom was running as fast as she could, knowing that her four-year-old daughter's life depended on it.

Melanie was going down the driveway, pushing along her doll buggy, completely unaware of the car that could have ended her life.

"Melanie! Stop right there!" Mom screamed as she watched the car come speeding up the road.

Melanie looked over at Mom and saw her running toward her. She must have thought her mom was playing a game, because she giggled and started running away. My dad, my two brothers and I were watching from the front deck, stunned.

As we all watched, my mom fell hard to the ground. Melanie looked back and saw Mom on the ground, unable to breathe. She started walking toward her, scared that Mom was hurt badly. The car passed our house. Two more steps toward the road and Melanie would have been hit.

My mom got up and picked up Melanie, holding her tight. When she finally caught her breath, she came up to the deck where we all were and said, "Who pushed me? Why did you push me?"

We looked at her with amazement and told her we hadn't moved. She kept saying that she had felt hands right on the middle of her back—and those hands shoved her HARD. At first, we all thought she was crazy. Now we believe that it was a guardian angel that pushed my mom to the ground. We realized that if my mom had kept running, Melanie would've kept running too, and she would have gone right out onto the road. The car would have ended her life. We now believe in guardian angels and believe that Melanie was very lucky that her guardian angel was looking out for her that afternoon.

I'm thankful that I have my little sister today. At times she is annoying, and I may call her names sometimes. But every time I get upset with her, I remember that day, and how Melanie was saved when my mom was pushed by an angel.

~Erin Carthew
Chicken Soup for the Preteen Soul 2

70

Mr. Oberley's Star

Silently, one by one, in the infinite meadows of heaven,
Blossomed the lovely stars, the forget-me-nots of the angels.
~Henry Wadsworth Longfellow, Evangeline

I was nine years old the last summer that we lived next to Mr. Oberley. By then, he was retired and living alone — if you could call sharing a house with about twenty-five cats living alone. Early in the morning, I often heard shouts from his porch.

"Where did you come from?" His voice shattered the morning quiet. "Go away, Kitty! The hotel is booked!"

I smiled, knowing it was another stray. Mr. Oberley grumbled and complained, but never once did he turn away a needy cat. Their happy mewing often drifted out his open windows. Mom and Dad called it "The Cat Chorus."

Mom told me Mr. Oberley used to be a veterinarian. Once, just for fun, he wrote a cookbook for cats. But now he spent his days in the garden, among the daffodils, his arthritic back as stiff as a board. He joked that he was too old to be good for anything but conducting The Cat Chorus.

Sometimes my parents would let me stay up late. One night, Mr. Oberley and I sat together, watching the night unfold. We breathed in the sweet perfume of lilacs as lightning bugs flickered like stardust strewn across the lawn. A parade of cats trampled over my stomach before scurrying into the purple dusk.

As the first star appeared, Mr. Oberley squinted into the sky.

"Life is so much larger than we can imagine," he said. He chuckled softly, rustling my hair. "Usually we think it's our problems that are so vast. Look, Cindy, sweetheart, look over there." He pointed to the largest and brightest star.

"One of these days, I'm going to climb that star and make it my swing," he said. "I'll ride it across the whole wide galaxy and see everything there is to see."

My first worry was, "But what if you fall?"

"I won't fall," he told me. "And just think, from the vantage point of my star I'll be able to watch you grow up. I'll even be able to hear the cats sing."

I thought long and hard about that. The following day, I told Mr. Oberley, in a most somber voice, that I did not want him to go off chasing stars.

"I'll miss you too much," I said. "And what about The Cat Chorus? The cats only sing when you're here."

It was true. Last year, when Mr. Oberley visited his sister, the cats had refused to sing at all. I bribed them with their favorite shrimp-flavored treats, but they didn't give one lousy meow... not until Mr. Oberley came back.

"I don't know," he said, tiredly. "Having a star to ride sounds pretty good when you have a body as old as mine."

Later that summer, Mr. Oberley became ill. His niece, Sarah, came to take care of him. The long, hot days passed slowly as I waited for him to get well again.

One day Mom and I brought him some chicken soup. I was shocked to see how thin he had become. He was almost too weak to lift his spoon. The worried cats serenaded him tirelessly, day and night.

The daffodils and lilac blossoms had wilted, but the roses were in full bloom the day Sarah knocked on our door.

"How is Mr. Oberley?" I asked right away.

His niece took a long, slow breath. "He told me to give you a message," she said finally. "He said you would know what it means."

"He found his star, didn't he?" I said, watching her eyes fill with tears. "Mr. Oberley went to ride on that great big old star."

Sarah nodded yes.

"And the cats?" I asked. "Who will take care of them?"

"I will," said Sarah. She planned to move into Mr. Oberley's house with her husband and young daughter, who was my age.

"Now you'll have a friend," she said.

"But Mr. Oberley is my friend," I insisted.

"Forever and always," said Sarah, wiping her eyes.

After Mr. Oberley's death, his cats refused to sing—except at night, after the first star lit the sky. And when that great big old star appeared, they sang until their hearts nearly burst. I knew then that it had to be true: Mr. Oberley was up on his star, just as he'd wanted.

~Cynthia Ross Cravit
Chicken Soup for the Preteen Soul

Daddy's Guardian Angel

My son commutes two hours to and from work each day and has to leave extremely early each morning. He never seems to get enough sleep, so I help by driving Airianna, his five-year-old daughter, to school.

One day she and I were discussing the importance of wearing a seat belt. I reminded her that recently a seat belt had saved her daddy's life when he was in a rollover accident.

"Your daddy always wears his seat belt," I told her. "With a seat belt and a prayer to God you are doubly protected. Every day Grandma says a prayer for his safety. I ask God to send his guardian angel to ride along with your daddy to watch over him and keep him safe while he drives."

She thought about this for a minute, then said, "Grandma, why couldn't the guardian angel just drive... and let Daddy sleep?"

~Christine M. Smith
Chicken Soup for the Christian Soul 2

Harry and George

Every year, starting on the day after Christmas, my sister and I looked forward to the fifteenth of June. That was the day our parents loaded up the car, and we moved to a ramshackle cottage on the bay for the rest of the summer. It was a child's idea of heaven on earth—late nights fishing on the wharf, barefoot days in bathing suits, sunning on boats, meals on a big, screened porch under lazy ceiling fans. Every summer seemed better than the last—until the summer we lost George.

George and his brother Harry were golden retrievers, and you never saw one without the other, whether they were crashing through tall saw grass or chasing bait-stealing herons off neighboring wharves. When they did get separated, Harry would bark until George found him. We all loved those dogs as if they were our own, but they really belonged to an old salt known to everyone as "the captain."

One afternoon during this particular summer, Harry and George lay down for a nap under some hydrangea bushes. After an hour or so, Harry woke up but George didn't. All the children, most of the mothers and even a few of the fathers could be seen sniffling and wiping away the tears when they heard Harry barking for his brother. The captain was almost as pitiful as Harry. Finally, Harry gave up barking altogether. Unfortunately when he quit barking, he also stopped eating. He wouldn't touch dog food, ignored his favorite doggy treats, even turned his nose up at a cheeseburger.

My sister and I were so worried that on the fifth night of Harry's fast, as we ate our supper of fried speckled trout, corn steaming on the cob and fresh tomatoes, I asked Mama what to do. She said to pray for an angel to help Harry.

That night I lay in bed under the slumber-inducing, back-and-forth breeze of an oscillating fan and pondered Harry's plight. I was pretty sure that angels dealt only with people and had certainly never heard of them involving themselves in dogs' problems. But just in case, I prayed myself to sleep: Please, God, send an angel to help Harry.

The next morning after breakfast Mama gave me a sausage with instructions to take it to Harry. I found him and the captain sitting morosely on the end of their wharf. I waved the sausage under Harry's nose, but he didn't blink. There's never an angel around when you need one, I thought. Harry got up and started toward the house. His huge head was so low it almost dragged on the wharf boards, and I could tell he was weak from not eating. The captain, watching Harry make his slow progress to the house, shook his old head and sighed.

A sudden splash in the water made us turn to see what kind of fish it was. It wasn't a fish, but the smiling face of a dolphin that broke the dark water, and even the captain had to smile back at her. She made a little dolphin squeak. A deep growl made me look up toward the house. Harry was on the deck, his ears all perked up. The dolphin rolled and splashed—as all dolphins do—then did something you often see trained dolphins do, but rarely get to see a wild bay dolphin do. Whoosh! Up she went like a rocket, silver and shining against the deep blue of the summer sky. The captain and I were clapping and cheering, we were so overcome at the sight. The next thing I knew, Harry came flying down the wharf barking his big, golden head off. When he was finally quiet, the dolphin looked the dog straight in the eye, said something in "dolphin" and swam away.

In all the excitement, I had dropped Mama's sausage. I watched in delight as Harry gobbled it up. The captain and I took him back to the house and fed him a giant bowl of dog food, then loaded him up with doggy treats.

The next morning Harry was waiting, and sure enough, the

dolphin came by. She blew air out of the top of her shining, gray head and smiled her dolphin smile. Harry began to bark like he had the day before and got a quick dolphin reply. Then off she went again, a smiling silver rocket.

Although I heard that the dolphin returned to visit Harry all through that summer, I never saw her again. But it hardly matters, since it was her very first visit that set Harry on the mend. When I told my sister the story, she decided that this qualified the dolphin as a pet and decided to name her Fishy. But I knew better: I called her Angel.

~Margaret P. Cunningham
Chicken Soup for the Dog Lover's Soul

73

Little Angel in Heaven

Two years ago, I met the most precious five-year-old in Hawaii, the only daughter of Keola and Lani. When I stood in the doorway to her room, her parents introduced me as their special friend.

Maile was on her bed, coloring pictures in a coloring book. Her eyes, rich with warmth and innocence, looked at me, and my heart melted as we exchanged greetings. She invited me to sit on her bed and color with her, and I accepted.

Maile had been battling leukemia for the past two years, and it had progressed beyond help three weeks before I was contacted by Hospice of Hilo, Hawaii.

We were silent, except for an occasional, "Please pass another crayon." I finished my masterpiece and watched Maile completing hers. As she finished, she sighed deeply and asked, "Are you here to help me die?"

Our eyes linked, and I asked, "Do you want help?"

She shook her head, "no," and began looking for two more blank pages for us to color, found the ones she liked and we began again. Coloring the trees green, Maile said, her eyes down, "Mommy and Daddy need help, though."

I continued coloring along with her and said, "Do you want me to help you help them?"

No words came back, but as a tear hit the page she was nodding her head, "yes."

I found her mother crying in the kitchen as she sipped a cup of tea. She said, "I can't let Maile go." As I hugged Lani, I reassured her that I would help her and her family through this hard time in their lives. She walked me out to my car and we found Keola aggressively sanding wood in his backyard with an almost uncontrollable runny nose. Having lost a daughter of my own, I recognized the silent pain held within their hearts.

Much of the time in my following visits to their home was spent with Maile, listening to her understanding of what was happening. She understood the doctors and nurses were no longer going to be poking her with needles or giving her medicine that made her sick. "One day I will go to sleep and never wake up, and the pain will go away then." That was the most important part—no more pain.

"Do you know God?" I asked her.

She began singing, "Jesus loves me this I know..."

I asked her what she thought heaven would be like, and she said, "My uncle and my friend Tommy from the hospital are there already, and I'm excited to be with them again."

But Maile had a very worrisome problem: "Mommy and Daddy cry a lot, and I don't want them to be sad anymore," she told me. We began to think of gifts she could leave them. She came up with the idea of taking out her first loose tooth.

"That's a special gift that I think they would really like," I said. "But we need to come up with something else your family can remember you by all their lives—not just Mommy and Daddy, but the grandmas, grandpas, uncles and aunties as well." She agreed.

With Maile's childlike connection with God in its purest form, I knew that her final gift to her family—which was for her to discover without my help—would be unique and special. Knowing she was okay, I spent many of my final visits with the family.

I posed the same question to Maile's family that I had asked her: "What will be your final gifts to her?" I wanted to involve all the family members and establish family rapport, too.

Their grief hindered their creative thoughts, so I mustered up the only idea God placed in my heart. "Suppose you men gather together and carve a casket out of koa wood with your loving hands." Koa wood is sacred to Hawaiians, and I knew it would have multiple meanings for them. The project would also unite them and give them strength. They jumped at the thought and agreed that the project would begin at Grandpa's house.

The women also struggled to think clearly about what they could give Maile. I saw a vision of a quilt made of all the special clothing pieces that had been worn and imbued with love by family members. I saw this colorful quilt surrounding and comforting Maile's little body in the koa casket. After many tears and hugs, the women agreed to begin the project at the other grandma's house.

With the projects assigned and support established among family members, I spent much of Maile's final few days with her while her parents and relatives were making their gifts.

Her days became quieter as she rested more. Her coloring book sat on the shelf with the crayons, never to be used again. As her breath became shallower, I had Lani and Keola take turns rocking their fragile child in their laps.

On my final visit, before I left Maile in the laps of her parents, I asked, "Have you thought of any special gift you want for your family?" Her big brown eyes looked up at me, then at her mommy and daddy. She said, "I want a baby brother or sister."

Both her parents were crying. Keola knelt beside Lani, who was holding Maile in her lap, and said, "Honey, we can't give you that gift."

She looked at them with a labored smile and said, "Not right now, but later. Then I can be the baby's angel, and watch over it and protect it."

I left the family alone that night. When I returned the next morning, Maile was in her bed, peaceful and with God, as family members surrounded her. Keola and Lani hugged me, and Keola opened his fisted hand, showing me his baby's first missing tooth. It fell out as they put her lifeless body back into her bed.

Her funeral was more special than I could have imagined. The quilt surrounding her little body was comforting and smelled like love. Loving hands also created the beautiful koa casket in which she rested. God had blessed this little family with a union that could not be torn apart.

And Maile's final gift? I got a call from Lani recently. They are expecting Maile's little angelic wings to go to work in June.

~Gail Eynon
Chicken Soup to Inspire the Body & Soul

74

The Snow Angel

Love the moment,
and the energy of that moment will spread beyond all boundaries.
~Corita Kent

Ever since I was little, my favorite season was winter. I loved to play in the snow and enjoy the hot chocolate.

Unfortunately, winter never gave me the special gift of snow on my birthday. The snow disappeared before my birthday and started after it.

I would ask my grandmother why it didn't snow on my birthday. She would laugh and tell me I asked too many questions. But one day, she promised that she would make it snow when I was enjoying life to the fullest. I thanked her and asked for snow on my next birthday.

That year, before my birthday, my grandmother died. I was at an emotional loss, but angry because she had promised me to make it snow. The day of my sixth birthday, I woke up and ran to my window, hoping to see just one snowflake.

Unfortunately, there was no snow. I cried and cried all day because my grandmother had let me down.

Before my birthday every year, I would pray for snow but it never came. I felt mad at my grandmother; she had broken a promise.

By my sixteenth birthday, I had lost all hope of getting my snow, even though I still wished for it. During my party, I had the best time ever! I enjoyed the company of my friends and family, and I was truly happy.

I was outside with a friend when she asked me if I was having a good time. I told her I was having the best time ever! I was enjoying life to the fullest. Then I saw the white snow falling all around. I became like a little child on Christmas morning as I ran around screaming and laughing. I was so excited that my friends looked at me as if I were crazy, and I think I was. They asked me if I had ever seen snow before, and I laughed and said that I had, but that this was special snow. They all laughed at me, but I didn't care.

When I got home, my grandpa told me he had a gift for me. I was confused because he had already given me my gift. He gave me a small white box that had snowflake wrapping on it. The box looked old, and it was turning a little yellow. I asked him what it was and he told me to stop asking so many questions and just open it. I did, and nestled in white paper was a crystal snowflake with a card that said, "Happy Birthday."

I asked my grandfather how this could be. He told me that it was my grandmother's final wish to give me this on my "sweet sixteenth." I cried and hugged him, although he didn't understand. I said a silent prayer to my smiling grandmother angel who I was certain was, and always had been, watching over me.

~Christine Fishlinger
Chicken Soup for the Preteen Soul

75

Daddy's Angels

Angels can fly directly into the heart of the matter.
~Author Unknown

"Dear Lord, could you please send two angels to protect my daddy? I don't mean to be selfish but, you see, he is six foot five. He may need the wings of both of them to completely cover him. Please let their wings shield him when the guns are fired and the rockets are shot. Let him know that he is protected and give him comfort. Amen."

I asked my girls to pray this prayer every day while my husband was gone, and I repeated a similar prayer many times throughout the day.

Two weeks after my husband's return from Baghdad, he told a story of how he returned to his trailer after midnight and felt that there was an intruder in his small living quarters. When his search revealed nothing, he prepared for bed with a great feeling of peace and comfort. One hour later he was awakened by the sound of rapid gunfire. Lying on his belly with his weapon drawn, he told us how he was never afraid.

My daughter asked him how this was possible.

My husband told her that he could feel someone in the room protecting him. Actually, he said, it felt more like two. My daughter's eyes grew wide as she looked at me and said quietly, "Daddy's angels."

This was the first my husband had heard of our special prayer for him.

~Tammy Ross
Chicken Soup for the Military Wife's Soul

76

A Matter of Believing

The guardian angels of life fly so high as to be beyond our sight,
but they are always looking down upon us.
~Jean Paul Richter

T he school bell rang loud and clear at the elementary school. Amidst much shouting and laughing, the children raced out the door for summer vacation. Johnny raced through the crowd to his bike, hopped on and headed home.

From nowhere, a car careened into him, knocking him off the bike and into the street, unconscious. The paramedics arrived and rushed him to the hospital, where doctors whispered behind closed doors and shook their heads solemnly. They had little hope the ten-year-old boy would make it.

News of the accident spread quickly. Teachers, friends and relatives came to the hospital to see their beloved Johnny and to pray and wait. He was conscious, but couldn't walk or talk. Johnny's mom stayed by his side day and night, praying and holding his little hand.

Slowly, he began to recover, trying to form words and even sitting up in bed. A nurse named Julie came by often to check on him and give him candy. But the doctors still doubted he would ever walk again.

Late one evening, Nurse Julie stopped in Johnny's room. She found him struggling to get out of bed. She rushed to help him, and soon Johnny's feet were on the floor. Julie looked him square in the eyes and said, "It's time for you to walk."

He took one step and stumbled. Julie reassured him: "Have faith, I'm here to help you. Believe you can do it, and you will." A few more steps led to a few more steps, and Johnny was walking. It was a miracle!

Johnny was standing by the window when his doctor came in. "How did you get over to the window?" he asked.

"Nurse Julie helped me," Johnny answered.

The doctor looked puzzled. "Who helped you?"

"Julie. She said all I had to do was believe, and I would walk again."

The doctor walked out of the room, mystified. There was no nurse named Julie. A thought crossed his mind. He shook it off. "No, I don't believe in angels." And he continued down the hall.

But it still puzzled him. He finally asked Johnny what the nurse looked like. From this description, he talked to the nurses, and learned that a nurse named Julie did work there—twenty-five years ago. After a bad accident she, also, was told she would never walk again. A few hours later, Julie died of heart failure.

The doctor talked with Johnny's parents, explaining the history of Nurse Julie. Johnny's mother smiled and said matter-of-factly, "Well, if God sent one of his angels, that's fine with me."

I met him at a charity bike-a-thon. After sharing his story with me, his faced beamed. "Today, I'm flying high because an angel of God touched me." I watched him ride, his muscles straining with the effort and his T-shirt blowing in the wind. He was on a bike again and truly flying high.

~Scot Thurman
Chicken Soup for the Nurse's Soul

77

River Baptism

The summer I turned thirteen, my family's vacation was a visit to our relatives in the mountains of North Carolina. My cousin Jim, who was my age, took me down to his favorite swimming hole along the river. It was a deep pool under a high canopy of leaves. From the top of a twenty-five-foot cliff, we looked down into the shimmering water and across to a sandy beach.

Standing beside us on the edge of that cliff grew a big white oak tree, with its roots sunk deep down into the rock. And hanging from a limb that stretched out at just the right height and angle was a rope swing.

"Look here," said Jim. "This is the way you do it. You got to get a running start. Then you grab the rope and swing out and up as high as you can, and then you let go and fall to the water. Here, I'll show you."

Jim made it look easy, and when his head surfaced in the bubbling water, he hollered up, "Now it's your turn!"

I was certain I was going to die, but at thirteen dying is better than looking bad. When I came up sputtering, Jim smiled approvingly, and we swam a few strokes to the beach, lay on the hot sand for a while, and then swam back across the pool to do it again.

Jim and all of his friends always wore the proper North Carolina swimming attire, because skinny-dipping was a time-honored tradition among boys throughout the mountain states. Sometimes I felt like I was a wild boy, or a beaver sliding through the water. Jim said he felt like an otter, since he loved to turn and twist in the deep pools and could swim underwater a long way.

Jim's family was Baptist. On Sunday, Jim's mom made us dress up in straight-jacket white shirts and stranglehold ties, marched us down the street and filed us into church.

"You must be baptized, by water and by the Spirit!" the preacher thundered. That water baptism sounded mighty good. I sat there dreaming of the river and waiting for the wonderful moment when the sermon would be over, and Jim and I could go running down the path to the river.

On the tails of the closing prayer, Jim and I flew out into the sunny day and home for a quick sandwich. Then we plunged down the trail into the woods alive with the hum of cicadas hanging thick in the branches of the burr oaks and hickories.

When we got within a hundred yards of the rope swing, Jim said, "I'll race you!"

"You got it!" I replied.

We dropped our clothes right there and tore down the trail to see who could get to the rope swing first. I was a fast runner, but Jim was faster. He pulled ahead of me and dove for the rope. With a shriek of victory, Jim swung out over the water and up to the very top of the arc. In perfect form, Jim let go of the rope and looked down to see where he was going to land.

But there—not twenty yards away on the beach—stood the preacher and two dozen of the faithful, performing a baptism. I could see they were looking straight up at Jim with their mouths wide open.

As fervently as Jim prayed to fly, he quickly descended from the heavens. Jim abandoned his plans for a graceful swan dive and instinctively assumed the cannonball position—known for its magnificent splash.

The whole congregation got baptized that day, but Jim never saw it. He broke his record for underwater swimming and was around the bend and out of sight while the congregation stood stunned and speechless on the shore.

"Don't worry, Jim," I consoled him later. "I'm sure everybody thought you were an angel, and besides, it turned out fine. You got the river dunking you wanted, and those folks will never forget that baptism."

Thinking about it now, I don't think there's much difference, anyway, between wild boys and angels, or between heaven and a rope swing on the river.

~Garth Gilchrist
Chicken Soup for the Nature Lover's Soul

78

Sister Said

Christmas is not a time nor a season, but a state of mind.
To cherish peace and goodwill, to be plenteous in mercy, is to
have the real spirit of Christmas.
~Calvin Coolidge

No two words in the English language could send our household into more of a tizzy than those two words, "Sister said." So when I announced shortly after Thanksgiving that the nuns at my elementary school said I was going to be one of the angels in the Christmas play, it set the wheels in motion for the most frenzied of activities.

My grandma rummaged through a trunk of yard goods, looking for the whitest of white scraps, while my father measured me shoulder to shoulder, neckline to shoe top. My mother searched the drawers and cupboards for the little bit of gold ribbon Sister said we were to wear around our waists. My father outlined wings on huge pieces of cardboard, wings that Sister said were to measure fourteen inches long and ten inches wide at the center.

My daily messages of "Sister said" brought occasional moans and groans from my dressmakers as plans were changed and sleeves had to cover our fingertips, not stop at the wrist as those on my robe did. Another day, Sister said the hem should be at least four inches deep and we should wear a pink slip under the robe, not a white one such as my grandma had just finished making.

When my brother Tom came home one night two weeks before

Christmas and said that his Sister had said that our family had to come to the Scout meeting that night, my father groaned the loudest and said, "But tonight I'm supposed to cut out those wings because Sister said Jeanie had to hand them in tomorrow for inspection!"

"Now, Raymond, you know perfectly well that I can cut out those wings," Grandma said. "You all go right ahead to that meeting, just like Sister said."

"Well, I don't know," my mother said. "You've been so tired lately. And you've taken that angel robe apart so many times the material is almost as worn as you."

"I'll be just fine," Grandma snapped. "Every stitch of the angel robe is made of love, and that's what keeps me going."

For the next few days and nights, my parents were too caught up with the Scouts' Christmas program to help much with the creation of my angel robe, so when late one Friday night, I said that Sister said the angels had to wear white shoes, my grandma promised, "We'll go right downtown tomorrow, Jeanie, just the two of us, and shop for those shoes. You parents have put enough wear and tear on their car for the time being."

Even though my mother exclaimed that the real wear and tear was more apparent on my grandmother, Grandma Thomas would hear none of it. Once again, she recited her line about every stitch of that robe being made of love.

Eight days before the play, Sister said it would be nice if all the angels had curls in their hair the night of the play, but not too many curls. Out came Grandma's bag of rags and each night before bedtime, she rolled up my hair, practicing, hoping to find that fine line between curly and not too curly. She listened patiently, too, as I sang "O Little Town of Bethlehem," a song Sister said we had to sing every night until we had the words down pat.

Each ensuing evening I had new and often contradictory tales of what Sister had said that day in regard to the angel robe. In their struggles to comply, my parents' nerves were often set on edge. Was it any wonder that when I came home four days before the play and tearfully said that Sister said I couldn't be an angel after all because I seemed too fat, my father thundered, "That does it! That does it! Too fat? Why, if you weighed an ounce less, you'd BE an angel, I fear. I do not ever want to hear 'Sister said' again in this house!"

"There must be some mistake," Grandma Thomas said softly.

"No, no! I know that's what Sister said," I cried.

"You march right up to Sister tomorrow, Jeanie," my mother said, "and get this straightened out. I'm sure there is some mistake. You are not too fat and you never will be."

"I can't do that," I sobbed. "Sister never makes mistakes."

"Perhaps if I went..." Grandma began, but my father said, "Absolutely not!"

"Jeanie must learn to stand on her own two feet," my mother said. "After all the work, all the love you put into that robe—why, I am sure there has been a mistake."

Thinking about all that love and how heartbroken my grandmother must have been kept me awake most of the night. The next morning I waited until the very last minute before leaving for school, hoping my grandmother would defy my parents and go with me. Or perhaps my father would not be as angry and would take matters into his own hands. Surely my mother would see I had not slept well. Maybe she would say, "You poor thing. You must stay home today. I will go talk to Sister myself."

But none of those dreams came true, and I ended up standing on my own two feet beside Sister's desk, asking, "Sister, why did you say I seemed too fat to be an angel?"

"Too fat!" Sister said, truly taken aback. "I never said—oh, I think I understand. Jeanie, I never said you seem too fat. I said you 'sing too flat.' Besides, I want you to be the narrator. You have a good strong voice and read very well. Will you do that part for me?"

Sing too flat! Not seem too fat! And now I was going to be narrator! The narrator's part was the best of the whole play!

"Oh, Sister," I said in a rush. "Oh, Sister, I'll do my very best. I'd much rather read than sing, you know."

"Don't I know!" Sister teased kindly.

"But... but, Sister," I asked, "What does the narrator wear?"

"Anything you want," Sister said. "You must have a special outfit you want to wear. Think it over and tell me about it when school is out."

I didn't need to think it over long, for school had barely begun when I knew the only outfit I wanted to wear. Now if only Sister would say yes, I prayed as the day dragged on.

When the bell rang at 3:30, I stood before Sister's desk once more.

"Have you decided on your outfit, Jeanie?" Sister asked as she straightened out her desktop.

"Yes, Sister, I have."

"And what is it made of? Cotton? Rayon? Velvet?"

Cotton? Rayon? Velvet? I didn't know! I only knew one thing my outfit was made of. Would Sister understand?

I drew a deep breath before I poured out the story of my outfit. At the story's end, I said, "So you see, Sister, all I know is that every stitch of my outfit is made of love. SO will that be okay?"

Sister bent down, picked me up and hugged me close as she tenderly whispered her reply.

My father wasn't home yet, so I could safely say "Sister said" without listening to him groan. It's too bad he wasn't there, because he didn't hear me shout as I came in the front door, "Sister said I can wear the angel robe! Sister said it's made of exactly what Christmas is made of! Lots and lots of love!"

And you know Sister. Sister never made a mistake.

~Jean Jeffrey Gietzen
Chicken Soup for the Grandma's Soul

A Child's Prayer

In my little bed I lie:
Heavenly Father, hear my cry;
Lord, keep Thou me through this night.
Bring me safe to morning light.
Amen.

Christian Kids

For Our Moms and Dads

*All kids need is a little help,
a little hope and somebody who believes in them.
~Earvin "Magic" Johnson*

79

Make a Wish, Mommy

Sometimes life's greatest lessons are the ones we would never be able to learn without difficult circumstances leading us there to them.

It was my twenty-eighth birthday, and I was depressed. Divorced, raising two children alone, and too poor to even afford a telephone, I was going through the most dark and depressing time in my life. I hadn't lived in Utah very long, and I was still trying to adjust to the snow, and this particular January was one of the most brutal in years.

The snow outside was literally thigh-high, and it was a daily struggle to leave the house, which added to my isolation. My son Nicholas was in kindergarten, and I was a junior at nearby Weber State University. I had taken the quarter off because my five-month-old, Maya, had been very ill, so I had little social interaction. It was a winter of loneliness for me, but also of incredible closeness with my children. My small son, with his enormous child-sized heart, taught me the greatest lesson.

The day before my birthday, I was a grouch. I was used to celebrating it with the friends I had moved away from. I was used to presents and phone calls, none of which I would be receiving this time. Feeling sorry for myself was becoming comfortable for me. Depression became so second-nature that I didn't even remember the happy, laughing person I used to be. I was so wrapped up in my own problems that I couldn't even see that the greatest joys, blessings and sources of laughter that I would ever know were right there in front of me.

Tucking the children into bed that night, I was in a cloud of hopelessness. My little Nick wrapped his chubby, six-year-old arms around my neck and said, "Tomorrow's your birthday, Mommy! I can't wait!" His blue eyes sparkled with an anticipation that mystified me.

Kissing his sweet rosy cheeks, I hoped that he didn't expect a birthday party to magically appear, like it did on his birthday. Life is so simple when you're six.

The next morning, I awoke before the children, and began making breakfast. Hearing noises in our tiny living room, I assumed Nick was up, and waited for him to come in to eat. Then I could hear Nick talking to Maya. He was sternly telling her to make Mommy smile today.

It suddenly hit me. Being so wrapped up in my misery, I didn't see how it affected my children. Even my little boy sensed I wasn't happy, and he was doing his best to do something about it. Tears of shame at my selfishness washed down my face. I knelt down in our little kitchen and asked for the strength to somehow find happiness again. I asked God to show me some beauty in my life. I asked Him to help me see, really see the blessings I did have.

Putting a smile on my face, I marched myself into the living room to hug my children. There sat Nick on the floor, Maya on her blanket next to him, and in front of them was a pile of presents. A birthday party for three.

I looked at the presents with disbelieving eyes, then looked back at my son. His face was gleeful at my shock. "I surprised you, Mommy, didn't I? Happy birthday!" He grinned his toothless, adorable grin.

Stunned, I knelt down next to him and with tears in my eyes, I asked him how in the world he had possibly found a way to get me presents. He reminded me of our trip to "All a Dollar Store." I suddenly remembered him telling me he was spending the allowance he had been saving for ages. I had laughed at his bulging pockets and remembered thinking that he walked like John Wayne, his pants loaded down with his life savings. I had almost chided him for spending everything he had so carefully saved, but thought better of it, and did my shopping while he did his.

Looking again at the beautiful pile of presents in front of me, I couldn't believe that my small, darling son had spent everything he had in his crayon bank on me. On his mom. What kind of kid goes without the toys he wanted so that he could buy his mom a pile of presents? There. I heard the voice in my heart: "I am showing you your blessings. How could you ever doubt them?" My prayers were being answered. No one was more blessed, and no one had more to be thankful for than I did. I had been so selfish and petty to feel unhappy with my life.

With tears flowing, I gently hugged my son and daughter and told them how lucky I was. At Nick's eager prompting, I carefully opened each present. A bracelet. A necklace. Another bracelet. Nail polish. Another bracelet. My favorite candy bars. Another bracelet. The thoughtful gifts, each wrapped in gift bags and wrapping paper purchased with a six-year-old's allowance, were the most perfect I've ever received. The final gift was his personal favorite. A wax birthday cake with the words "I love you" painted in fake frosting across the top.

"You have to have a birthday cake, Mom," my oh-so-wise little one informed me.

"It's the most beautiful cake I've ever seen," I told him. And it was. He then sang "Happy Birthday" to me in his sweet little boy voice that melted my heart and brought on more tears. "Make a wish, Mommy," he insisted.

I looked into my little boy's shining blue eyes and couldn't think of a single thing to wish for. "I already got my wish," I whispered through the tears. "I have you."

~Susan Farr Fahncke
Chicken Soup for the Christian Woman's Soul

80

One Mother's Dream

For as long as I can remember, I dreamed of holding a baby. When I was a child, she was an infant-sized doll. If I could sit still, I was allowed to hold my baby sister, then, three years later, my brother. In summer, I rocked a large zucchini with button eyes from Grandma's garden. When the neighborhood gang played house in our backyard, I was always Mom—and a bit bossy! Acting as Mother Mary in the annual La Posada at church, I felt honored to be carrying Baby Jesus.

As I grew older, with each romance I dreamed of the day when I would hold a baby and birth a family. I wept barren tears in my mid-twenties during years of discerning a celibate religious vocation, and later, while in a relationship with a man who didn't want to marry. I held babies I loved deeply... first a goddaughter, then a nephew, all the while smiling with joy, wondering when my time would come. I continued to dream and started to pray.

At thirty-one, the dream began in earnest. Together with Jim, my new husband—literally the man next door—I imagined the day we would hold our child, fantasizing perfect names and even beginning to purchase necessary baby gear. Month after month after month, tears flowed like clockwork. I held another nephew, then a niece, then a second goddaughter. Well-intentioned friends said things such as: "Just relax." "Get away for a romantic weekend." "If you adopt, you'll get pregnant for sure." "Fall on your knees and pray more." As if I hadn't already prayed, and tried everything I could think of! I was angry and sad. In prayer, I let God know it. After all, I was working in church ministry serving the Lord. I deserved my dream. I began to wonder if I was paying a price for past sins.

But the God I encountered in prayer was suffering with me, not condemning me. Barrenness has a powerful precedent in scripture. Stories of Sarah, Rachel and Elizabeth brought me renewed hope. I just knew a baby and family was God's good and creative dream in me. How could it be denied? I heard God's word in Psalm 46: "Be still and know that I am God." Yet, year after year my healthy, strong, vibrant body betrayed me.

Jim and I spent considerable time contemplating fertility treatments, sperm donors, domestic and international infant adoption, and our limited finances. When a notice in our church bulletin listed a phone number with a request for foster adoptive parents, we just wanted to eliminate a choice we didn't think was a fit for us. Thus, one hot July evening, we sat on our porch with a caseworker from the local foster adoption agency. The three of us sat on our deck, overlooking a Colorado lake, with a little rowboat moored on the shore, where Jim spent most of his leisure time fishing.

As our conversation progressed, the caseworker asked, "Are you certain you want to adopt an infant?"

I replied, "Yes."

A little later in the conversation, the same question. My answer remained, "Yes."

Finally, again, "Are you certain you want an infant?"

I looked into her eyes. "What are you thinking? That's the third time you've asked me the same question."

"Well," she answered, "if you were to adopt an older child you could continue working." I just stared at her. "And," she continued, "I know a seven-year-old boy in town who loves to fish and desperately needs a strong father and forever family."

I didn't move. The next thing I knew my six-foot-five husband was towering over us, practically shouting, "That's the right age for me!"

I sat stunned. Birds chirped in the trees. I listened to my heart beat wildly.

So be it.

One month later, just in time for third grade, our son-to-be spent his first night in our home.

Nothing prepared me for parenting a little boy who had lived in nine foster homes. The warm fuzzies I had anticipated were non-existent. Somewhere along the way I neglected to comprehend that foster children like Justin already had birth parents, a family and past experiences that shaped their lives. Bonding and attachment might not happen, maybe couldn't. I discovered my own worst behaviors were not unlike Justin's: anger at not being listened to, not having my needs met. Odd that as an adult I had the same feelings as the child in my home.

I slowly learned to understand the gift of being a lifesaver for a young boy—and he became a lifesaver of sorts for me, too, as I grew into fuller maturity, discovering within myself reservoirs of patience and wisdom. My prayer was simple: to love him as Jesus.

Together we learned the safety of boundaries. We talked about feelings, listened to one other. Justin began to grow with our focused, consistent attention, meals and bedtimes. Learning about Jesus, he discovered he could be loved no matter what. I felt happiness that he felt safe enough to throw a temper tantrum. He explored personal interests, caught fish and gained confidence. Through prayer, I learned to love him as if I had birthed him myself. God softened my heart and taught me generosity.

One afternoon after an emotional meltdown, Justin asked if he could sit on my lap. Though his legs and arms were a bit long, I snuggled him closely against me. Looking beyond my shoulder, he cautiously asked, "If you had been my birth mom, what would you have done?"

Realizing he wanted to hear a different version of his own tumultuous childhood, I said softly, "I would have held you every day, rocking you just like this, and told you stories, real and imaginary. You would have known you were safe and loved, no matter what." I stopped talking, feeling the weight of his body against mine, then continued, "And you know what? We can still do that, even though your elbow is poking my side!"

We chuckled together and after a minute of rocking, the air hushed. He turned, looking me straight in the eyes, and asked, "Could you tell me a story now?"

My blinking eyelids pushed back tears. Smiling at him, I began: "A long, long time ago, a little girl dreamed of being a mom and holding a little boy on her lap...." His hand gripped mine tightly. Breathing slow and steady, he listened intently, never taking his eyes from mine.

In the coming months Justin often asked to sit on my lap, and we discovered how much we both needed each other. Later that year, after his legal adoption, I received an unexpected valentine: "Dear Mom, Thank you so much for taking care of me over all these years and making sure that I have food to eat and that I have a roof over my head. I also love having a very loving and caring person such as you."

Not words I ever expected I'd receive from a child. But still more powerful to me than an actual, "I love you, Mommy," which I suspect I'll never hear.

Justin is now in his teens and an only child. I have learned the fierce love that I am certain Mary shared with her son two thousand years ago. Jesus has taught me to welcome and love the orphan. Just last week, at five-foot-nine, Justin gave me a hug, and looking down at me, asked, "Do you remember when I was small enough to fit in your lap?"

I smiled a "yes" into his eyes and offered a silent prayer of gratitude to be living a mother's dream.

~Pegge Bernecker
Chicken Soup for the Christian Soul 2

81

Mother's Day Flowers

Blessed be the hand that prepares a pleasure for a child,
for there is no saying when and where it may bloom forth.
~Douglas Jerrold

When my husband calmly announced that, after eleven years of marriage, he had filed for a divorce and was moving out, my first thought was for my children. My son was just five, and my daughter, four. Could I hold us together and give them a sense of family? Could I, as a single parent, maintain our home and teach them the ethics and values I knew they would need in life? All I knew was that I had to try.

So every Sunday, we attended church. During the week, I made time to review their homework with them, and we often discussed why it was important to do the right things. This took time and energy when I had little to spare, and worse, it was hard to tell if I was really reaching them.

One Mother's Day, two years after the divorce, as we walked into church, I noticed carts of beautiful flowers in little pots on either side of the altar. During the service, the pastor told us that he thought motherhood was one of the toughest jobs in life, and deserved recognition and reward. He then asked every child to come forward to pick out a beautiful flower and present it to his or her mother as a symbol of how much she was loved and appreciated.

My son and daughter, hand in hand, went up the aisle with the other children. Together they considered which plant to bring back to me. We had certainly survived some hard times, and this little bit of appreciation was just what I needed. I looked at the beautiful begonias, the golden marigolds and purple pansies, and started planning where I could plant whichever one they chose for me, for surely they would bring me a beautiful bloom to show their love.

My children took their assignment seriously, and looked over every pot on all the carts. Long after the other children had returned to their seats, and presented the other mothers with a beautiful potted flower, my two were still making their selection. Finally, with a joyful exclamation, they made their selection from the back of one of the carts. With exuberant smiles lighting their faces, they proudly proceeded down the aisle to where I was seated and presented me with the plant they had chosen as their Mother's Day gift of appreciation.

I stared in amazement at the broken, bedraggled, sickly looking stick being held out to me by my son. Mortified, I accepted the pot from him. They had obviously chosen the smallest, sickest plant — it didn't even have a bloom on it. Looking down at their smiling faces, I saw their pride in this choice, and knowing how long it took them to choose this particular plant, I smiled and accepted their gift.

But then I had to ask — out of all those beautiful flowers — what had made them pick this particular plant to give to me?

With great pride, my son said, "This one looked like it needed you, Mom."

As tears flowed down my face, I hugged both children close. They had just given me the greatest Mother's Day gift I could ever have imagined. My hard work and sacrifices had not been in vain — they would grow up just fine.

~Patricia A. Rinaldi
Chicken Soup for the Mother's Soul 2

82

The Birthday

Prayer does not change God,
but it changes him who prays.
~Søren Kierkegaard

"Hurry, Mom, hurry! Blow out the candles!" my four-year-old daughter, Abigail, shouted, tugging on my shirt. "Make a prayer," she reminded, her brown eyes alight with childish wonder.

"Make a prayer?" her grandmother asked. "What's that?"

"Silly Grammy!" Abigail laughed, covering her mouth. "We say prayers instead of wishes! It's easy!"

The lights dimmed and the candles flickered. Several witty birthday cards on aging were propped beside the cake. Just last month, my older brother refused to celebrate his fortieth birthday. He had not wanted to be reminded that he was getting older. I closed my eyes and breathed deeply. How many people, including myself, did that each year?

My daughter slipped her hand into my pocket, her tiny fingers finding mine. I rubbed her soft skin and sighed.

Memories of my friend, Susie, flooded me. Mother of two and married for over twenty years, Susie had been young and vibrant. She'd had a welcoming grin, a kind heart—and breast cancer. Violently sick from chemotherapy, she had lost her hair and begun a journey of pain and endurance.

Her husband, desperate for a medical breakthrough, had

arranged experimental procedures, but nothing worked and her condition worsened. Time passed, but Susie refused to give up.

Those who knew her best began to doubt her life-and-death decisions. "Why is she doing this to herself?" they'd often asked. "She and her family are going to have to accept the inevitable. She's going to die. She should stop the treatments and live the rest of her days as best she can. Can't she see that?"

I had joined together with a prayer partner, and we had diligently lifted Susie in prayer from the onset of her cancer. Everyone who loved Susie wanted what was best for her. Some chose the "live your remaining days free of medical services" approach. Others continued helping her find new alternatives. Whatever their advice, Susie never wavered from her path—doing whatever she had committed to do in order to beat the disease. She continued medical treatment though her doctors told her there was little hope.

During Susie's struggle, at night when I cradled my newborn son, I often thought of her family that would be left behind if she died. Maybe it was because of how I loved my own children and husband that her battle affected me so greatly.

Looking at life through Susie's eyes, a new humility and appreciation for each new day surrounded me. When my husband kissed me as he left for work, I'd linger in his arms a little longer. Every night, I'd kneel beside my children's sleeping figures and study their angelic faces, not wanting to take one second for granted. Soon, I began to ache for Susie, and during that time I realized why she'd continued on with such passion.

Susie knew the secret of life. And that secret, simply, was life itself.

She wanted another opportunity to laugh and smack her husband's hand as he pinched her when she walked past. She wanted to witness her daughter's high school graduation and her son's first prom. She wanted to see the glory of another sunrise and wanted to be in the world when her first grandchild entered it. Life was not a mystery but a miracle. And Susie knew that, right up until the moment when, on a crisp winter day, she died.

"Mama," Abigail said, pointing to the candles. "Hurry, they're melting!"

My husband, holding our precious son, Simeon, caught my eyes from across the table. He kissed the top of Simeon's head, then smiled at me. Butterflies fluttered in my stomach. Those whom I loved most were near.

Because of Susie's zest for life and faith in God, I've never seen birthdays in the same way again. Anxiety didn't flood me at my first wrinkles. And since Susie's death, I've never bought an insulting birthday card again. Instead, I've embraced the joys and trials of getting older. After all, each birthday is one more year that I've experienced life's many jewels, ranging from my children wrestling with my husband to me being awakened by a bird's morning song.

"Hurry, Mama! Hurry!" Abigail pleaded. "I'll help you blow them out!"

My son giggled, waving his hand at me, and my husband winked. "Let's do it," I told my daughter. We filled our cheeks with air and blew out the candles. The smoke traveled upward.

"Look, Mama! Look!" Abigail shouted, pointing a finger towards the ceiling. "The smoke's carrying your prayer to heaven! It's gonna be answered!"

Bending down, I cupped Abigail's beautiful face. Her eyes were beaming, and I inhaled the sweet scent that was hers exclusively. "It already has been, honey," I whispered, thanking Jesus for another year. "It already has been."

~Karen Majoris-Garrison
Chicken Soup for the Christian Soul 2

Letting Them Go

Dad, your guiding hand on my shoulder
will remain with me forever.
~Author Unknown

The preparation was always exhausting, for me anyway. Of course, most of the work fell on me — and my darling wife who makes sure we don't forget anything: preparing menus, shopping for supplies, inspecting camping gear, restringing fishing reels, organizing and restocking tackle boxes, making lists and checking them twice, and making sure it all gets loaded into the van. All of this preparation was for our annual father/son canoeing and fishing adventure. We both looked forward to this trip and the time we could spend together. We were always diligent. We never embarked on our adventures unprepared. As the final preparations were concluded, an irony flashed through my mind: All of the planning and all of the work end up with us letting them go.

The smallmouth bass in the Ozark Mountain streams we fished were a treat to catch, for us and for many other anglers. But they were particularly susceptible to fishing pressures, so I instructed my son about catch and release. I taught him about the joy of letting them go, watching them swim away so they could come to us again another day, bigger and stronger.

This year my son was intent on exerting his independence. After a little refresher on knot tying, he successfully attached his hook to the end of his line and slipped on his bait of choice. We pushed the canoe into the river, and the adventure began. It was not long before the fish began to bite. It was time for more lessons. On each cast I offered a little advice, and help when he asked for it.

"Reel up the slack before you set the hook, son."

"Keep your rod tip up after you set the hook. Don't let any slack in the line."

"Don't reel against the drag. Let the fish take the line."

"Leave enough line so you can reach down and lip the fish, son. There you go. Now grab him quick! Don't be afraid."

"Now, leave slack in the line when you are taking the hook out. Work quickly so you don't hurt the fish."

"Here, son, let me help you with that."

As the day wore on, he needed less and less help. Eventually, I remained silent as he hooked a nice smallmouth and let him pull against the drag. He played the fish well. As the fish tired, he gently brought it to the canoe, lipped the fish out of the water, removed the hook, admired it for a moment and let it go.

As we watched the fish swim away through the crystal-clear water, my son exclaimed, "I did it, Dad! I did it all by myself! I even let it go!"

All of the preparation, all of the work, all of the instruction, just to let them go. But there was joy in letting them go, as the smile on my son's face attested.

One week later we were going canoeing with the church youth group. My son was now old enough to be a "youth," and this was his first trip with them. A lot seemed to have changed in the span of one week. My son wanted to pack his things all by himself. He didn't mind my being around, so long as I acted like I didn't know him. He even rode in a canoe with someone else. I was glad he blended in with the group so well.

As I reflected on my son's growing independence, the irony flashed through my mind again:

All of the planning, the work, the instruction, the protection and all of the love end up with us letting them go. But there is joy in letting them go.

I hope I can remember that.

~Gary Usery
Chicken Soup for the Fisherman's Soul

Table of Plenty

I believe in prayer.
It's the best way we have to draw strength from heaven.
~Josephine Baker

When our family sits at the table for a meal, I am reminded of how blessed we are to give grace, eat, drink and share our assemblage under one roof.

There was a time in our lives when internal circumstances led to our family being separated from one another.

Many summers ago, when our daughter was five years old, my husband and I decided to disunite after thirteen years of marriage. We both felt more affected by the worse than the better.

I filed for divorce, obtained legal guardianship of our daughter and ventured to a town about fifty miles north of the city where my husband resided.

It was not an easy time because I had been a stay-at-home mom for several years, and had very little money. We stayed with relatives of my husband's for a while. Then we moved into an apartment over a cake shop, which was one block from where my daughter attended school.

Meanwhile, my daughter and I began visiting a large church in the center of town. The more we visited, the more determined I was for us to return there.

One Sunday, as I listened to the angelic voices of the choir that echoed from the rear balcony of the church, the Holy Spirit touched my heart and soul with such magnitude that I felt compelled to become a member.

I wanted my daughter to be baptized in this particular faith. I also wanted her to grow in the knowledge that, although her parents were apart, we dearly loved her and, most importantly, so did God.

During the same period I obtained an education grant and enrolled in a computer class so I could find a job to support us. It had been years since I was in a classroom all day, so it took all I had to concentrate and persevere, but I knew that with God's help it would be done.

Each day before I drove my daughter to school and hurried to my class, I prayed, "Dear Heavenly Father, please help me find the strength and courage I need to get through another day. I pray that You will wrap Your loving arms of protection around my daughter and me, so that we may be reunited by the end of the day—alive and well. Amen."

As my spirituality grew, so did the positive factors in my life. I was blessed with an internship during the two semesters I was a student. I wrote an essay for the Soroptimist Club and won an award.

By Thanksgiving, there was much to be thankful for: our new friends, and the kindness they gave to us as mentors, neighbors and parishioners.

I was receiving child support payments and was thankful to God, the state and my estranged husband for the help. He had always been a responsible and devoted father, and I could tell by his phone conversations that God was also at work in his life. For the first time in many years, I sensed in him a genuine sensitivity and concern for my total well-being.

One night at bedtime, I overheard my daughter pray, "God—please let me see my daddy on Christmas, and let my mommy and daddy be together again. Amen."

The prayer brought on a flow of emotion that I had tried desperately to suppress. As I silently sobbed, I repeated her prayer.

The next day my husband phoned to let me know he had shopped for the presents our daughter had requested for Christmas. At that point, I invited him to join us at the apartment for the holidays.

When I hung up, I had ambiguous thoughts about seeing him, and wondered if I had been too impulsive. While I was pleased that his presence would be an answer to our daughter's prayer, I was also worried that it would have the potential to evoke an upsurge of negative feelings between us again.

The church asked if it could provide my daughter and me with Christmas gifts. I turned them down, not because I was proud or ungrateful, but because I felt God would provide us with the gifts for which we had prayed.

On Christmas, my husband and I communicated without blame or consternation. We laughed about things that no longer had any significance, and calmly discussed everything that did. We related to each other with greater respect. This time there was clarity in our individual purpose, credulity within our joint understanding and unity in our mission as parents. Our family of three shared in the spirits of hope, joy and gratitude that holy season.

As the months progressed into the next year, our daughter had her first communion. After the sacrament, a photo was taken of our family outside the church. In the picture, there is a statue of St. Joseph with his arm extended toward us, in a surrounding halo of light. I perceived the anomaly in the picture to be a sign that God was still answering our prayers, and that He wanted us to be a real family again.

After almost two years of a second courtship—which included commutes, a wealth of letters and phone calls, bouquets of flowers, restaurant dinners, counseling and church visits—my husband and I rebuilt our marriage. This time, we based it on faith, love, respect and patience.

The day before school began in the fall, my daughter and I moved back to the city and reunited with my husband as a family—in our new home.

Sure, there are still some challenges, but they don't seem as insurmountable anymore. We live one day at a time, grateful to God for all blessings great and small, and for His forgiveness of our failings.

We give you thanks, almighty God,
for these and all your gifts
which we have received
through Christ our Lord. Amen.

~Stephani Marlow James
Chicken Soup for the Christian Soul 2

85

Mommy's Moon

I was twenty years old when my wife died, leaving behind only a sparkling memory of her touch and a beautiful baby girl named Aurora. We called her Rory for short, because I always liked the name Rory, and through constant use, I had gotten my way.

Rory grew quickly, and like all bright-eyed children, she led me through a range of emotions that parents often experience with these beautiful, frustrating little bundles of tears and wonder. But something was coming, and I wasn't sure I could deal with it.

"She's going to ask questions." I heard over and over again from my well-meaning friends. It was usually backed up with either, "It's going to be hard," or "I wouldn't want to have to answer them."

Rory was stumbling on unsure baby legs toward that fateful day, and I was dreading every moment of it. When she was asleep or off at a garage sale with her grandparents, I would sit in my room and plan strategies, writing down the things I wanted to say to her. Every carefully worded speech I prepared ended up at the bottom of the wastebasket, or shredded on the floor, as I became more convinced with each passing day that I would blow it and say something stupid.

We were sitting on the front porch one brisk summer night, watching the cars whiz past the house, and I was telling Rory about how interesting it was that every car that went past contained people with a different story to tell. Rory was drinking from her juice cup and not really listening, a skill she'd developed from my constant need to talk to her.

She turned on my lap then, and asked a question.

"Daddy, where is my mommy?"

I stalled. My heart was pounding, and I began to fumble. I was at a loss for words. What do I say? How do I make this one better? I couldn't think. My mouth was dry; I felt like I was chewing on cotton balls.

"She's in heaven," I said stupidly. I'm not a religious man, but it was the only thing I could think of.

Rory thought this over for a moment. "Is that in Canada?"

I almost smiled. We had been discussing Santa Claus earlier, and I was informing her of his Canadian nationality, as the North Pole was in Canadian territory. As far as Rory knew, everything was in Canada.

"No, honey," I said, holding her close to me. "I think it's way up in the sky, past all the stars, even beyond outer space."

Rory looked up at the night sky, and her eyes gravitated toward the big yellow moon hanging in front of us. Suddenly, her eyes brightened.

"The moon!" she squealed.

"Yup. A big old yellow moon," I said. "Rory, did you know that those dark spots are mountains and valleys?" Ever the educator. Like I said, Rory learned how to ignore me out of necessity.

"Mommy's moon," she said, still smiling.

"What was that?" I asked, confused.

"Mommy's on the moon, where she can see me," Rory replied. I gasped. Her logic amazed me sometimes.

"What is she doing up there?" I asked.

"Fixing my broken toys. I hope she comes back someday."

And that was that. Leaving me speechless, she went back to her juice cup.

I like to tell myself that I am responsible for my daughter's imagination. I also like to tell myself that my little girl will always be a little girl. Somehow, I don't really think either is true. I do believe, however, that adults complicate things that don't need to be so complicated.

For me, it was coming to terms with mortality and loss. For Rory, it was as easy as looking up into the night sky.

~J. W. Schnarr
Chicken Soup for the Single Parent's Soul

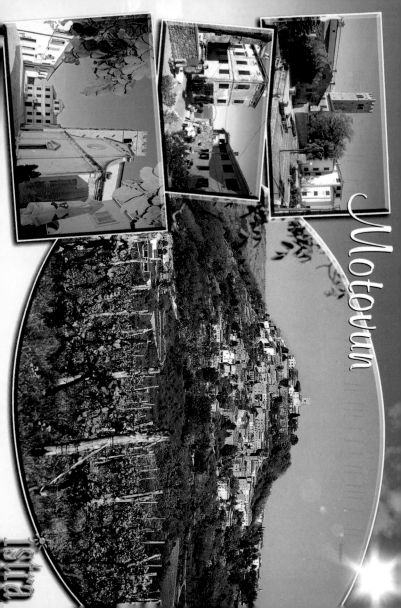

Motovun

Istra

Hrvatska golupka (*Hemaris croatica*)

HRVATSKA Republika

ⓗHP

2012

4.60

Tisak MORE • Rijeka • 051-624-464 • 051-624-177

CROATIA

PLITVIČKA JEZERA
06 06 13 12
53231

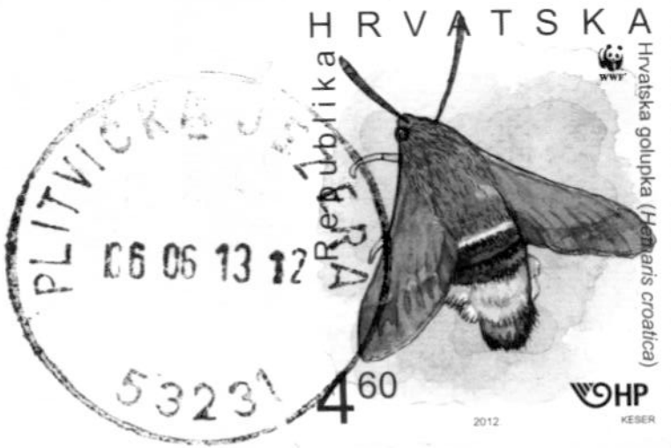

KYLER SORBER
1556 DUNKIRK RD.
TMR, QC H3R-3K3
CANADA

Hey Kyler - Pliz card
w/ photo to Mario &
Ondrette - been driving
over a week now and
feel I'm really for a rest.
In Slovenia - walked to
Vintgar Gorge - awesome
waterfalls, tiny chapels,
old cemeteries - over the
top great (5 hrs got lost)
Graham + Gail

The Lord's Prayer for Children

Our Father who art in heaven;
Hallowed be Thy Name;
Thy kingdom come;
Thy will be done on earth as it is in heaven;
Give us this day our daily bread;
And forgive us our trespasses as we forgive those who trespass against us;
And lead us not into temptation;
But deliver us from evil;
For Thine is the kingdom, and the power, and the glory, forever and ever.
Amen.

Christian Kids

Miracles Happen

For every mountain there is a miracle.
~ Robert H. Schuller

86

Covered

For He shall give his angels charge over thee,
to keep thee in all thy ways.
~Psalm 91:11

The day began like most days; I was running behind. After wolfing down breakfast, I ran out the door and down the street to my friend Teresa's house, only to find she wasn't going to school that day.

I knew if I went back for Mom, I would be late for school, so I ignored her warnings about the dangers of being at the bus stop alone. If I'd had a clue as to what was in store for me, I would have chosen to be late.

As it was, the bus itself was late, so I sat on the grass under a tree and opened a book. I got so into what I was reading, that I didn't pay much attention to the men in the pickup as they passed by, or when they stopped up the road and backed up. They caught my attention when they spoke to me, but I didn't understand what they said. I stood up and asked, "Pardon me?"

The truck held two men who were in their mid-twenties. The driver had dark hair and a tattoo on the arm he had hanging out the window; the other man had long blond hair.

I knew not to speak to strangers, but I asked again, "Pardon me? I didn't understand what you said."

The driver asked, "Have you seen a black lab running loose?

He disappeared out of our yard last night, and I can't find him anywhere."

While he was talking, something in the back of my mind told me I shouldn't be having this conversation at all. Finally, a bell went off in my mind and I remembered Mom and Dad having Mr. Jay come into our karate class and act out this very same scenario with all the younger students.

It was like déjà vu. The man in the truck uttered the very same words Mr. Jay had used during our self-defense class, "How about coming over here so I can show you his picture. That way you can let me know if you see him. Maybe you will see him while you're on the bus, or something."

Under the tree, I was well away from the road, but I still began to back up.

"Come on, it will only take a minute to look. What if it was your dog, wouldn't you want somebody to help you find him?"

My emphatic "No! You look for your own dog" wasn't the answer he was looking for, and when the driver first opened his door, I was shocked. No one in class had ever said someone would actually get out of their vehicle and come after me. They did always have a saying in class though, "He who runs away, lives to fight another day."

I ran.

When I looked back, the blond guy had slid over to the steering wheel and was driving on the road parallel to me while the other guy was gaining ground behind me. It was then that I really started to get scared.

I tried to pray, but all that would run through my head was, Oh God! Oh God! Please don't let him get me!

When the man latched onto the neck of my T-shirt and pulled me backward, I couldn't scream, claw, bite, punch or kick, because I froze.

It was only when he let go of my shirt and grabbed my wrist that I was once again able to move. We had covered wrist grabs many times, and thankfully, lessons that had been repeatedly practiced became instinctual.

I stepped back and executed the twisting yank against his thumb that also caused my upper body to twist away from him. When I realized it had worked, I almost froze again, but instead, I finished the technique they had taught me.

Using the torque of my twisted body, I swung back around at the man and landed a back fist to his face. Between the torque, the adrenaline and my height, I made a solid connection that made his nose bleed. I allowed my body to continue on past with the back fist and gave the strongest spinning back kick I could to the man's knees.

With blood running down his face and hopping on one leg, the guy began to curse me, but I didn't wait around to hear much. I ran across the field, crawled through the fence of a horse farm, ran past the horses and on to the closest house. Luckily, I knew the people who lived there. From there, I called the police and then my mom.

When Mom heard what had happened, she began to cry and shake. It wasn't until we got to the sheriff's office and I told them my story that I began to cry, too.

Two weeks later, the paper reported the abduction of a twelve-year-old girl not far from our home who was taken by two men in a truck that matched the description I had given the deputy. I often wonder if some martial arts training could have helped to save her.

Later on I heard Mom and Dad discussing what had happened. I heard my mom say to him, "All those years of karate really helped her defend herself when she really needed it. But, knowing what happened to that other girl, I think Victoria had a little extra help that day. I believe that God covered her back, too."

~Victoria Perry as told by Tenna Perry
Chicken Soup for the Preteen Soul 2

87

Our Little Pink Blanket

I was having a normal conversation with my four-year-old daughter about various things when suddenly she announced, "I saw Jesus, Mommy!"

"Oh you did? Where did you see him, Lauren?" I asked, expecting to hear church or Sunday school as her answer.

"In heaven, when I was sick," she stated matter-of-factly.

My mind drifted back to days I usually try to forget....

Lauren, our second daughter, was determined to be born early. My husband Keith and I were expecting twins, and I had miscarried one twin at six weeks. I was then put on bed rest for six weeks to keep Lauren in tow until her May 19th due date. On February 7, 1989, the excitement started—premature labor. We went to the emergency room at the local hospital where the doctor transferred me to a larger hospital with a neonatal unit. As I was being transferred out I overheard him say, "The baby will probably be born dead."

We arrived at the new hospital expecting bad news and were thrilled to hear our chances were fifty-fifty. I was twenty-five weeks along in the pregnancy, and I was hoping to hold out until week thirty-four. I did not like the idea of being confined to bed one hundred miles from home, with a two-and-a-half-year-old daughter and a husband waiting for me there. But I knew I had to do everything possible to increase our baby's chances.

Eight days had come and gone with no problems when my husband called to check on us and tell me he was coming for an unplanned visit.

Round two then began. Lauren's heart rate flattened out and the pain began. They wheeled me to surgery for an emergency C-section, and Lauren was born at twenty-seven weeks old, just as Keith arrived. She was so tiny—two pounds, twelve ounces and only sixteen inches long. Her frail body was strapped down, tubes dangling out of her everywhere. We only saw her seconds before she was whisked away. The doctors told us she was very big for her age, but a very sick little girl. She had hemorrhaging in her head, and her lungs were not developed.

At about 4 A.M., I received a call from a doctor stating they had to insert two chest tubes into Lauren. It seems her lungs were leaking, endangering her heart. "She is a very sick little girl," the doctor stated once again. Still, somehow I knew she'd be all right.

I was dismissed from the hospital and told I had to go home and rest. It broke my heart to leave our daughter in the ICU. We visited twice a week and called at least two times a day. How I ached to hold and rock her. The doctors and nurses were wonderful, filling us in on every little detail. Lauren was a real fighter. She constantly pulled out her tubes and they had to put mittens on her hands. I remember thinking, "She's going to make it." I just knew it.

After a few more setbacks, and a lot of prayers and love, we finally took Lauren home—one month earlier than the doctors had anticipated. As Keith held Lauren in his arms, I began packing. Among her many tiny Cabbage Patch preemie dresses was a small pink blanket.

"This pink blanket is not ours," I informed the nurse.

"Yes, I think it is," she answered.

"No, I would have remembered buying such a warm, fuzzy, tiny pink blanket," I insisted.

"No, you did not buy it," the nurse admitted, then slowly explained. "When a baby is not expected to make it, we wrap them in this blanket and let the parents hold them one last time."

Keith and I stared at each other and then Lauren. She was truly our miracle baby. We continued to pack her belongings and I cried most of the way home—it was all over now....

"Mommy, I said I saw Jesus in heaven when I was sick!" Lauren repeated.

"What did He say? What did He do?" I quizzed my four-year-old child.

"I went up to heaven when I was very sick in the hospital. Jesus walked towards me and held me," she answered as if it were yesterday. "He then told me I should go back. Jesus said 'You will be all right. Go back.' So I said bye and came back."

And so she did.

~Sandy Deters
Chicken Soup for the Christian Woman's Soul

88

Abigail's Dove

Pay attention to your dreams—
God's angels often speak directly to our hearts when we are asleep.
~ The Angels' Little Instruction Book
by Eileen Elias Freeman

I t had been the worst snowstorm in ten years, and I'd been caught in it. After hearing earlier that it was supposed to snow later in the night, I had volunteered at our church to take groceries and medical prescriptions to elderly members in need. Since my husband was away on business, I called my mother and she immediately came over to my house to watch my three-year-old daughter, Abigail.

"Can't someone else help those people?" she had asked me, concerned for my safety. "I have a bad feeling about this, and it looks like it might snow at any minute."

I glanced out the window and had to admit that the sky looked threatening. I began to feel uncertain.

"Mama will be okay," my daughter smiled, taking her grandmother's hand. "She likes helping people. Besides, I'll be praying for her!"

My heart swelled at her words. We had such a close relationship that sometimes when I breathed, it was as though Abigail exhaled. I decided then that I had to act on what I'd been instilling in my daughter: that sometimes we just have to step out in faith and believe that God will keep us safe. Kissing my mother and daughter goodbye,

I set out to make my rounds. On my last stop, the snow began to fall.

"You shouldn't have come here," Bill Watkins, a ninety-two-year-old member of our congregation, scolded. He coughed, trying to get out of bed, but the effort proved too taxing. Giving up, he settled back onto the pillows. "I told the pastor that I didn't expect anyone to come to the boonies for me."

"Nonsense," I grinned, positioning snacks and drinks by his bed. Beneath his gruff exterior, Bill was sweet as candy. His heart medication had to be taken every day, and living on a modest income without any surviving family members, he needed as much help as possible.

"Well, look what your stubbornness brought you," he said, pointing to the snow-covered road outside the window. His fingers clasped my hand. "Stay here, Karen. I want you safe."

I kissed the top of his head but decided to brave the road conditions. It would be worse later, I reasoned.

"I'll be okay," I told him, remembering my sweet daughter's words before I left. Thoughts of Abigail made me more determined to get home. I missed her already.

I got into my Volkswagen and gradually tried making it down the steep hill. Remembering old instructions about driving in the snow, I kept the compact car in second gear. The wind increased, creating waves of blinding white. As I squinted through the windshield, holding my breath, I screamed and jerked the wheel, narrowly missing the deer that stood frozen by my headlights.

The Volkswagen hit the embankment, plummeted off the side of the road, and skidded to the bottom of a ravine below. When the rolling motion finally stopped, I opened my eyes and realized that I had been unconscious for some time. Night had arrived—and with it the forecasted accumulation of snow. Panicking, I tried opening the door, but it wouldn't budge against the resisting snow. Sliding over to the passenger's door, I realized that the door had been jammed shut by a tree. I turned the key to start the engine, but the battery was dead. My hopes of rolling down the power windows to crawl out vanished.

Without heat and adequate clothing, I curled up on the back seat and waited for help.

The frigid air enveloped me. Shivering, I chastised myself for not preparing for a circumstance like this. My toes and fingers were already numb. An eternity seemed to pass, and as I listened to the wind and snow hitting against the car, I prayed for my family, who would be sick with worry by now. Abigail would probably be drawing pictures for me when I arrived home. Since she'd been old enough to hold a crayon, she'd drawn pictures to brighten the days of her loved ones.

To calm my growing concern about my safety, I closed my eyes and concentrated on pleasant thoughts. Drifting into sleep, I saw Abigail. Abigail in the warm sunlight, laughing as she held out a beautiful white dove to me. The dove's graceful, serene presence and the love shining in my daughter's eyes filled me with peace.

The night grew colder, and as I floated in and out of consciousness, I fixed my mind on the image of Abigail and her dove. Together, they kept me company throughout the night. Hours later, as the first rays of daybreak appeared, I heard tapping on my window. Relieved to see an emergency rescue team, my stiff lips tried to smile as they hoisted me onto a stretcher and into an ambulance. At the hospital, I was treated for mild frostbite and a head wound before being told I'd have to stay overnight for observation. Anxious to see my family, I propped myself up on the bed pillows and waited impatiently.

Before long, the door opened and my mother burst into the room. "We were so worried about you!" she cried, rushing over to hug me. "I knew you were in trouble! Mothers sense these kinds of things." Her maternal instincts surfaced as she appraised the food tray nearby. "Your tea is cold! I'll be right back."

Seizing the opportunity to have me all to herself, Abigail climbed onto the bed and buried her face in my neck. I scooped her closer. "I've missed you so much," I murmured softly, brushing a silky strand of hair from her face. "And what have you been doing while I've been away?"

"Oh, I forgot!" she exclaimed, jumping out of my arms to grab a large tube of construction paper nearby. "I drew this for you last night when we didn't know where you were. I thought you might've been scared, and I wanted you to feel better."

As if it were a treasure map, I unrolled it and oohed and aahed over the images. "Well, that's our car," I said, pointing to the red square. "And that's me," I laughed, touching my fingertips to a stick person with long hair. "But what am I holding?"

Abigail's eyes brightened as she pushed her fingertip to the small object on the paper. "That's God's spirit," she said excitedly. "I drew it as a dove like I saw in Sunday school." She pressed her soft lips against my cheek and added, "I didn't want you to be alone, Mama, and so I gave you the best friend I could think of."

"Oh, darling," I exclaimed, recalling the white dove that had given me comfort in the darkest of nights. "Your dove was with me." Taking her hand, I marveled at the heavenly bond between mothers and daughters.

"And what are you two looking at?" my mother interrupted, placing a steaming cup of tea on the nightstand. She started to move away, but I grabbed her hand and brought it between Abigail's and mine. It was a remarkable feeling, this incredible connection of three generations.

"We're looking at the love that flows between us," I whispered, kissing the top of my daughter's head as I met my mother's understanding eyes. Returning my gaze to Abigail's picture, I studied the beautiful bird that had, on such a dismal night, connected my daughter's heart with mine.

Years later, that extraordinary event in our mother-daughter relationship became known as the "miracle." The miracle of Abigail's dove.

~Karen Majoris-Garrison
Chicken Soup for the Mother & Daughter Soul

89

The Almost-Missed Miracle

Mother love is the fuel that enables a normal human being
to do the impossible.
~Marion C. Garretty

"The photo of your daughter has arrived. Come right over!" announced our adoption agency on the phone. Within minutes, we were driving, drunk with anticipation, our hearts dancing out of our chests, toward this magnificent moment.

After fifteen torturous months of waiting, we had our first look at the thumbnail-size, black-and-white photo of the little girl from China destined to be our daughter. "She is," I sighed, "a black-and-white portrait of innocence."

"She has a cleft palate," the worker reported. "There will be no way to determine the severity of her condition or how many surgeries she might need until you have her examined." He asked, "Will you accept this match?"

My mind floated back to the intense crucible we had faced in our journey to adopt. Halfway through the process, the Chinese government shocked us by decreeing that families who had children didn't qualify to adopt a healthy child. With two teenage children, this new twist meant we could only adopt a child with special medical needs. And we wouldn't know the "minor" medical condition until we were matched.

I felt betrayed by this change of contract. I remember collapsing in the newly pastel-decorated nursery, drooping like the pink bunny in the rocking chair next to me. I wept over the injustice. It had been hard enough at our ages to rally the courage to adopt a healthy child and to ignore the raised eyebrows and disdainful comments about our plans. Our trek through the minefields of fear had intensified exponentially. Admittedly not the nurse type, I imagined all kinds of horrible medical conditions we might face. What a slap in the face in the middle of a path already fraught with uncertainty and raw emotion.

"I just want my baby!" I cried, trying to grapple with both fear and fury. I wasn't up to handling the emotional nausea and extra financial burden that I sensed was shadowing my adoption fantasies. There were hundreds of thousands of healthy abandoned girls in China needing families. Why this ridiculous red tape? I fumed. I halfway understood why several families dropped out of the process at this point, disgusted by this new obstacle. "God, help me process this," I agonized.

I traced the hard steps that had brought me to this juncture. I pondered the raw facts that had moved me in the beginning. The "one child" law for population control had caused a holocaust of baby girls in China. Everyone wanted a son for financial security and to carry on their family name. Girls that escaped abortion and made it through the birth canal faced another horror: total abandonment.

Rocking with the bunny on my lap, my self-pity began to diminish as my focus turned outward. I pictured new mothers throughout China, just hours after cutting the umbilical cord, being forced to do the unthinkable. I imagined their tears as they secretly and gently laid their bundled little girls somewhere out in the open, hoping that the cries of their delicate offspring would be heard... that someone would deliver them to a government welfare institute. Their desperation engulfed me as I envisioned them giving their final kiss.

"How could I turn back now?" I avowed. "Some precious, tiny girl has miraculously survived the gauntlet of life thus far and awaits my loving arms....Will I, too, forsake her because she's not perfect?"

Even my young teenagers understood that love required sacrifice. To help us raise the money we needed, they joined my husband on an excruciating, 101-mile walk across Death Valley, getting sponsors per mile. "We didn't mind the blisters and pain, Mom, as long as we thought about rescuing our little sister," they reported, having grown up a year in just one week. "We walked through the valley of death to give her a chance at life."

Rehearsing all of these moments brought my struggle with selfishness and fear to an end. My husband confirmed our direction. "Maybe we are the only way this little girl can ever get the medical help she needs," he tenderly concluded. His selfless words calmed the remaining storm inside me. Perfect love had cast out fear. Quitting now would only hurt our daughter; she was the one being imprisoned by these restrictions. And love isn't love if it doesn't pay a price. Didn't I learn that from Jesus?

"Yes!" I blurted out loudly to our agency worker. "Absolutely!"

I was elated that we had settled the issue months earlier.

"You'll fly to meet her in two weeks," he announced to our utter shock.

Our hearts nearly stopped when we spied the Chinese nannies filing into our Nanchang City hotel lobby, carrying little bundles. All ten anxious families in our group had paced the halls for the last hour in anticipation of this thrilling delivery. We'd all waited, pregnant with a dream of a daughter for well over a year, but this last hour of labor was the most acute. This labor of the heart in an adoptive parent is as intense as physical child labor, and the moment of delivery almost more exhilarating.

"Porter," a man called out, signaling that it was our turn to come face-to-face with our baby. I was ecstatic as he placed a tiny, fragile-as-porcelain masterpiece of a child into my arms. Her familiar black eyes studied me back, and in a holy moment our hearts attached as mother and child.

I tenderly stroked her shaved head, covered with insect bites and scratches. "She is beautiful," we marveled. She silently, compliantly watched us pass her back and forth, mother to father, then brother to sister. Her ebony eyes were beckoning, as if to say, "Take me, I'm yours."

Morning light revealed a wonder that overwhelmed us all, an almost-missed miracle. The doctor announced that her palate was absolutely perfect. There would be no need for surgeries and lifelong speech therapy after all. The Great Physician had taken care of all that on His own.

~Claudia Porter
Chicken Soup for the Christian Soul 2

90

The Red Sled

I t was the day after Thanksgiving 2004, and all four of our kids were home together for the first time in a while. The house was alive with the sounds of our college-age kids teasing their little brother, Zach. The smell of holiday cooking filled the house. Outside, a fresh blanket of snow created a Norman Rockwell winter scene.

A substantial coating of snow is pretty rare by Thanksgiving, so twelve-year-old Zach pestered his two older brothers to take him sledding. Zach is a very persistent young man. In fact, after months of Zach badgering us for a cell phone, I had just recently relented and bought him one. Zach's persistent nature again paid off, and he, Jake and Mike took their sleds for an afternoon on the hills.

Marilee and I were in the midst of preparing supper and cleaning up after the tornado of the kids when the phone rang. It was Michael, our oldest, calling on Zach's cell phone. He asked if there were any Band-Aids in the car because Jake had cut himself sledding. I told him where they might be in the car and hung up. Just in case he was unable to find any, I laid a couple of Band-Aids on the table, ready to deliver if needed. Sure enough, the phone rang a few minutes later. "Dad," Mike stammered in apparent panic, "you need to get here right away. Jake is really hurt! He can't move!"

With a mother's intuition, Marilee knew before I said a word that there was something wrong.

"Where are you?" I asked Michael, trying to stay calm.

"I don't know," Mike replied. "Jake drove and I wasn't paying attention to where we were going."

I ran through a list of potential sledding spots in the area, but none sounded right to Michael. "Do you remember anything you passed on the way?" I asked.

"Groveland School," was all he could remember. I hung up and called 911. I asked dispatch to send an ambulance to the Groveland school parking lot, and Marilee and I jumped in the car.

We arrived at the school only moments before the ambulance and police. I explained our dilemma. Neither the police nor the emergency medical technicians could think of any sledding hills in the immediate area. I called Mike again and told him we were at Groveland with the ambulance and asked him if he could see a main road.

"I can't see any main road. It's all residential, but I can hear the sirens," he said.

If he could hear the sirens, we must be close, so I told him, "Try to flag us down!"

We headed east, hoping to spot them, with the police and ambulance following close behind. We drove just a few blocks when I saw something to our left.

Marilee said, "Someone is waving us down holding a red sled."

I looked left and saw no sign of the kids, but turned into a residential area, not really knowing where I was heading but knowing it was where I had to go. As we cleared the last house, I spotted the car. Then I saw them: three kids huddled by a wall at the base of the hill.

We ran to the unforgettable scene, followed by the ambulance and police. It appeared Jake had crashed the sled headfirst into the wall. The goose egg over his right eye was the size of a tennis ball and bleeding. He was conscious, but incoherent. He didn't know where he was, what day it was or what holiday we had just celebrated.

The EMTs secured his neck with a brace, gingerly lifted him onto a backboard, and rushed him to the hospital. After extensive X-rays of his head and neck, the doctor came in with the news. Jake had a bad concussion and a broken vertebra in his neck. It was hard to tell the extent of the damage until the swelling subsided, but he was able to move his legs and arms, though he had lost strength in his arms. The hospital rigged him up with a brace from his waist to his neck, and we settled in for the evening, awaiting more X-rays to determine the extent of his injuries and prognosis for recovery.

Over the next few days, family and friends lending prayers and support joined us at the hospital. We even got a surprise visit and prayers from Archbishop Flynn, who happened to be visiting someone else. The doctor finally came in and told us Jake would not need surgery but would need to continue to wear the brace.

On a follow-up visit, however, the doctor noticed Jake continuing to lose strength on his right side, so he ordered a CT scan. On Christmas Eve, we got the results: The damage was more extensive than the doctors had thought; that's why Jake was losing strength in his arms. They recommended surgery soon.

I don't remember much about Christmas Eve services that night, other than the love and support we received from the St. Therese Church choir where we sing.

The surgery was performed a few days later. Doctors inserted a titanium plate into the front of his neck to fuse the break. It was the longest six hours of my life. The doctor met with us afterward and assured us the procedure had gone well, though the damage was much worse than originally expected. "In fact," he said, "I have never seen a break this bad before where the patient survived." It was then that I lost it. God surely has something in the future for Jake and was not ready to take him.

Our family spent New Year's Eve in the hospital while Jake recovered, and finally we had time to recollect the events on the day of the accident. We shuddered to think of what could have happened if we had not gotten there with the ambulance when we did and if Jake had tried to move with a broken neck. Marilee remarked how fortunate it was that the EMT crew had been so careful... and how lucky it was that Zach had brought his new cell phone to the hill.

"Who brings a cell phone sledding?" we teased.

"And how good it was that Zach flagged us down with the red sled when we were trying to find you," Marilee said.

At this, both Mike and Zach looked at us with an odd expression. "Mom, we didn't flag you down, and we didn't have a red sled. We were the only ones at that hill sledding that day."

We all sat in stunned silence for a long while, coming to the realization that they were not alone on the hill that day. Jake's recovery had been nothing short of a miracle, thanks to the fast and conscientious work of the ambulance crew, the doctors at the hospital, and to his guardian angel... with the red sled.

~Dave Mahler
Chicken Soup for the Christian Soul 2

A Child's Prayer

Dear Father in heaven,
Look down from above;
Bless papa and mama,
And those whom I love.
May angels guard over
My slumbers, and when
The morning is breaking,
Awake me.
Amen.

Christian Kids

The Wisdom of Children

*Grown-ups never understand anything for themselves,
and it is tiresome for children to be always and forever
explaining things to them.*
~Antoine de Saint-Exupéry,
The Little Prince

91

You Are Never Too Young to Take a Stand

If we are ever in doubt about what to do, it is a good rule to ask ourselves
what we shall wish on the morrow that we had done.
~John Lubbock

When I was eleven, I looked older than I was; in fact, I looked like I was about fifteen or sixteen. I felt older than most of my classmates, and I just never fit in. I had always been tall for my age too, and that really didn't help. Most of the kids I hung out with were at least two years ahead of me in school. One day I reached a turning point when I realized that it isn't your age that makes you mature. It is a personal thing.

One of my best friends, Linda, asked me to go to the high school football game with her. Of course I went, not only because I loved hanging out with her but because I also had the biggest crush on her older brother. When we got to the game, I didn't see too many people I knew from school, but Linda had a lot of friends there. I thought it was so awesome that she had as many friends as she did, and I wished I was more like her. She was fun, and she had a great personality.

The game was winding down, and our team was losing big time.

A lot of people had already left the game because it was so obvious that we weren't going to win. A large group of girls came by and saw Linda and asked her to come over and talk to them. She told me she would be right back and went and sat with them.

After a few minutes passed, she turned and yelled for me to come down and sit with them too. I did, never thinking it would be a big deal. After a while, they all started smoking, and they offered Linda a cigarette. These were girls from her neighborhood, and I guess she wanted them to think of her as being tough, so she accepted.

She asked, "What about my friend?" and they said, "Sure, would you like a cigarette?" At that moment, I felt so shocked, so embarrassed and so young. These girls are only thirteen, I thought, with a shock. Do two years make such a huge difference? Only two years, but they were far beyond me, or so I thought to myself.

I was humiliated. I knew my parents trusted me to make right choices, or else they would have never let me go to the game. Of course, they trusted Linda too—she was older and supposedly looking out for me.

It seemed like hours passed in that short minute, with all the thoughts going through my head: Should I take a cigarette? Will they laugh at me and make fun of me if I don't? Will they want to beat me up because they'll think that I think I am too good to take what they have offered me? Finally, with all those thoughts racing through my brain, I just said, "No. Thank you, but I don't smoke." Then I got up and went back to the seat where we were originally sitting and just sat there in the stands all by myself.

Linda finished her cigarette and came up to where I was sitting and sat down by me. After the game, we went on as if nothing had happened. That was fine with me—I just wanted to go home and cry. It may sound silly now, but that is how I felt.

Several months passed and things went on as usual. Then one Sunday at our church youth group, we had a special service, and a lot of people were giving testimonies—it was just such an inspirational service. After the service was over, Linda came over to where I was standing and cornered me. She told me that she needed to tell me something.

"I just wanted to tell you what an inspiration you were to me when you were offered a cigarette, and everyone around you was smoking—including me—and you said no... and you stood by what you knew was right for you. It meant a lot to me, and I will never forget it."

I was so stunned. I never realized that when I had taken my stand and said no, the decision I had made would influence someone else—even someone older than I was.

Later in life, I realized that saying no to something as simple as a cigarette made me stronger and more able to stand up and say no to other things as time went by. I was offered so much more while hanging out with my peers as I got older.

At eleven, I learned that when you think you are all alone, sitting by yourself, others are watching what you are doing. Your actions may help other people take a stand for what they believe in when they are not strong enough to do it alone.

~Maudie Conrad
Chicken Soup for the Girl's Soul

92

Straight to the Heart

But Jesus called to them and said,
"Let the little children come to me,
and do not forbid them;
for of such is the kingdom of God."
~Luke 18:16

It was my three-year-old granddaughter, Jani, who gave me the answer to a question I'd been puzzling over.

I was visiting both of my daughters in the city that day and had taken the youngest grandchild for a walk. It was only by chance that we came upon that little park, complete with tiny hills and lovely greenery. It was like a little hideaway that not a soul knew was there. Even the sounds of traffic were blocked out.

Jani was enjoying the swing, and I sat back to watch her from a wooden bench flanked by shrubs. That was when I felt something indescribable yet so peaceful. What was that?

I knew I'd felt something like this before at our little country home, but even there I was unable to really identify it. That indescribable "feeling" was the reason we ended up buying the place.

We had been looking for an affordable home in the country and finally discovered an old farmhouse on an acre and a half thirty minutes from the city. The house had been built as a one-room schoolhouse in 1911. The basement was still a dirt cellar.

Looking at this old place and thinking of giving up my beautiful home in the city with wall-to-wall carpets, a lovely fireplace and a bay window was a bit of a downer. I just didn't know if I could do it. Then we walked out across the land, and that beautiful feeling hit me. I commented to my husband, Shawn, "It feels so good here."

We looked through the old place and once again walked out in the yard, and as we traveled down a wee slope to an enclosure, that wondrous feeling again came upon me. "Shawn, I can't describe it, but it feels so good here!" I guess I told him that at least three or four times that day.

In the weeks and months that followed our purchase of the home, I received that feeling each time I walked in my enclosed "secret garden."

But I was not the only one to feel this warm energy. When we had company I encouraged each person to spend some alone time in the secret garden, and every single one reported the same warm, good feeling came over them. But what was it?

Now here I was in a park, and I had that same lovely, indescribable feeling.

I called over to my rambunctious little granddaughter. "Jani, come over here and sit with Grandma."

She climbed up on the park bench and managed to slow down her little energetic body long enough to listen.

"Jani, will you sit here with me and just close your eyes and see if you feel anything?"

Bless her, she didn't question my weird request; she merely closed her eyes and sat perfectly still. I waited to see if she would experience what I did. And then I kept waiting, as she seemed in no hurry to open her eyes. Strange inactivity for such a lively little bundle of energy!

Finally I could wait no longer. "Jani?" I touched her shoulder gently, encouraging her to open her eyes. As she did, I asked, "Jani, did you feel anything?"

Trust a child to cut through all the fuss and head straight for the heart. She broke out with a beautiful, radiant smile, and she said, "Oh Gamma, it feels like God giving me a hug!"

~Ellie Braun-Haley
Chicken Soup for the Christian Soul 2

93

Without You

Love is missing someone whenever you're apart,
but somehow feeling warm inside because you're close in heart.
~Kay Knudsen

We were all saddened and angry at losing Daddy, but the hardest hit was our three-year-old son, Patrick. He had established a unique bond with his grandfather from the moment he could hold onto the elder's hand and take his first steps. Then, in those final days, he spent hours playing hide-and-seek around the bedroom door, finally coming to let Grampa hold him tight with a paralyzed arm.

Patrick was the most insistent of our four children when it came to talking about Grampa no longer being in his life. My mother tried to soothe him but couldn't find the words. Following the funeral and return to the city where we lived, Patrick could speak of nothing else. We were required to repeat the explanation that Grampa's heart got tired and decided to stop working. "Like the ol' tick-tock in Grampa's room?" he asked. The answer was yes. His three-year-old mind still wasn't satisfied, especially when his older sister said that Grampa was gone forever. The confusion and wondering were too much.

Together one day, rolling out snickerdoodles on the kitchen table, Patrick blurted out another question, "Will I see Forever someday, like Grampa?" Tears welled up in my eyes as I explained that yes, someday he would join Grampa, but not for a long, long time. "I don't want Grampa in Forever!" Patrick cried out. "I want him here RIGHT NOW!"

I had to admit that I wanted that, too. In desperate prayer, I asked for some kind of wisdom and guidance concerning this dear child's struggle with his grievous loss. There just had to be a way for him to understand the faith I held onto in times of distress.

Groping for words, I reminded Patrick of how very much Grampa had loved him physically; of all the laughs and winks, the hugs and kisses they had shared. Oh, yes, Patrick smiled, remembering them. "Well," I said, "there are times when I can almost feel those hugs he gave and all the love Grampa gave us. Sometimes it seems like his love is still around us, like a blanket on a cold night."

"Like HOW? I wanna feel it, too." He was insistent.

"Okay," I said, "when you ride your trike down the driveway, I stand at the door and wave and say out loud, 'Patrick, I love you.' You hear me and call back to say that you love me, too. You ride farther down the sidewalk, past the Ketelsen's big tree where I can't see you. But I can still say, 'Patrick, I love you.' You can't hear me, but if you think about it, you know that when I go back to the kitchen dishes, I can say it again with you still not hearing, but it's there in the air where I said it. You can go pedaling all the way to the corner, and while you're doing it, you can say ever so softly, 'Mommy, I love you.' And if I think about it, I can feel your loving without hearing you say it. I can still feel it all around me. Now, I think that's the way Grampa is still around us and with us with his love that didn't stop when his heart did. Even if we can't hear it, we can feel it all the time."

Patrick was very quiet, thinking there in the kitchen with me that day. And I remember that he didn't pester us with questions as much, even when my mother came to spend a few days. When Patrick and I took her to the bus station for her trip home, she couldn't hold back the tears. They flowed freely while Patrick held her hand and watched closely.

"Why you cryin', Gramma?" he asked. When her answer came that she would miss us all so very much, he said something we didn't understand at first. "Don't be lonesome, Gramma. 'Member, I wuv you wiffout YOU."

"Whatever does he mean?" my mother queried, and for a second I had to rack my brain. Suddenly, it dawned on me, recalling our snickerdoodle talk. Patrick really had understood what I'd spoken of and now was putting it into words a three-year-old could understand. A remarkable answer to prayer.

Ever afterward, my mother put at the close of her letters or telephone conversations, "Remember, I love you without you!" That saying has become a family trademark when we are apart from each other, thanks to a little boy's persistence and insight.

Her grandson is now in his midlife, and she nearing 102, but they still end their letters using their "without you" love.

~Alice Ann Knisely
Chicken Soup to Inspire a Woman's Soul

Tammy's Trauma

Sometimes someone says something really small,
and it just fits right into this empty place in. your heart
~From the television show My So-Called Life

Tammy was a cheerful, determined, resourceful and loving kindergartener. She smiled a lot. When her father picked up Tammy at the kindergarten door, she would jump into her father's arms and wrap her legs around the man like a toddler would. Tammy's love for her father bubbled up and spilled over like the foam of root beer running down the side of the glass.

I spent many special moments hugging Tammy, providing snacks (since she rarely brought one from home) and just plain loving her. Then, one horrible day, her father committed suicide. Tammy was out of school for several days.

I remember entering the floral shop and ordering a fruit basket to be sent to Tammy's house. With tears streaming down my face, I said to the young man behind the counter, "Please make this a children's fruit basket. Four children under the age of eight have lost their father. Make this basket as joyous as you possibly can, so if their mother cannot attend to them, they can just reach up on the counter and grab something good to eat."

I was tormented about what I should do to prepare for Tammy's return to school. I wanted to make the whole thing go away, just like a bad dream. I decided not to mention anything about it to the class. My intuition told me that I would have to respond to whatever

Tammy brought with her into our classroom family. I couldn't possibly prepare the class because I had no idea what had actually happened, and I didn't know what Tammy had been told. I prayed for guidance.

When Tammy returned to school, we sat for our opening meeting as we always did. At first, she didn't mention anything about her father. I prayed. After fifteen minutes, she said, "Mrs. DeLucia, my daddy died."

"I know, Tammy. I'm so sorry."

She continued by clutching both her hands around her little neck and choking out these words: "He took a rope and did this until his face turned red."

The class sat speechless.

I managed to utter, "Who told you this?"

She responded, "My grandma."

Then, from behind Tammy, came the tender and caring arm of Sarah. She rested it gently on Tammy's shoulder. She spoke spontaneously, "It's okay, Tammy. Even though you'll never see him again, he'll always live in your heart."

Goosebumps covered my entire body as I heard myself say, "Tell her again, Sarah." She obediently repeated the words, and across Tammy's face came a smile that I can't even describe.

God had truly answered my prayers. Without any forewarning, Sarah's genuine and sincere compassion had rescued us all in a moment of need. Nothing I could have said would have had the power and magnificence that came through the arm and wise words of one five-year-old and into the heart of another.

~Maureen Murphy DeLucia
Chicken Soup for the Soul Stories for a Better World

The Breathin' Part

When my beloved Mama Farley died at age ninety, Don and I decided that five-year-old Holly and six-year-old Jay would attend the Kentucky funeral with us. During the long drive south, we talked about heaven and told our children that Mama—the part we couldn't see—was already with the Lord. Then I, a veteran of Southern funerals, told them about the part they would see. She'd be lying in a big box, called a casket, surrounded by flowers. A lot of people would be in the room, I said, and many would be crying because Mama Farley couldn't talk to them anymore.

Then remembering previous funerals, I explained that some people would touch her hands or kiss her forehead. Don and I stressed that no one would make them kiss her, but they could touch her hands if they wanted to.

I talked about the sad hymns the people would sing, what the minister would do and even about the procession to the cemetery after her adult grandsons carried the casket to the big car called a hearse. Then, most important of all, we asked if they had any questions. Jay wondered about practical matters, such as how they put the casket in the ground, but Holly just stared at me, her eyes round with silent wondering.

When we arrived at the funeral home, we held the children's hands and walked into the flowered area. I studied Mama Farley's dear, ancient face and thought of the godly example she'd been throughout my childhood. I remembered the family unity during our farm days and longed for a skillet full of her incredible biscuits. I thought of her faith-filled, pragmatic view of life. Still years away in my memories, I was startled by Holly's question.

"Is Mama breathing?" she whispered.

We hadn't anticipated that question, and it required more than just a quick, "No, of course not." Suddenly this business of explaining death to myself had become difficult. How could I make a child grasp what I couldn't?

"Well, Holly..." I stalled, searching for something both simple and theologically sound.

Jay then turned from flipping the casket handles to face his little sister. "No, Holly, she's not breathing. Remember? The breathin' part's in heaven."

~Sandra P. Aldrich
Chicken Soup for the Christian Woman's Soul

The Empty Hook

The soul is healed by being with children.
~Fyodor Dostoevsky

My parents shared a love of the outdoors, especially fishing. We lived in New York City, and opportunities to pursue these passions were few. When I was ten years old, my father decided we would spend part of our summer on the eastern end of Long Island. I was overjoyed at the thought of being out of the hot city and spending quality time with my beloved parents. Dad rented a small cottage on the bay that included the use of a rowboat. Each morning we would push off and row to an inlet where we fished from the shore. My dad also had a handmade crab trap, and mother dug for clams in the sand with her toes.

Directly across the way was a vast estate, and tied to its dock was an enormous yacht. My mother referred to it as the "Miniature Queen Mary." Every day a very well-dressed older man was helped out to the end of the dock by a servant who set up a chair for him and handed him his fishing pole. We could tell by the thick dark glasses he wore and the way he was guided out onto the dock that he was blind.

I watched the man with great interest. He sat for hours, never reeling in his fishing line to see if he had caught anything. My parents agreed if we owned such a magnificent yacht, we would be out on it, fishing every day. The man was quite a mystery to me, and I hoped to get his attention by calling out to him every day as we left for home. "Bye mister, see you tomorrow!" I would yell. He never answered.

My curiosity grew with each passing day, and when I couldn't take it anymore, I set out on a mission. I was allowed to ride my bike after dinner one warm evening. I rode out toward the inlet, which didn't appear to be that far away; however, it took nearly an hour of riding before I sighted the old man's house. I stopped on the side of the road when I heard a car pull up behind me and watched as the driver got out and opened the back door for the passenger. It was the older man whom I had watched fishing every day.

He told me I was trespassing on private property. I apologized, but continued by saying, "Sir, I came out here to say hello to you in person. I watch you fish every day from the other side of the inlet and you never catch a thing. I thought I could help you." The man cut me off with his laughter.

"How old are you, child?" he asked.

"I'm ten years old and my name is Anne and I love to fish and my parents love to fish and we live in the city and...." Once again I was stopped by his very hearty laugh.

"Young lady, you're quite a chatterbox. It's getting very late. I think we'd better get you home to your parents before they start to worry about you."

My bike was loaded into the trunk and I arrived home that evening in a shiny black limousine. My parents, both in shock, but grateful for my return, invited the gentleman in for coffee and dessert, and he accepted. He sat in our small kitchen eating my mother's homemade crumb cake and told us the story of his life.

He had been blinded in a terrible accident that years ago had taken the life of his wife and his only child, a son. Although a man of wealth, nothing mattered to him after the accident. He sold his business, shunned the rest of his family and friends, and became a recluse. He said that he had bought the yacht for his son who loved to fish, and added that when his son died, he vowed never to take the boat out, and never go fishing again.

I had been listening quietly, but at this point I couldn't help myself and blurted out, "But mister, I see you fishing on your dock every day!"

My parents gave me the look that told me I should have remained silent.

The man said, "You're right, Anne. You do see me with a fishing pole in my hand every day, but I never put any bait on my hook. I just sit on the dock and reflect on the times when fishing meant so much to me and my family."

I thought for a moment, then said, "I bet your son is very sad when he looks down from heaven and sees you so unhappy."

This time my parents hushed me with more than a look.

After a long pause the man said, "Your daughter's right. What an old fool I've been."

A few days later, the limousine arrived for us, and we spent the day on the yacht on beautiful Long Island Sound—FISHING. It was a day not to be forgotten. That night I thought about the smile on the man's face when I thanked him.

"No," he said, "I must thank you, as today was my happiest day in years." I gave him a big hug and he hugged me back.

Years have come and gone since that day. Life has many pleasures for me today. I don't get to go fishing very often, but I have a very full schedule. I have a wonderful husband, children and grandchildren, and I reside on Long Island. I hold fast to a lesson that I learned when I was just ten years old. Life is what you make of it. I treasure a picture that sits on my desk, faded with age, but a joy to behold. It shows a man smiling and holding a very large fish that he had just caught. The words written under the photo make me smile even after all these years. It simply says, "To Anne—Life will never be an empty hook again. THANK YOU!"

~Anne Carter
Chicken Soup for the Fisherman's Soul

A Child's Prayer

We thank Thee, heav'nly Father,
For ev'ry earthly good,
For life, and health, and clothing,
And for our daily food.

O give us hearts to thank Thee,
For ev'ry blessing sent,
And whatsoe'er Thou sendest
Make us therewith content.

Christian Kids

We Believe

But Jesus said,
Suffer little children,
and forbid them not, to come to me:
for of such is the kingdom of heaven.
~Matthew 19:14

97

Children's Eyes

What kind of world is it my friend
that little children see?
I wonder if they see God first
because they just believe?

Do they see strength in caring eyes
who watch them as they play --
or maybe love through gentle hands
that guide them on their way?

Do you think they dream of future times
when they would be a king --
or just enjoy their present life
while with their friends they sing?

Do they see the acts of kindness
done for people who are poor?
Is the very best in everyone
what they are looking for?

And when the day is over,
as they close their eyes to sleep,
do they look forward to tomorrow

with its promises to keep?

If this is what the children see,
then it should be no surprise,
the world would be a better place
if we all had children's eyes.

~Tom Krause
Chicken Soup for the Teenage Soul III

98

An Act of Faith

When my son Luke was small, he liked to sit on my lap and watch television. Sometimes he'd point out what he thought belonged to the real world—auto accidents, fires, Joe Montana, astronauts—and what did not. Big Bird, for instance, belonged to the world of make-believe. But so did dinosaurs.

Luke had trouble understanding how dinosaurs could be considered real if they were not around anymore. My explanation that they were once alive but had all died long ago perplexed and annoyed him.

One day Mawmaw, his great-grandmother, sent him a drawing of a cat with a note that suggested he color it.

He finished this project the very day it arrived and then climbed into my chair to show it to me. The cat was red, blue and green.

"I've never seen such a colorful cat," I said.

"'Course not," he said. "He's mine and Mawmaw's," as though that somehow explained things. He nestled against me and I clicked on the TV to a retrospective of the life of John Kennedy.

As a picture of young JFK at the tiller of a small sailboat appeared, Luke asked, "Who is that man?"

"It's John Kennedy. He was president of the United States."

"Where is he?"

"He's dead now."

Luke looked at my face to see if I could be teasing. "Is he all dead?"

"Yes."

There was a short silence. Then he asked, "His feet are dead?"

"Yes."

"Is his head dead?"

"Yes."

This last question was followed by a long, thoughtful pause. Then Luke finally said, "Well, he certainly talks very well."

Though I tried not to, I laughed—partly because he did seem to speak very well, for a dead person, that is, and partly because Luke had been so earnest in examining the problem.

After the JFK incident, Luke seemed haunted by the problem that death presented. Thereafter, almost every walk in the woods became a search for something dead—a field mouse, a raccoon or perhaps a bird. He would squat down on his haunches over the find and sometimes make up stories about what the animal had been doing when it died. Sometimes we held small funerals.

I was concerned, of course. The concept of death was a very large one for a three-year-old to understand.

One day in the woods, we found a few tawny tufts of rabbit fur. Luke rolled it around with a sassafras twig. "This was Peter Rabbit," he said. "He was going home to his house when a fox ate him up. He is in a fox now."

"But Peter Rabbit lives in the world of make-believe," I said, "and this was a real rabbit."

"I know that." he said. "I was just seeing." I think he meant that he was making up a story that would somehow let things turn out in a way he could understand.

I explained that most people thought only your body died. That you had another part, called a spirit, which survived. We didn't know that for sure, I said. But if you believed something deep inside—even though you couldn't prove it—that was called faith and that helped you to understand many things.

This produced amazement. "You are in two parts?" he said.

"Not exactly." I now knew I was in for it. His inquiry into these new ideas lasted about a week. On another of our walks, I showed him a butterfly cocoon that had once housed a pupa. I told him a caterpillar had spun that cocoon and eventually had emerged as a totally different creature—a butterfly. He accepted that easily because he had seen it happen on a nature show.

He said, "But you can still see the real butterfly. He goes places. You can touch him. If you're dead, people can only see you on TV."

"That's true," I said. "But you can see dead people in your head—in your imagination."

He thought long about that one. Finally, he asked how that could possibly be. I told him to close his eyes and imagine someone who was not with us. His friend, Charlie, for instance. "Can you imagine Charlie?"

He squealed with delight. "No! No! But I can hear him!"

"Well, it's like that. People who aren't with you right at the moment sort of hang around with you for as long as you remember them."

"But I can play with Charlie."

"Yes."

"And I couldn't go play with the bunny. Because he's dead."

"Yes, that's right."

Luke's preoccupation continued for another few days. But soon his attention switched to his upcoming birthday party, and he did not speak of his deep concern about death again.

About a year and a half later, Mawmaw died. Our southern family's custom is to lay out our kin at home, so my father's mother had a wake. When Luke insisted he be allowed to go, my wife and I thought that might be a good idea.

Mawmaw's house overflowed with guests and food and talk. She had lived a long, rich life, so there was none of the kind of wretched grief that attends early or unexpected deaths. People remembered her joy, her amazing personal strength, her humor and her kindness.

We let Luke go about as he pleased—talking with relatives, eating, getting praised and playing with his cousins. Then, at almost the last possible moment, he asked me to take him into the room where Mawmaw lay.

I took his hand and led him to stand beside his great-grandmother's bier. He was too small to see anything but flowers, so I picked him up and held him on my hip. He took a long look and then said, "Okay, Dad."

I put him down, and we walked out of the room down the long hallway toward the kitchen. Before we got there, he pulled me into a small room where my grandmother had once pressed flowers or done needlework. Looking solemnly at me, he whispered, "Dad, that is not Mawmaw."

"What do you mean?"

"It isn't," he said. "She is not in there."

"Then where is she?" I asked.

"Talking somewhere."

"Why do you think that?" I knelt down and put my hand on his shoulder.

"I just know. That's all. I just know." There was a long pause as we looked at each other. Finally he took a deep breath and said with more seriousness than I had ever seen in him, "Is that faith?"

"Yes, Son."

"Well, then that's how I know. That's what I got."

I looked at him with awe and joy, realizing he had just found one of the most powerful resources of the heart—a guide other than his mother or me. He had found a way of understanding that would be with him for the rest of his life, even in the valley of the shadow.

I suddenly felt deeply relieved and grateful in a way I had not anticipated when that day began. I looked at Luke smiling at me, and then we walked down the hall, hand in hand, to find something to eat and perhaps tell a story of our own.

~Walter W. Meade
Chicken Soup for the Unsinkable Soul

99

God on Her Side

One important key to success is self-confidence.
An important key to self-confidence is preparation.
~Arthur Ashe

I was only five years old. People think that children don't remember things from such an early age, but when I live to be one hundred, I will remember that day as if it were yesterday.

It seemed like we were sitting for hours in the emergency room, waiting for our turn to see the doctor. It had been my mother and me for as long as I can remember. My father and mother separated when I was a baby. I didn't like doctors or hospitals much, so my mom did her best to keep me happy and occupied while we waited. She did a good job of hiding how very awful she felt. We sang and played little games. She had called my grandparents, and they were on their way, but they were delayed in traffic.

Finally they called my mother's name, and we were taken to a small bed with curtains all around it. The nurse asked my mother to change into a gown and to lie down. After she lay down, I quickly jumped on her tummy and straddled her with a leg on each side. We continued to sing and play our games while we waited for the doctor. Mom had had pants on before she was asked to change, but now with the hospital gown on, her leg could be seen, but I could not see it because I was looking into her face.

When the doctor finally came, he opened the curtain. I did not see his face; he was not there long enough for me to even turn my head. He said, "Oh my god!" Then he closed the curtain and left. A few moments later, he returned with not one, but five doctors. I will always remember the looks on their faces. They were looks of extreme terror. Then came the next words, "You have a flesh-eating disease, and unless we cut off your leg in the next ten minutes, you will die." Then they closed the curtain and left just as fast as they had appeared.

My mother tried her best to change the subject. She asked me about school, my friends, my cat. I wanted to be brave for Mommy, but I couldn't. The tears started coming faster and faster, and I could not control them.

When my grandparents arrived a few minutes later, they thought at first that something had happened to me, because when they opened the curtain I was crying and my mother was trying her best to comfort me. Now that I am older, I wonder how in the world she managed to comfort me, when her whole world was crashing in around her.

The nurse asked my grandparents to take me away from my mother, and the three of us left her and went to a private waiting area. All I could think about was how the doctor said my mother could die in ten minutes.

I know every child thinks his or her mother is special, but mine is especially so. Ever since I had been born, we had spent every moment we could together. My mother has two artificial hips and has a hard time doing things, but that has never stopped her. She just figured out how she can do things in a different way, even if it meant she went to bed in pain. She never wanted to let me down. I know that now—I didn't know that then. She was my rock, my hero, my champion, my best friend, and I was terrified that she was going to die.

The doctors came into the little room where the nurse had put us, to explain the situation to my grandparents and to ask my grandparents to talk to my mother. She had given them permission to take out the part of the leg that was infected, but they were not allowed to cut her leg off. The doctors told my grandparents that this would not be enough and that she would die that night if they were not allowed to cut off the entire leg at the hip.

This all seemed like a dream. Again, in front of me, they said the same thing, "Your daughter is going to die if we do not cut off her leg." My grandparents had a lot of questions, but the doctor said there wasn't enough time to answer them. They were already preparing my mother for surgery.

I thought back to the day before, when my mother had been outside with me. We had played hide and seek with our duck, Crackers. Crackers loved to hide, and when we found her, she would quack and quack and quack. It was May, and the weather was beautiful in California where we lived. We were in the process of repainting our entire home inside. I helped paint each room with a roller. We wanted to make it our home; a place that the two of us created with love. She had been fine all that day. What had happened? I only knew that she got a high fever, and it did not go away. She had not shown me her leg, swollen all over with bright red spots and one big bump with a big white circle on the top. I only caught sight of it as the nurse was taking me from her lap.

My grandparents told the doctor that they could not help him. My mother was forty-one years old, and they could not make her cut her leg off if she did not want to. I did not understand this as a five-year-old. They were her parents. Why couldn't they tell her what to do? She always told me to do what was right. Why couldn't they tell her what was right? I just wanted her to live. I wanted my mommy.

Before she was taken to the operating room, my mommy insisted she see me. Instead of being worried about herself, she was worried about me. She was angry with the doctors for saying she was going to die while I was right there on her lap. She wanted to see me to tell me something before she went in for the surgery.

So the nurse came to get me but asked my grandparents to stay behind. There I was, holding the hand of a stranger, going down what seemed to be the longest hall in the world. There were no other beds in the hall. Just one. And on it was my mother. She greeted me with a big smile. There were no tears in her eyes or on her face. She asked the nurse to pick me up and put me on her chest. I remember that the nurse said no. But my mother insisted. There I lay, on top of my mother. I could feel her heart beating. I could smell her smell, the one I had always known. It was comforting.

She looked me straight in the eyes and told me these special words. "I have told you before, Ashleigh, that you are my gift from God." She had told me that story since the day I was born. My mother was told that she could never have children. She had had a condition called endometriosis, and she had had many surgeries due to complications from the condition. Her doctor told her she could never have children, but she wanted me so very badly.

On the night I was conceived, she said a prayer over and over to God, begging him for the chance to be a mother. When her cycle did not come, she called her doctor and asked for a blood test, but he refused. He said she could not possibly be pregnant and told her it was a "hysterical pregnancy." He explained that he thought it was because she wanted me so badly, she just had the symptoms of being pregnant. Another month went by and my mother took a home pregnancy test. She said it seemed like forever before the results showed in the window of the test stick (she still has the stick, framed on the wall). It said she was pregnant! Again she called her doctor. He still refused to do the blood test.

Another month went by and finally the doctor agreed to see her. He did not want to perform a blood test for her though, because he was sure that she was not pregnant. Instead he did an exam. My mother said the look on his face was priceless. He said, "I don't know how you did it, but you are indeed pregnant!" My mother promptly told him she had prayed for me.

So there I was, lying on my mother, feeling calm but not really understanding why. She used to say a prayer to me every night before we said our other prayers together. She said she heard it in the movie *Yentl*, and it had stayed with her. She recited the prayer to me again as we lay there together, in that long hallway with the nurse standing next to us. And then she told me, "Ashleigh, I don't want you to worry. I am not going to have my leg cut off, and I am not going to die."

"But, Mommy," I remember saying, "the doctor said you would die unless he cuts it off."

"He is a doctor, Ashleigh. He is not God. God gave you to me as a special gift. The doctor does not know that. But I know that God is not going to take me away from the special little girl he gave me. He knows you need me here right now. He can wait a little longer for me in heaven."

The nurse was crying, but I wasn't. My mother was right; we had God on our side. So from that very moment on, I was fine.

When I returned to my grandparents, the doctors were still begging them to "talk some sense" into my mother. My mother had told my grandparents, too, that God was not going to let her die. When the doctors left the room, you could tell that they were exasperated.

My mom was in surgery for hours, and my grandparents tried their best to keep me busy as we all waited. I know now that they must have been crazy with worry, but they didn't show it to me. We went to the cafeteria where I had some ice cream, and we waited and waited... and waited.

Finally, one of the doctors appeared in the little waiting room. He told us that the surgery was over. They did not cut off her leg, although they had to take a lot out of the front of it.

It has been six years now since that day. On the wall in our house is a paper. The paper reads, "We told her we had to cut off her leg or she would die. The patient states that God would not let this happen." My mother and I smile each time she walks past that paper, on her own two legs. We even smile as we look at the scar on the front of her leg that also serves as a reminder. A reminder to us of a gift from God—me—and how important he knew it was for me and my mom to be together a little while longer.

~Ashleigh Figler-Ehrlich
Chicken Soup for the Girl's Soul

100

The Smell of Rain

A cold March wind danced around Dallas as the doctor walked into Diana Blessing's small hospital room. It was the dead of night and she was still groggy from surgery. Her husband, David, held her as they braced themselves for the latest news.

That rainy afternoon, March 10, 1991, complications had forced Diana, only twenty-four weeks pregnant, to undergo emergency surgery. At twelve inches long and weighing only one pound, nine ounces, Danae Lu arrived by cesarean delivery.

They already knew she was perilously premature. Still, the doctor's soft words dropped like bombs. "I don't think she's going to make it," he said as kindly as he could. "There's only a 10 percent chance she will live through the night. If by some slim chance she does make it, her future could be a very cruel one." Numb with disbelief, David and Diana listened as the doctor described the devastating problems Danae could face if she survived.

She would probably never walk, or talk, or see. She would be prone to other catastrophic conditions from cerebral palsy to complete mental retardation, and on and on. Through the dark hours of morning as Danae held onto life by the thinnest thread, Diana slipped in and out of drugged sleep. But she was determined that their daughter would live to be a happy, healthy young girl. David, fully awake, knew he must confront his wife with the inevitable.

David told Diana that they needed to talk about funeral arrangements. But Diana said, "No, that is not going to happen. No way! I don't care what the doctors say; Danae is not going to die. One day she will be just fine and she will be home with us."

As if willed to live by Diana's determination, Danae clung to life hour after hour. But as those first rainy days passed, a new agony set in for David and Diana. Because Danae's underdeveloped nervous system was essentially "raw," the least kiss or caress only intensified her discomfort, so they couldn't even cradle their tiny baby. All they could do, as Danae struggled beneath the ultraviolet light, was to pray that God would stay close to their precious little girl.

At last, when Danae was two months old, her parents were able to hold her for the first time. Two months later, she went home from the hospital just as her mother predicted, even though doctors grimly warned that her chances of leading a normal life were almost zero.

Today, five years later, Danae is a petite but feisty young girl with glittering gray eyes and an unquenchable zest for life. She shows no sign of any mental or physical impairment. But that happy ending is not the end of the story.

One blistering summer afternoon in 1996 in Irving, Texas, Danae was sitting in her mother's lap at the ball park where her brother's baseball team was practicing. As always, Danae was busy chattering when she suddenly fell silent. Hugging her arms across her chest, Danae asked her mom, "Do you smell that?"

Smelling the air and detecting a thunderstorm approaching, Diana replied, "Yes, it smells like rain."

Danae closed her eyes again and asked, "Do you smell that?"

Once again her mother replied, "Yes, I think we're about to get wet, it smells like rain."

Caught in the moment, Danae shook her head, patted her thin shoulder and loudly announced, "No, it smells like him. It smells like God when you lay your head on His chest."

Tears blurred Diana's eyes as Danae happily hopped down to play with the other children before the rain came. Her daughter's words confirmed what Diana and the rest of the Blessing family had known all along. During those long days and nights of the first two months of her life, when her nerves were too sensitive to be touched, God was holding Danae on his chest, and it is His scent that she remembers so well.

~Nancy Miller
Chicken Soup for the Christian Family Soul

Grandma's Garden

Anyone can count the seeds in an apple.
Only God can count all the apples in one seed.
~Robert H. Schuller

I watched my grandma hoe the clay soil in my garden.

"Don't see how you grow anything in this," she mused.

"Colorado soil can't compare to yours in Iowa, Grandma!" I stared at her in awe, capturing the moment in my memory forever. Wisps of her silvery hair sneaked from beneath her headscarf as her thin torso bent down to pull a fistful of bindweed.

"This stuff will grow anywhere," she laughed. "Even in this soil!"

Although she lived alone on the Iowa farm she and Grandpa had settled a half century ago, she still maintained a garden that could sustain most of Benton County! Some of my favorite summer childhood days had been spent in her garden helping her pull up plants she identified as weeds, or planting vegetables and flowers. She had taught me that gardening wasn't only about cultivating plants, it was about cultivating faith. Each seed planted was proof of that. When I was seven, I asked, "Grandma, how do the seeds know to grow the roots down and the green part up?"

"Faith," was her answer.

When I grew up and married, my husband recognized the impression Grandma's dirt left under my fingernails and in my heart. He supported my dream to live outside the city, and our two-acre plot had a horse, dog, cat, rabbit, six hens and, of course, a large garden. I was privileged and overjoyed to have Grandma working in it.

Grandma leaned the hoe next to a fence post and walked to my flower bed to help me plant the daisies she'd brought from her garden to mine. She didn't know I was watching as she patted the dirt around the base of a plant. Waving her hand in the sign of a cross above it, she whispered, "God bless you, grow." I'd almost forgotten that garden blessing from my youth. Ten years later, those daisies still flourish.

Grandma is tending God's garden now but still influences me daily. Whenever I tuck a seedling into the earth, I trace a small cross above it in the air and say, "God bless you, grow."

And in quiet times, I can still hear her blessing, nurturing my faith. "God bless you, grow."

~LeAnn Thieman
Chicken Soup for the Golden Soul

A Child's Prayer

Lord Jesus,
look down from heaven upon my friend and soon
make her well again.
Thou canst do all things;
hear my prayer!
Amen.

~Share with Us~
~More Chicken Soup~
~About the Authors~
~Acknowledgments~

Share with Us

W e would like to know how these stories affected you and which ones were your favorites. Please e-mail us and let us know.

We also would like to share your stories with future readers. You may be able to help another reader, and become a published author at the same time. Please send us your own stories and poems for our future books. Some of our past contributors have launched writing and speaking careers from the publication of their stories in our books!

Your stories have the best chance of being used if you submit them through our web site, at:

www.chickensoup.com

If you do not have access to the Internet, you may submit your stories by mail or by facsimile. Please do not send us any book manuscripts, unless through a literary agent, as these will be automatically discarded.

Chicken Soup for the Soul
P.O. Box 700
Cos Cob, CT 06807-0700
Fax 203-861-7194

More for Christian Kids & Families

Chicken Soup for the Kid's Soul
1-55874-609-9
Chicken Soup for the Kid's Soul 2
0-7573-0405-2
Chicken Soup for the Child's Soul
0-7573-0589-X
Chicken Soup for the Preteen Soul
1-55874-800-8
Chicken Soup for the Preteen Soul 2
0-7573-0150-9
Chicken Soup for the Girl's Soul
0-7573-0313-7
Chicken Soup for the Teenage Soul
1-55874-463-0
Chicken Soup for the Teenage Soul II
1-55874-616-1
Chicken Soup for the Teenage Soul III
1-55874-761-3
Chicken Soup for the Teenage Soul IV
0-7573-0233-5
Chicken Soup for the Teenage Soul on Tough Stuff
1-55874-942-X
Chicken Soup for the Christian Teenage Soul
0-7573-0095-2
Chicken Soup for the Christian Soul
1-55874-501-7
Chicken Soup for the Christian Family Soul
1-55874-714-1
Chicken Soup for the Christian Woman's Soul
0-7573-0018-9
Chicken Soup for the Christian Soul II
0-7573-0320-X

Christmas Cheer

Everyone loves Christmas and the holiday season. We reunite scattered family members, watch the wonder in a child's eyes, and feel the joy of giving gifts. The rituals of the holiday season give a rhythm to the years and create a foundation for our lives, as we gather with family, with our communities at church, at school, and even at the mall, to share the special spirit of the season, brightening those long winter days.

Teens Talk Middle School

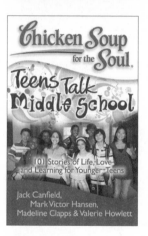

This "support group in a book" is specifically geared to middle school students ages eleven to fourteen — the ones still worrying about puberty, cliques, discovering the opposite sex, and figuring out who they are. Stories cover regrets and lessons learned, love and "like," popularity, friendship, tough issues such as divorce, illness, and death, failure and rising above it, embarrassing moments, bullying, and finding something you're passionate about.

Teens Talk High School

This book focuses on issues specific to high school age kids, ages fourteen to eighteen — sports and clubs, religion and faith, driving, curfews, growing up, self-image and self-acceptance, dating and sex, family relationships, friends, divorce, illness, death, pregnancy, drinking, failure, and preparing for life after high school. High school students will find comfort and inspiration in the words of this book, referring to it through all four years of their high school experience, like a portable support group.

Our
101
BEST
STORIES

*C*heck out our
great books fo

Christian Teen Talk

Devout Christian teens care about their connection and relationship with God, but they are also experiencing all the ups and downs of teenage life. This book provides support to teens who care about their faith but are trying to navigate their teenage years. This book includes 101 heartfelt, true stories about love, compassion, loss, forgiveness, friends, school, and faith. It also covers tough issues such as self-destructive behavior, substance abuse, teen pregnancy, and divorce.

Stories of Faith

This is the first Chicken Soup book to focus specifically on stories of faith, including 101 of the best stories from Chicken Soup's library on faith, hope, miracles, and devotion. These true stories written by regular people tell of prayers answered miraculously, amazing coincidences, rediscovered faith, and the serenity that comes from believing in a greater power, appealing to Christians and those of other faiths, and everyone who seeks enlightenment and inspiration through a good story.

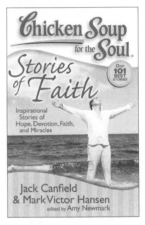

Living Catholic Faith

This is Chicken Soup for the Soul's first book written just for Catholics. From the once-a-year attendee at Christmas Mass, to the church volunteer and daily worshipper. 101 spirit-filled stories written by Catholics of all ages, this book covers the gamut, including stories about growing up Catholic to stories about sacraments and miracles. These stories bestow happiness, hope, and healing to everyone in all stages of life and faith.

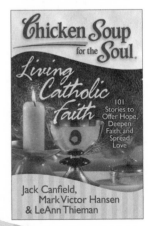

Families

Who Is
Jack Canfield?

J ack Canfield is the co-creator and editor of the *Chicken Soup for the Soul* series, which *Time* magazine has called "the publishing phenomenon of the decade." Jack is also the co-author of eight other bestselling books including *The Success Principles™: How to Get from Where You Are to Where You Want to Be, Dare to Win, The Aladdin Factor, You've Got to Read This Book,* and *The Power of Focus: How to Hit Your Business and Personal and Financial Targets with Absolute Certainty.*

Jack has recently developed a telephone coaching program and an online coaching program based on his most recent book *The Success Principles.* He also offers a seven-day *Breakthrough to Success* seminar every summer, which attracts 400 people from fifteen countries around the world.

Jack is the CEO of the Canfield Training Group in Santa Barbara, California, and founder of the Foundation for Self-Esteem in Culver City, California. He has conducted intensive personal and professional development seminars on the principles of success for over a million people in twenty-three countries. Jack is a dynamic keynote speaker and he has spoken to hundreds of thousands of others at more than 1,000 corporations, universities, professional conferences and conventions, and has been seen by millions more on national television shows such as *The Today Show, Fox and Friends, Inside Edition, Hard Copy, CNN's Talk Back Live, 20/20, Eye to Eye,* and the *NBC Nightly News* and the *CBS Evening News.*

Jack is the recipient of many awards and honors, including three honorary doctorates and a *Guinness World Records Certificate* for having seven books from the *Chicken Soup for the Soul* series appearing on the *New York Times* bestseller list on May 24, 1998.

To write to Jack or for inquiries about Jack as a speaker, his coaching programs, trainings or seminars, use the following contact information:

Jack Canfield
The Canfield Companies
P.O. Box 30880 • Santa Barbara, CA 93130
phone: 805-563-2935 • fax: 805-563-2945
E-mail: info@jackcanfield.com
www.jackcanfield.com

Who Is
Mark Victor Hansen?

Mark Victor Hansen is the co-founder of *Chicken Soup for the Soul*, along with Jack Canfield. He is also a sought-after keynote speaker, bestselling author, and marketing maven. For more than thirty years, Mark has focused solely on helping people from all walks of life reshape their personal vision of what's possible. His powerful messages of possibility, opportunity, and action have created powerful change in thousands of organizations and millions of individuals worldwide.

Mark's credentials include a lifetime of entrepreneurial success. He is a prolific writer with many bestselling books, such as *The One Minute Millionaire*, *Cracking the Millionaire Code*, *How to Make the Rest of Your Life the Best of Your Life*, *The Power of Focus*, *The Aladdin Factor*, and *Dare to Win*, in addition to the *Chicken Soup for the Soul* series. Mark has had a profound influence in the field of human potential through his library of audios, videos, and articles in the areas of big thinking, sales achievement, wealth building, publishing success, and personal and professional development.

Mark is the founder of the *MEGA Seminar Series*. *MEGA Book Marketing University* and *Building Your MEGA Speaking Empire* are annual conferences where Mark coaches and teaches new and aspiring authors, speakers, and experts on building lucrative publishing and speaking careers. Other MEGA events include *MEGA Info-Marketing* and *My MEGA Life*.

He has appeared on *Oprah*, *CNN*, and *The Today Show*. He has been quoted in *Time*, *U.S. News & World Report*, *USA Today*, *New York Times*, and *Entrepreneur* and has had countless radio interviews, assuring our planet's people that "You can easily create the life you deserve."

As a philanthropist and humanitarian, Mark works tirelessly for organizations such as Habitat for Humanity, American Red Cross, March of Dimes, Childhelp USA, and many others. He is the recipient of numerous awards that honor his entrepreneurial spirit, philanthropic heart, and business acumen. He is a lifetime member of the Horatio Alger Association of Distinguished Americans, an organization that honored Mark with the prestigious Horatio Alger Award for his extraordinary life achievements.

Mark Victor Hansen is an enthusiastic crusader of what's possible and is driven to make the world a better place.

Mark Victor Hansen & Associates, Inc.

P.O. Box 7665 • Newport Beach, CA 92658

phone: 949-764-2640 • fax: 949-722-6912

www.markvictorhansen.com

Who Is
Amy Newmark?

Amy Newmark was recently named publisher of Chicken Soup for the Soul, after a thirty-year career as a writer, speaker, financial analyst, and business executive in the worlds of finance and telecommunications.

Amy is a graduate of Harvard College, where she majored in Portuguese, minored in French, and traveled extensively. She is also the mother of two children in college and has two grown stepchildren.

After a long career writing books on telecommunications, voluminous financial reports, business plans, and corporate press releases, Chicken Soup for the Soul is a breath of fresh air for Amy. She has fallen in love with Chicken Soup for the Soul and its life-changing books, and found it a true pleasure to conceptualize, compile, and edit the "101 Best Stories" books for our readers.

The best way to contact Chicken Soup for the Soul is through our web site, at www.chickensoup.com. This will always get the fastest attention.

If you do not have access to the Internet, please contact us by mail or by facsimile.

Chicken Soup for the Soul
P.O. Box 700
Cos Cob, CT 06807-0700
Fax 203-861-7194

Thank You!

Our first thanks go to our loyal readers who have inspired the entire Chicken Soup team for the past fifteen years. Your appreciative letters and emails have reminded us why we work so hard on these books.

We owe huge thanks to all of our contributors as well. We know that you pour your hearts and souls into the stories and poems that you share with us, and ultimately with each other. We appreciate your willingness to open up your lives to other Chicken Soup readers.

We can only publish a small percentage of the stories that are submitted, but we read every single one and even the ones that do not appear in a book have an influence on us and on the final manuscripts.

As always, we would like to thank the entire staff of Chicken Soup for the Soul for their help on this project and the 101 Best series in general.

Among our California staff, we would especially like to single out the following people:

- D'ette Corona, our Assistant Publisher, who is the heart and soul of the Chicken Soup publishing operation, and who put together the first draft of this manuscript

- Barbara LoMonaco, our Webmaster and Chicken Soup for the Soul Editor, for invaluable assistance in obtaining the fabulous quotations that add depth and meaning to this book

- Patty Hansen for her extra special help with the permissions for these fabulous stories and for her amazing knowledge of the Chicken Soup library

- and Patti Clement for her help with permissions and other organizational matters.

In our Connecticut office, we would like to thank our able editors, Valerie Howlett and Madeline Clapps, for their assistance in setting up our new offices, editing, and helping us put together the best possible books.

We would also like to thank our master of design, Creative Director and book producer Brian Taylor at Pneuma Books, for his brilliant vision for our covers and interiors.

Finally, none of this would be possible without the business and creative leadership of our CEO, Bill Rouhana, and our president, Bob Jacobs.

Chicken Soup
www.chickensoup.com
for the Soul